Ready Notes

for use with

Fundamentals Of Investments:
Valuation & Management

Second Edition

Charles J. Corrado
University of Auckland- New Zealand

Bradford D. Jordan
University of Kentucky

Prepared by
Yee- Tien Fu
Stanford University

McGraw-Hill
Irwin

Boston   Burr Ridge, IL   Dubuque, IA   Madison, WI   New York   San Francisco   St. Louis
Bangkok   Bogotá   Caracas   Kuala Lumpur   Lisbon   London   Madrid   Mexico City
Milan   Montreal   New Delhi   Santiago   Seoul   Singapore   Sydney   Taipei   Toronto

Ready Notes for use with
FUNDAMENTALS OF INVESTMENTS: VALUATION AND MANAGEMENT
Charles J. Corrado, Bradford D. Jordan

1 2 3 4 5 6 7 8 9 0 BKM/BKM 0 9 8 7 6 5 4 3 2 1

ISBN 0-07-244341-3

www.mhhe.com

1

Chapter

A Brief History of Risk and Return

Fundamentals *of* Investments
Valuation & Management
second edition

Charles J. Corrado   Bradford D. Jordan

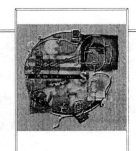

McGraw Hill / Irwin   *Slides by Yee-Tien (Ted) Fu*

Who Wants To Be A Millionaire?

A Brief History of Risk and Return

Goal Our goal in this chapter is to see what financial market history can tell us about risk and return.

- Two key observations emerge.

  ① There is a reward for bearing risk, and at least on average, that reward has been substantial.

  ② Greater rewards are accompanied by greater risks.

Returns

 Total dollar return

The return on an investment measured in dollars that accounts for all cash flows and capital gains or losses.

Example

$$\text{Total dollar return on stock} = \text{Dividend income} + \text{Capital gain (or loss)}$$

Returns

 Total percent return
The return on an investment measured as a
% of the originally invested sum that
accounts for all cash flows and capital gains
or losses.
It is the return for *each dollar* invested.

Example

$$\text{Percent return on stock} = \text{Dividend yield} + \text{Capital gains yield}$$

$$\text{or} \quad \frac{\text{Total dollar return}}{\text{Beginning stock price}}$$

Returns

Example: Calculating Returns

- Suppose you invested $1,000 in a stock at $25 per
  share. After one year, the price increases to $35. For
  each share, you also received $2 in dividends.

- Dividend yield = $2 / $25 = 8%

- Capital gains yield = ($35 − $25) / $25 = 40%

- Total percentage return = 8% + 40% = 48%

- Total dollar return = 48% of $1,000 = $480

- At the end of the year, the value of your $1,000
  investment is $1,480.

Work the Web

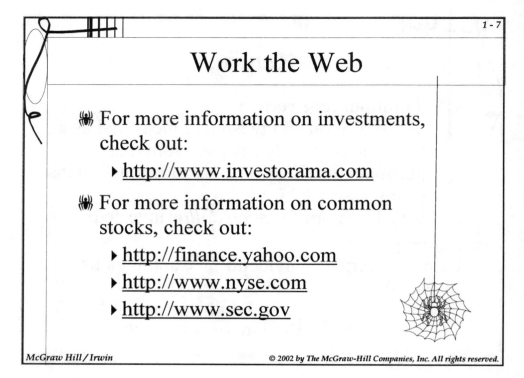

- 🕸 For more information on investments, check out:
    - ▸ http://www.investorama.com
- 🕸 For more information on common stocks, check out:
    - ▸ http://finance.yahoo.com
    - ▸ http://www.nyse.com
    - ▸ http://www.sec.gov

McGraw Hill / Irwin

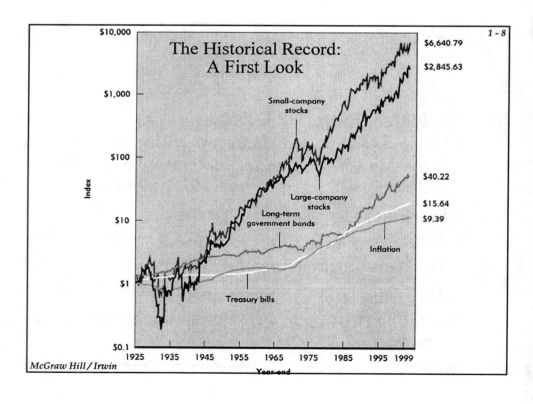

McGraw Hill / Irwin

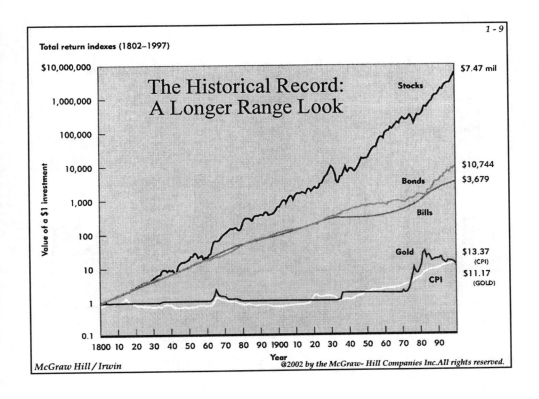

Total return indexes (1802–1997)

The Historical Record:
A Longer Range Look

The Historical Record: A Closer Look

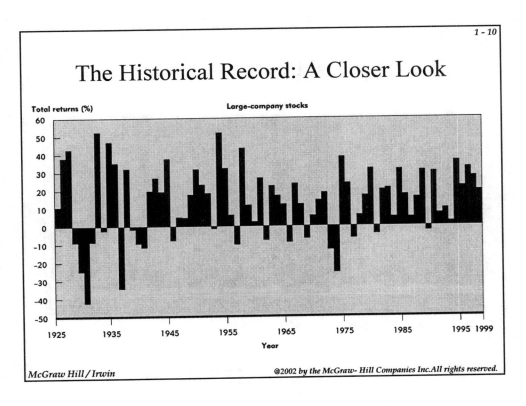

The Historical Record: A Closer Look

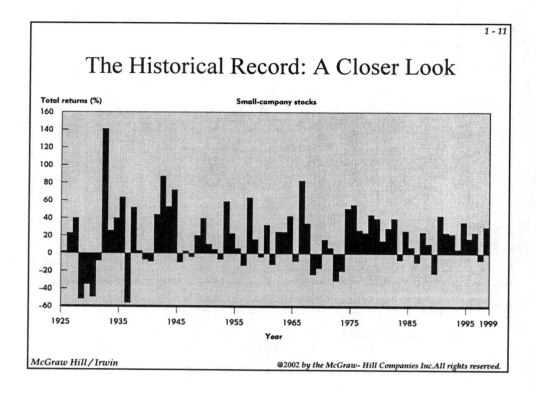

The Historical Record: A Closer Look

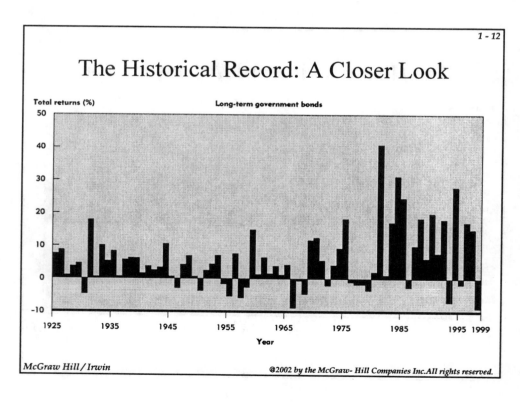

The Historical Record: A Closer Look

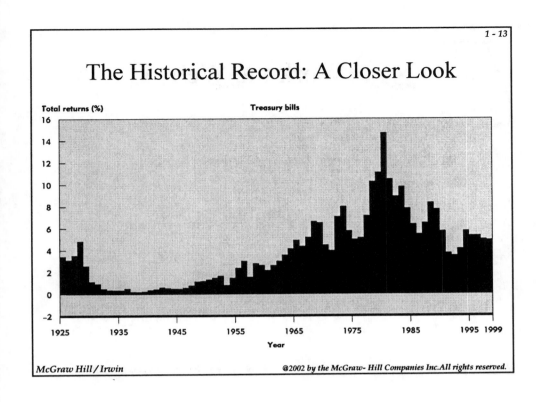

The Historical Record: A Closer Look

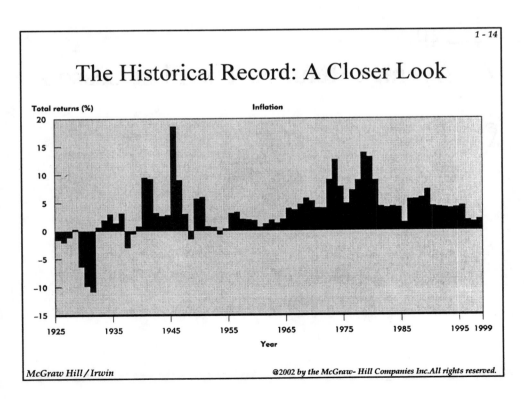

Work the Web

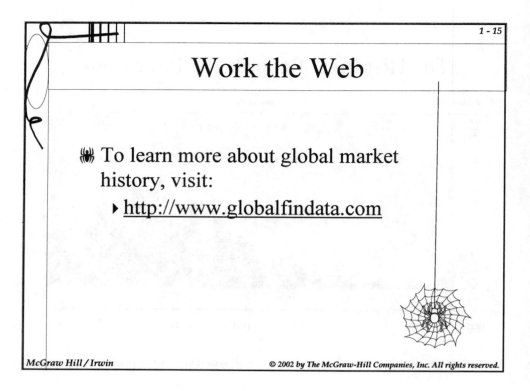

🕷 To learn more about global market history, visit:

▸ http://www.globalfindata.com

Average Returns: The First Lesson

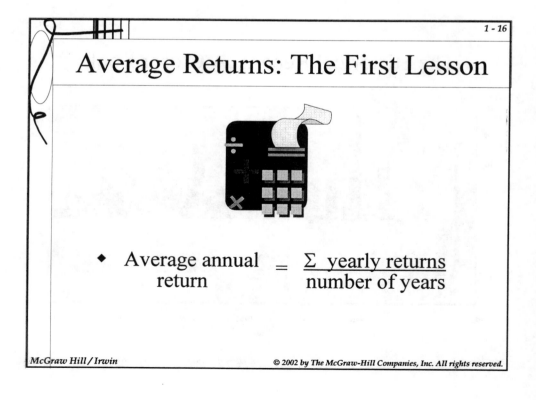

◆ Average annual return $= \dfrac{\Sigma \text{ yearly returns}}{\text{number of years}}$

Average Returns: The First Lesson

Average Annual Returns: 1926–99			
Investment	Average Return	Maximum	Minimum
Large stocks	13.3%	53.99%	−43.34%
Small stocks	17.6	142.87	−58.01
Long-term corporate bonds	5.9	43.79	−8.09
Long-term government bonds	5.5	40.35	−9.19
U.S. Treasury bills	3.8	14.71	−0.02
Inflation	3.2	13.31	−10.30

Source: *Stocks, Bonds, Bills, and Inflation Yearbook*™, Ibbotson Associates, Inc., Chicago (annually updates work by Roger G. Ibbotson and Rex A. Sinquefield). All rights reserved.

Average Returns: The First Lesson

 Risk-free rate
The rate of return on a riskless investment.

 Risk premium
The extra return on a risky asset over the risk-free rate; the reward for bearing risk.

Average Returns: The First Lesson

Average Annual Returns and Risk Premiums: 1926–99		
Investment	Average Return	Risk Premium
Large stocks	13.3%	9.5%
Small stocks	17.6	13.8
Long-term corporate bonds	5.9	2.1
Long-term government bonds	5.5	1.7
U.S. Treasury bills	3.8	0.0

Source: *Stocks, Bonds, Bills, and Inflation Yearbook*™, Ibbotson Associates, Inc., Chicago (annually updates work by Roger G. Ibbotson and Rex A. Sinquefield). All rights reserved.

Average Returns: The First Lesson

The First Lesson

- There is a reward, on average, for bearing risk.

Return Variability: The Second Lesson

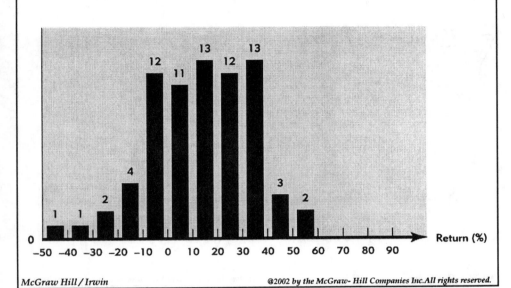

Return Variability: The Second Lesson

 Variance
A common measure of volatility.

 Standard deviation
The square root of the variance.

 Normal distribution
A symmetric, bell-shaped frequency distribution that is completely defined by its average and standard deviation.

Return Variability: The Second Lesson

Variance of return

$$Var(R) = 6^2 = \frac{\sum_{i=1}^{N}(R_i - \overline{R})^2}{N-1}$$

where N is the number of returns

Standard deviation of return

$$SD(R) = 6 = \sqrt{Var(R)}$$

Return Variability: The Second Lesson

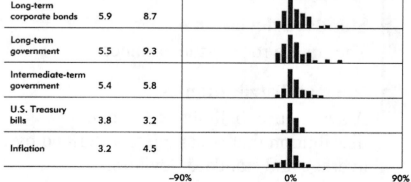

Series	Average Return	Standard Deviation	Distribution
Large-company stocks	13.3%	20.1%	
Small-company stocks	17.6	33.6	
Long-term corporate bonds	5.9	8.7	
Long-term government	5.5	9.3	
Intermediate-term government	5.4	5.8	
U.S. Treasury bills	3.8	3.2	
Inflation	3.2	4.5	

−90%   0%   90%

*The 1933 small-company stock total return was 142.9 percent.

Return Variability: The Second Lesson

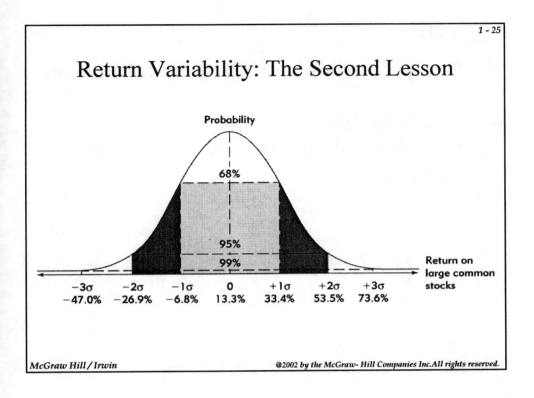

Work the Web

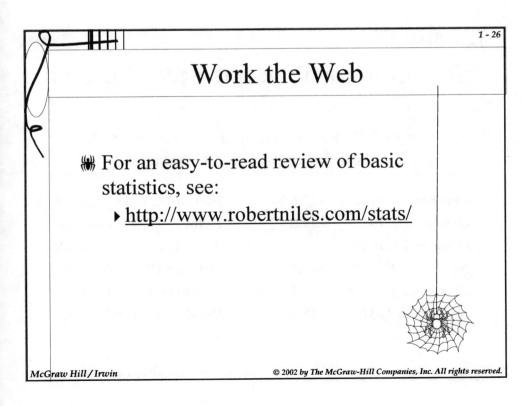

🕷 For an easy-to-read review of basic statistics, see:

▸ http://www.robertniles.com/stats/

Return Variability: The Second Lesson

The Second Lesson

* The greater the potential reward, the greater the risk.

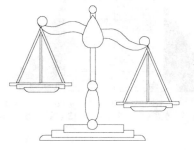

Return Variability: The Second Lesson

Top 12 One-Day Percentage Changes in the Dow Jones Industrial Average

October 19, 1987	- 22.6 %	March 14, 1907	- 8.3 %
October 28, 1929	- 12.8	October 26, 1987	- 8.0
October 29, 1929	- 11.7	July 21, 1933	- 7.8
November 6, 1929	- 9.9	October 18, 1937	- 7.7
December 18, 1899	- 8.7	February 1, 1917	- 7.2
August 12, 1932	- 8.4	October 27, 1997	- 7.2

Risk and Return

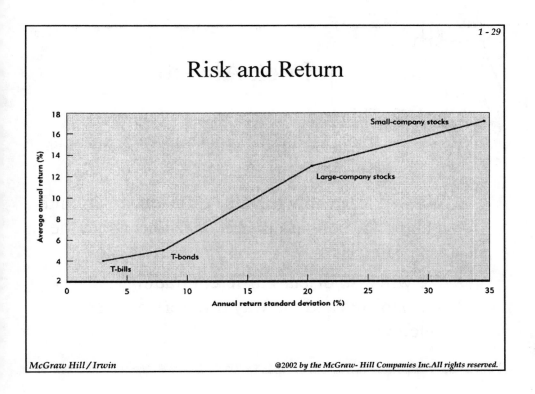

Risk and Return

- The risk-free rate represents compensation for just waiting. So, it is often called the *time value of money*.
- If we are willing to bear risk, then we can expect to earn a risk premium, at least on average.
- Further, the more risk we are willing to bear, the greater is that risk premium.

A Look Ahead

 This text focuses exclusively on financial assets: stocks, bonds, options, and futures.

- We will learn how to value different assets and make informed, intelligent decisions about the associated risks.
- We will also discuss different trading mechanisms and the way different markets function.

Chapter Review

- **Returns**
  - Dollar Returns
  - Percentage Returns
- **The Historical Record**
  - A First Look
  - A Longer Range Look
  - A Closer Look

Chapter Review

- ◆ Average Returns: The First Lesson
  - → Calculating Average Returns
  - → Average Returns: The Historical Record
  - → Risk Premiums
  - → The First Lesson

Chapter Review

- ◆ Return Variability: The Second Lesson
  - → Frequency Distributions and Variability
  - → The Historical Variance and Standard Deviation
  - → The Historical Record
  - → Normal Distribution
  - → The Second Lesson
- ◆ Risk and Return
  - → The Risk-Return Trade-Off
  - → A Look Ahead

2
Chapter

Buying and Selling Securities

Fundamentals
of Investments
Valuation & Management
second edition

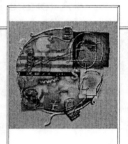

Charles J. Corrado   Bradford D. Jordan

First you buy a stock.

First you buy a stock.
If it goes up, sell it. If it doesn't go up, don't buy it.

– Will Rogers

Buying and Selling Securities

 Goal This chapter covers the basics of the investing process.

♦ We begin by describing how you go about buying and selling securities such as stocks and bonds.

♦ Then we outline some important considerations and constraints to keep in mind as you get more involved in the investing process.

Getting Started

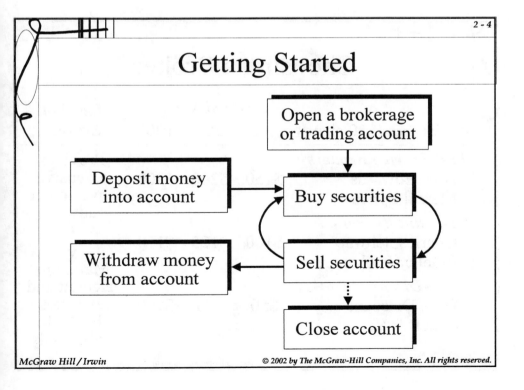

Choosing a Broker

- ◆ Brokers are traditionally divided into three groups.
  - ① full-service brokers
  - ② discount brokers
  - ③ deep-discount brokers

- ◆ These three groups can be distinguished by the level of service provided, as well as the resulting commissions charged.

Choosing a Broker

# of shares ($50/share)	Commissions			Level of Service
	200	500	1000	
Full-Service Brokers				Provides extensive investment advice
A.G. Edwards	$150	$200	$300	
Merrill Lynch				
Discount Brokers				
Charles Schwab	$100	$125	$150	
Fidelity Brokerage				
Deep-Discount Brokers				Maintains account and executes buy/sell orders only
Olde Discount	$50	$75	$100	
Quick & Reilly				

Choosing a Broker

- ◆ However, as the brokerage industry becomes more competitive, the differences among the broker types seem to be blurring.
- ◆ Another important change is the rapid growth of *online brokers*, also known as e-brokers or cyberbrokers.
- ◆ Online investing has fundamentally changed the discount and deep-discount brokerage industry by slashing costs dramatically.

Choosing a Broker

Broker	Commission for Simple Trade
Charles Schwab http://www.schwab.com	$29.95, up to 1000 shares
Fidelity Investments http://www.fidelity.com	$25, up to 1000 shares
CSFBdirect http://www.csfbdirect.com	$20, up to 1000 shares
E*Trade http://www.etrade.com	$14.95, up to 5000 shares
TD Waterhouse http://www.tdwaterhouse.com	$12, up to 5000 shares
Ameritrade http://www.ameritrade.com	$8, no share limits

Work the Web

 Which online broker is the best?
See ratings at:
- ▸ http://www.gomez.com

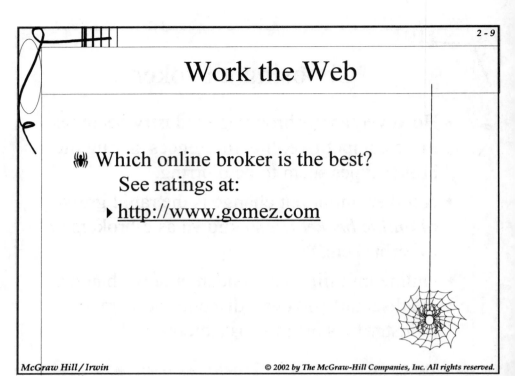

Security Investors Protection Corporation

Security Investors Protection Corporation (SIPC)
Insurance fund covering investors' brokerage accounts with member firms.

- ◆ Most brokerage firms belong to the SIPC, which insures each account for up to $500,000 in cash and securities, with a $100,000 cash maximum.

- ◆ Note that SIPC does not guarantee the value of any security.

Broker-Customer Relations

- There are several important things to keep in mind when dealing with a broker.

  ① Any advice you receive is *not* guaranteed.

  ② Your broker works as your agent and has a legal duty to act in your best interest. On the other hand, brokerage firms are in the business of generating brokerage commissions.

  ③ Your account agreement will probably specify that any disputes will be settled by arbitration and that the arbitration is final and binding.

Work the Web

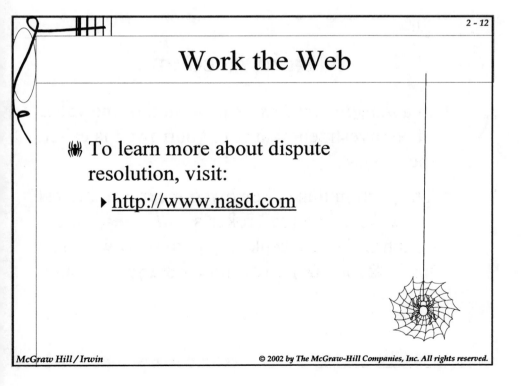

- To learn more about dispute resolution, visit:
  - http://www.nasd.com

Brokerage Accounts

 Cash account
A brokerage account in which all transactions are made on a strictly cash basis.

 Margin account
A brokerage account in which, subject to limits, securities can be bought and sold on credit.

Margin Accounts

- In a *margin purchase*, the portion of the value of an investment that is *not* borrowed is called the *margin*.

- The portion that is borrowed incurs an interest that is based on the broker's *call money rate*, which is the rate brokers pay to borrow bank funds for lending to customer margin accounts.

Margin Accounts

Example: The Account Balance Sheet

- You want to buy 1000 Wal-Mart shares at $24 per share. You put up $18,000 and borrow the rest.
  - ✧ Amount borrowed = $24,000 − $18,000 = $6,000
  - ✧ Margin = $18,000 / $24,000 = 75%

Assets		Liabilities & Account Equity	
1000 WM shares	$24,000	Margin loan	$ 6,000
		Account equity	18,000
Total	$24,000	Total	$24,000

Margin Accounts

- In a margin purchase, the minimum margin that must be supplied is called the *initial margin*.

- The *maintenance margin* is the minimum margin that must be present at all times in a margin account.

- When the margin drops below the maintenance margin, the broker may demand for more funds. This is known as a *margin call*.

Margin Accounts

Example: Margin Requirements

- Your account requires an initial margin of 50% and a maintenance margin of 30%. Stock A is selling at $50 per share. You have $20,000, and you want to buy as much of stock A as you possibly can.
- ✧ You may buy up to $20,000 / 0.5 = $40,000 worth of shares.

Assets		Liabilities & Account Equity	
800 A shares	$40,000	Margin loan	$20,000
		Account equity	20,000
Total	$40,000	Total	$40,000

Margin Accounts

Example: Margin Requirements

- After your purchase, the share price of stock A falls to $35 per share.

Assets		Liabilities & Account Equity	
800 A shares	$28,000	Margin loan	$20,000
		Account equity	8,000
Total	$28,000	Total	$28,000

- ✧ New margin = $8,000 / $28,000 = 28.6% < 30% Therefore, you are subject to a margin call.

Margin Accounts

- ◆ Margin is a form of *financial leverage*.
  - → When you borrow money to make an investment, the impact is to magnify both your gains and your losses.

A Note on Annualizing Returns

- ◆ To compare investments, we will usually need to express returns on a per-year, or *annualized*, basis.

- ◆ Such a return is often called an *effective annual return (EAR)*.

- ◆ $1 + EAR = (1 + \text{holding period \% return})^m$

  where m is the number of holding periods in a year.

Hypothecation and Street Name Registration

 Hypothecation

Pledging securities as a collateral against a loan, so that the securities can be sold by the broker if the customer is unwilling or unable to meet a margin call.

 Street name registration

An arrangement under which a broker is the registered owner of a security.

The account holder is the "beneficial owner."

Other Account Issues

- Trading accounts can also be differentiated by the ways they are managed.
  - → *Advisory account* - You pay someone else to make buy and sell decisions on your behalf.
  - → *Wrap account* - All the expenses associated with your account are "wrapped" into a single fee.
  - → *Discretionary account* - You simply authorize your broker to trade for you.
  - → *Asset management account* - Provide for complete money management, including check-writing privileges, credit cards, and margin loans.

Other Account Issues

- To invest in financial securities, a brokerage account is not a necessity.
    - → One alternative is to buy securities directly from the issuer.
    - → Another alternative is to invest in *mutual funds*.

Short Sales

Short sale
A sale in which the seller does not actually own the security that is sold.

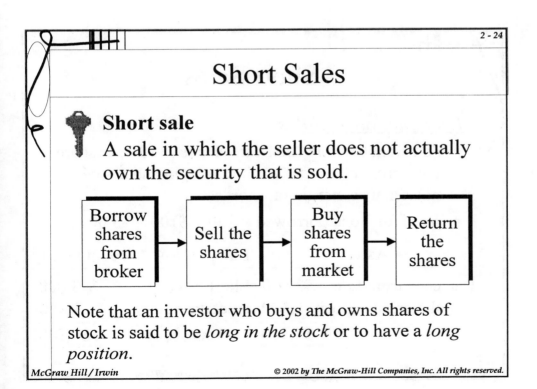

Note that an investor who buys and owns shares of stock is said to be *long in the stock* or to have a *long position*.

Short Sales

- ◆ An investor with a long position benefits from price increases.

- ◆ On the other hand, an investor with a short position benefits from price decreases.

Short Sales

Example: Short Sales

- ◆ You want to short 100 Sears shares at $30 per share. Your broker has a 50% initial margin and a 40% maintenance margin on short sales.
- ◇ Worth of stock borrowed = $30 × $100 = $3,000

Assets		Liabilities & Account Equity	
Proceeds from sale	$3,000	Short position	$ 3,000
Initial margin deposit	1,500	Account equity	1,500
Total	$4,500	Total	$4,500

Short Sales

Example: Short Sales ...*continued*

◆ Scenario 1: The stock price falls to $20 per share.

Assets		Liabilities & Account Equity	
Proceeds from sale	$3,000	Short position	$ 2,000
Initial margin deposit	1,500	Account equity	2,500
Total	$4,500	Total	$4,500

◇ New margin = $2,500 / $2,000 = 125%

Short Sales

Example: Short Sales ...*continued*

◆ Scenario 2: The stock price rises to $40 per share.

Assets		Liabilities & Account Equity	
Proceeds from sale	$3,000	Short position	$ 4,000
Initial margin deposit	1,500	Account equity	500
Total	$4,500	Total	$4,500

◇ New margin = $500 / $4,000 = 12.5% < 40%
  Therefore, you are subject to a margin call.

Short Sales

 Short interest
The amount of common stock held in short positions.

- ◆ In practice, short selling is quite common and a substantial volume of stock sales are initiated by short sellers.

- ◆ Note that with a short position, you may lose more than your total investment, as there is no limit to how high the stock price may rise.

Work the Web

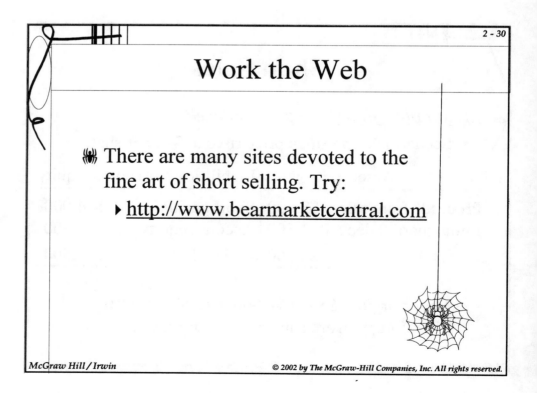 There are many sites devoted to the fine art of short selling. Try:

- ▶ http://www.bearmarketcentral.com

Risk and Return

◆ In formulating investment objectives, the individual must balance return objectives with risk tolerance.

Work the Web

🕷 How risk-averse are you?
  Take a test at:
  ‣ http://www.investorama.com/calc

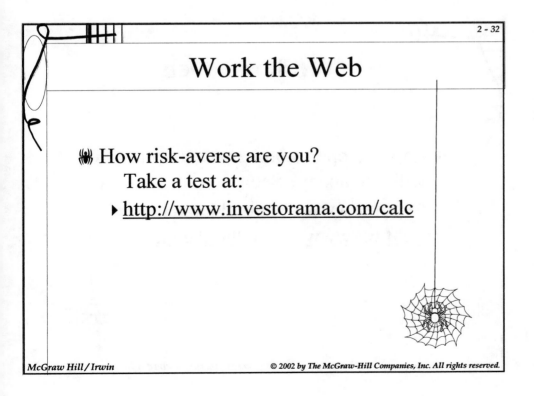

Investor Constraints

- *Resources.* What is the minimum sum needed? What are the associated costs?
- *Horizon.* When do you need the money?
- *Liquidity.* How high is the possibility that you need to sell the asset quickly?
- *Taxes.* Which tax bracket are you in?
- *Special circumstances.* Does your company provide any incentive? What are your regulatory and legal restrictions?

Work the Web

- Can you open a brokerage account with no money? See:
    - http://www.sharebuilder.com
    - http://www.buyandhold.com

Strategies and Policies

- *Investment management.* Should you manage your investments yourself?
- *Market timing.* Should you try to buy and sell in anticipation of the future direction of the market?

Strategies and Policies

- *Asset allocation.* How should you distribute your investment funds across the different classes of assets?
- *Security selection.* Within each class, which specific securities should you buy?

Chapter Review

- ◆ Getting Started
  - → Choosing a Broker
  - → Online Brokers
  - → Security Investors Protection Corporation
  - → Broker-Customer Relations

Chapter Review

- ◆ Brokerage Accounts
  - → Cash Accounts
  - → Margin Accounts
  - → A Note on Annualizing Returns
  - → Hypothecation and Street Name Registration
  - → Other Account Issues

Chapter Review

- ◆ Short Sales
  - → Basics of a Short Sale
  - → Some Details

- ◆ Investor Objectives, Constraints, and Strategies
  - → Risk and Return
  - → Investor Constraints
  - → Strategies and Policies

3

Chapter

Security Types

Fundamentals
of Investments
Valuation & Management
second edition

Charles J. Corrado Bradford D. Jordan

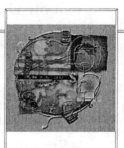

Security Types

Goal Our goal in this chapter is to introduce the different types of securities that are routinely bought and sold in financial markets around the world.

♦ For each security type, we will examine:
 ① its distinguishing characteristics,
 ② the potential gains and losses from owning it, and
 ③ how its prices are quoted in the financial press.

Classifying Securities

Basic Types	Major Subtypes
Interest-bearing	Money market instruments Fixed-income securities
Equities	Common stock Preferred stock
Derivatives	Options Futures

Interest-Bearing Assets

 Money market instruments
Short-term debt obligations of large corporations and governments that mature in a year or less.

 Fixed-income securities
Longer-term debt obligations, often of corporations or governments, that promise to make fixed payments according to a preset schedule.

Money Market Instruments

- *Examples:* U.S. Treasury bills (T-bills), bank certificates of deposit (CDs), corporate and municipal money market instruments.
- *Potential gains/losses:* Fixed future payment, except when the borrower defaults.
- *Price quotations:* Usually, the instruments are sold on a *discount basis*, and only the interest rates are quoted. So, some calculation is necessary to convert the rates to prices.

Fixed-Income Securities

- *Examples:* U.S. Treasury notes, corporate bonds, car loans, student loans.
- *Potential gains/losses:*
  - → Fixed coupon payments and final payment at maturity, except when the borrower defaults.
  - → Possibility of gain/loss from fall/rise in interest rates.
  - → Can be quite illiquid.

Fixed-Income Securities

♦ *Price quotations:*

AT&T, the issuer of the bond.

The bond will mature in the year 2022.

BONDS	CUR YLD.	VOL	CLOSE	NET CHG.
NEW YORK BONDS				
Corporation Bonds				
ATT 73/407	7.8	56	100	+ 1/4
ATT 81/822	8.6	433	94 1/8	+ 5/8
ATT 81/824	8.7	453	93 3/4	−

The bond's annual coupon rate. You will receive 81/8% of the bond's face value each year in 2 semiannual coupon payments.

Fixed-Income Securities

♦ *Price quotations:*

$$\text{Current yield} = \frac{\text{annual coupon}}{\text{current price}}$$

The closing price for the day is 94.125% of face value.

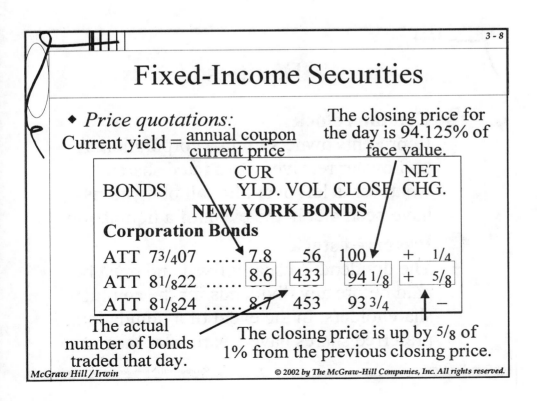

BONDS	CUR YLD.	VOL	CLOSE	NET CHG.
NEW YORK BONDS				
Corporation Bonds				
ATT 73/407	7.8	56	100	+ 1/4
ATT 81/822	8.6	433	94 1/8	+ 5/8
ATT 81/824	8.7	453	93 3/4	−

The actual number of bonds traded that day.

The closing price is up by 5/8 of 1% from the previous closing price.

Work the Web

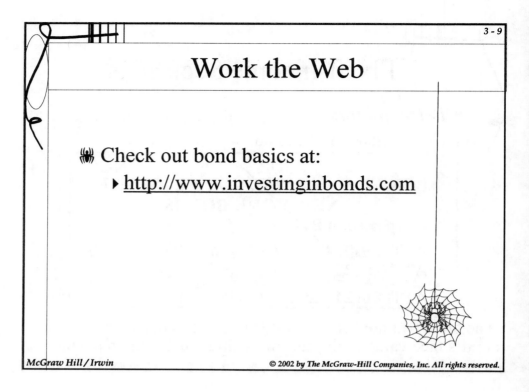

🕷 Check out bond basics at:
- ▸ http://www.investinginbonds.com

Equities

 Common stock
Represents ownership in a corporation. A part owner receives a pro rated share of whatever is left over after all obligations have been met in the event of a liquidation.

 Preferred stock
The dividend is usually fixed and must be paid before any dividends for the common shareholders. In the event of a liquidation, preferred shares have a particular face value.

Common Stock

- *Examples:* IBM shares, Microsoft shares, etc.
- *Potential gains/losses:*
  - → Many companies pay cash dividends to their shareholders. However, neither the timing nor the amount of any dividend is guaranteed.
  - → The stock value may rise or fall depending on the prospects for the company and market-wide circumstances.

Preferred Stock

- *Example:* Citigroup preferred stock.
- *Potential gains/losses:*
  - → Dividends are "promised." However, there is no legal requirement that the dividends be paid, as long as no common dividends are distributed.
  - → The stock value may rise or fall depending on the prospects for the company and market-wide circumstances.

Equities : *Price quotations*

NEW YORK STOCK EXCHANGE COMPOSITE TRANSACTIONS

Thursday, June 28, 2001

	YTD %CHG	52 WEEKS HI	LO	STOCK (SYM)	DIV	YLD %	PE	VOL 100S	LAST	NET CHG
+	80.4	24.10	7	Circorlnt **CIR**	.15	.8	22	425	18.04	−0.31
+	280.2	17.50	3.06	CircCtyCmx **KMX**		...	28	1328	14.97	−0.04
+	46.5	38.69	8.69	CircCty **CC** x	.07	.4	34	12240	16.85	−0.12
+	1.2	59.13	39	Citigroup **C** s	.56	1.1	20	109610	51.70	−0.45
−	10.8	19	11.28	CtznComm **CZN**	j	...	dd	12329	11.71	+0.02
▼−	2.7	25.81	24.54	CitizensComm **CZB** n		...	...	1251	24.80	+0.22
+	12.9	45	30.75	CityNtl **CYN**	.74	1.7	16	1726	43.81	+0.41
+	3.7	24.94 ♣	15.63	ClairStrs **CLE**	.16	.9	13	1805	18.60	+0.55
+	22.0	26.85 ♣	16.88	CLARCOR **CLC**	.47	1.9	15	423	25.23	−0.22
+	9.7	8.15	5.13	ClarCmrd A **CLR**	.80	10.1	12	5	7.95	−0.01
+	35.7	15.80	7.94	ClaytnHms **CMH**	.06	.4	18	3457	15.60	+0.10
+	23.9	85.81	43.88	ClearChanl **CCU**		...	dd	20489	60.01	+1.03
−	17.6	28.25 ♣	16.66	CLECO **CNL** s	.87	3.9	17	727	22.56	+0.41
−	14.4	27.25	13.69	ClvlndClfs **CLF**	.40	2.2	17	2494	18.46	−0.64
−	3.1	48.63	28.38	Clorox **CLX**	.84	2.4	22	4917	34.39	−0.48

McGraw Hill / Irwin

Work the Web

- Are you a *Foolish* investor? Go to "Fool School" at:
  - http://www.fool.com
- You can also learn more about the "ticker tape" at:
  - http://www.stocktickercompany.com
- and create your own ticker at:
  - http://www.cnbc.com

McGraw Hill / Irwin

Derivatives

 Primary asset
Security originally sold by a business or government to raise money.

 Derivative asset
A financial asset that is derived from an existing traded asset rather than issued by a business or government to raise capital. More generally, any financial asset that is not a primary asset.

Derivatives

 Futures contract
An agreement made today regarding the terms of a trade that will take place later.

 Option contract
An agreement that gives the owner the right, but not the obligation, to buy or sell a specific asset at a specified price for a set period of time.

Futures Contracts

- *Examples:* financial futures, commodity futures.
- *Potential gains/losses:*
  - → At maturity, you gain if your contracted price is better than the market price of the underlying asset, and vice versa.
  - → If you sell your contract before its maturity, you may gain or lose depending on the market price for the contract.
  - → Note that enormous gains/losses are possible.

McGraw Hill / Irwin

Futures Contracts

- *Price quotations:*

FUTURES PRICES

Monday, November 6, 2000

INTEREST RATE

	OPEN	HIGH	LOW	SETTLE	CHANGE	LIFETIME HIGH	LIFETIME LOW	OPEN INT.
Treasury Bonds (CBT)-$100,000; pts 32nds of 100%								
Dec	99-01	99-06	98-16	98-25	– 8	101-11	88-13	406,955
Mr01	99-04	99-06	98-17	98-25	– 9	101-11	88-06	17,055
June	...	...	...	98-21	– 9	100-08	96-21	156

Est vol 175,000; vol Fri 313,212; open int 424,399, +3,206.

McGraw Hill / Irwin

Work the Web

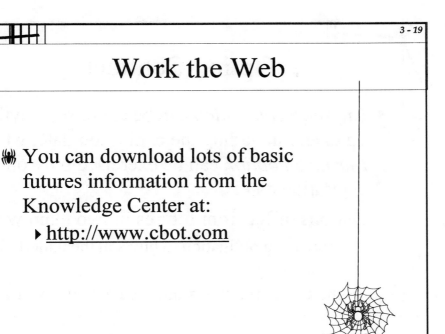

🕷 You can download lots of basic
futures information from the
Knowledge Center at:
  ▸ http://www.cbot.com

Option Contracts

- A *call option* gives the owner the right, but not
  the obligation, to *buy* an asset, while a *put
  option* gives the owner the right, but not the
  obligation, to *sell* an asset.
- The price you pay to buy an option is called
  the *option premium*.
- The specified price at which the underlying
  asset can be bought or sold is called the *strike
  price*, or *exercise price*.

Option Contracts

- ◆ An *American option* can be exercised anytime up to and including the expiration date, while a *European option* can be exercised only on the expiration date.
- ◆ Options differ from futures in two main ways:
  - ① There is no obligation to buy/sell the underlying asset.
  - ② There is a premium associated with the contract.

Option Contracts

- ◆ *Potential gains/losses:*
  - → Buyers gain if the strike price is better than the market price, and if the difference is greater than the option premium. In the worst case, buyers lose the entire premium.
  - → Sellers gain the premium if the market price is better than strike price. Here, the gain is limited but the loss is not.

Option Contracts

• *Price quotations:*

LISTED OPTIONS QUOTATIONS

Monday, November 6, 2000

OPTION/STRIKE	EXP.	CALL VOL.	CALL LAST	PUT VOL.	PUT LAST
AmOnline 30	Jan	10	26^{50}	767	0^{20}
55^{60} 40	Nov	13	16^{40}	1156	0^{10}
55^{60} 40	Jan	20	17	262	0^{70}
55^{60} 42^{50}	Nov	23	13	920	0^{15}
55^{60} 45	Nov	162	11^{10}	684	0^{25}
55^{60} 50	Nov	4271	6^{50}	1952	0^{55}
55^{60} 50	Dec	183	7^{50}	258	1^{50}
55^{60} 50	Jan	346	8^{70}	2109	2^{50}
55^{60} 55	Nov	8567	2^{50}	843	1^{75}
55^{60} 55	Dec	516	4^{40}	191	3^{20}
55^{60} 55	Jan	366	5^{70}	829	4^{30}
55^{60} 55	Apr	73	8^{90}	288	6^{10}
55^{60} 60	Nov	5601	0^{65}	103	4^{40}
55^{60} 60	Dec	4282	2^{05}	55	6
55^{60} 60	Jan	1258	3^{60}	44	7
55^{60} 65	Nov	798	0^{20}	90	9
55^{60} 65	Dec	1245	0^{90}	57	9^{70}
55^{60} 65	Jan	1758	2^{10}	18	10^{30}
55^{60} 70	Jan	637	1^{15}	...	...
55^{60} 75	Jan	293	2^{05}	...	...
55^{60} 80	Apr	1197	1^{70}	...	...

McGraw Hill / Irwin

Investing in Stocks versus Options

Example:

• Suppose you have $10,000 for investments. Macron Technology is selling at $50 per share.

◇ Number of shares bought = $10,000 / $50 = 200

◇ If Macron is selling for $55 per share 3 months later, gain = ($55 × 200) − $10,000 = $1,000

◇ If Macron is selling for $45 per share 3 months later, gain = ($45 × 200) − $10,000 = − $1,000

McGraw Hill / Irwin

Investing in Stocks versus Options

Example: ...*continued*

- A call option with a $50 strike price and 3 months to maturity is also available at a premium of $4.
  - ⟡ A call contract costs $4 × 100 = $400, so number of contracts bought = $10,000 / $400 = 25 (for 25 × 100 = 2500 shares)
  - ⟡ If Macron is selling for $55 per share 3 months later, gain = {($55 − $50) × 2500} − $10,000 = $2,500
  - ⟡ If Macron is selling for $45 per share 3 months later, gain = ($0 × 2500) − $10,000 = − $10,000

Chapter Review

- Classifying Securities
- Interest-Bearing Assets
  - → Money Market Instruments
  - → Fixed-Income Securities
- Equities
  - → Common Stock
  - → Preferred Stock
  - → Common and Preferred Stock Price Quotes

Chapter Review

- ◆ Derivatives
  - → Futures Contracts
  - → Futures Price Quotes
  - → Gains and Losses on Futures Contracts
- ◆ Option Contracts
  - → Option Terminology
  - → Options versus Futures
  - → Option Price Quotes
  - → Gains and Losses on Option Contracts
  - → Investing in Stocks versus Options

4

Chapter

Mutual Funds

Fundamentals
of Investments
Valuation & Management
second edition

Charles J. Corrado   Bradford D. Jordan

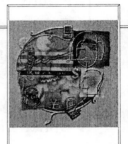

McGraw Hill / Irwin

Mutual Funds

Goal   Our goal in this chapter is to understand the different types of mutual funds, their risks, and returns.

- Investors added $363 billion in net new funds to mutual funds in 1999, and by the end of the year, mutual fund assets totaled $6.85 *trillion*. These were estimated to be owned by

83 million Americans.

McGraw Hill / Irwin

Mutual Funds

- Mutual funds are simply a means of combining or pooling the funds of a large group of investors.

- The buy and sell decisions for the resulting pool are then made by a fund manager, who is compensated for the service provided.

- Like commercial banks and life insurance companies, mutual funds are a form of financial intermediary.

Investment Companies and Fund Types

Investment company
A business that specializes in pooling funds from individual investors and investing them.

Open-end fund
An investment company that stands ready to buy and sell shares at any time.

Closed-end fund
An investment company with a fixed number of shares that are bought and sold only in the open stock market.

Investment Companies and Fund Types

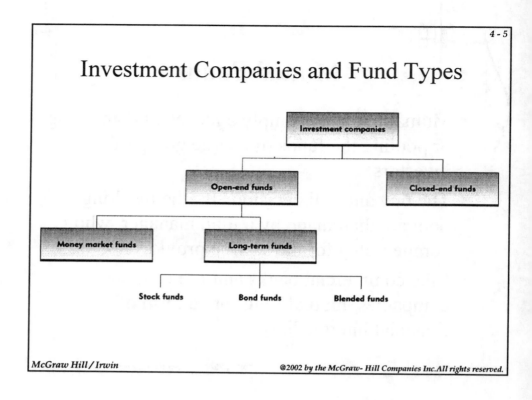

Investment Companies and Fund Types

Net asset value

The value of the assets held by a mutual fund, divided by the number of shares. Abbreviated NAV.

♦ Shares in an open-end fund are worth their NAV, because the fund stands ready to redeem their shares at any time.

♦ In contrast, the shares of closed-end funds may or may not be equal to their NAV.

Work the Web

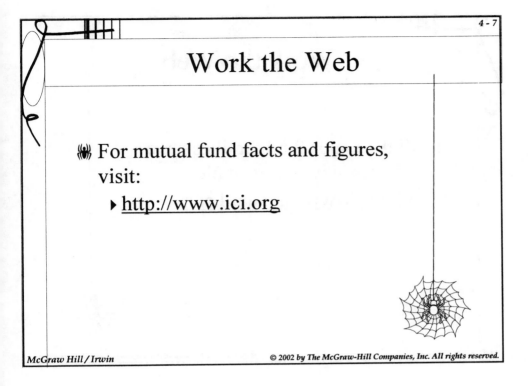

🕷 For mutual fund facts and figures, visit:

  ▸ http://www.ici.org

Mutual Fund Operations

Organization and Creation

- A mutual fund is simply a corporation. It is owned by shareholders, who elect a board of directors.
- Most mutual funds are created by investment advisory firms (such as Fidelity Investments), or brokerage firms with investment advisory operations (such as Merrill Lynch).
- These firms wish to manage the funds to earn fees.

Work the Web

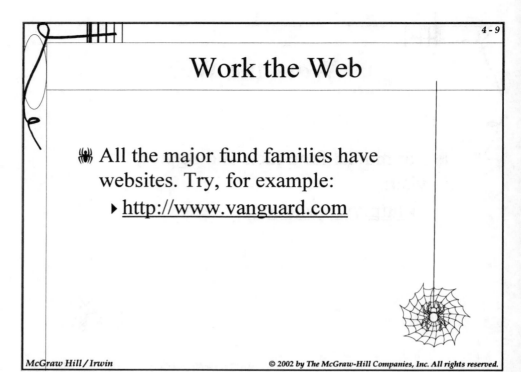

All the major fund families have websites. Try, for example:

▸ http://www.vanguard.com

Mutual Fund Operations

Taxation of Investment Companies

♦ An investment company that
  ① holds almost all its assets as investments in stocks, bonds, and other securities,
  ② uses no more than 5% of its assets when acquiring a particular security, and
  ③ passes through all realized investment income to fund shareholders,

  is treated as a "regulated investment company" for tax purposes and does not need to pay taxes on its investment income.

Mutual Fund Operations

The Fund Prospectus and Annual Report

- Mutual funds are required by law to supply a prospectus to any investor who wishes to purchase shares.
- Mutual funds must also provide an annual report to their shareholders.

Mutual Fund Costs and Fees

Types of Expenses and Fees

① *Sales charges or "loads."* Front-end loads are charges levied on purchases, while back-end loads are charges levied on redemptions.

② *12b-1 fees.* SEC Rule 12b-1 allows funds to spend up to 1% of fund assets annually to cover distribution and marketing costs.

③ *Management fees.* Usually based on fund size, performance, etc.

Mutual Fund Costs and Fees

Types of Expenses and Fees ...*continued*

④ *Trading costs.* This is related to the fund's turnover.

Mutual Fund Costs and Fees

Expense Reporting

◆ Mutual funds are required to report expenses in a fairly standardized way in the prospectus.

　① Shareholder transaction expenses - loads and deferred sales charges.

　② Fund operating expenses - management and 12b-1 fees, legal, accounting, and reporting costs, director fees.

　③ Hypothetical example showing the total expense you would pay over time per $10,000 invested.

Mutual Fund Costs & Fees

Fidelity

Retirement Growth

Fund

Prospectus

Expenses

Expenses

Shareholder transaction expenses are charges you pay when you buy or sell shares of a fund.

Maximum sales charge on purchases and reinvested dividends	None
Deferred sales charge on redemptions	None
Exchange fee	None

Annual fund operating expenses are paid out of the fund's assets. The fund pays a management fee that varies based on its performance. It also incurs other expenses for services such as maintaining shareholder records and furnishing shareholder statements and fund reports. The fund's expenses are factored into its share price or dividends and are not charged directly to shareholder accounts.

The following are projections based on historical expenses and are calculated as a percentage of average net assets.

Management fee	.40%
12b-1 fee	None
Other expenses	.22%
Total fund operating expenses	.62%

Examples: Let's say, hypothetically, that the fund's annual return is 5% and that its operating expenses are exactly as just described. For every $10,000 you invested, here's how much you would pay in total expenses if you close your account after the number of years indicated:

After 1 year	$63
After 3 years	$199
After 5 years	$346
After 10 years	$774

These examples illustrate the effect of expenses, but are not meant to suggest actual or expected costs or returns, all of which may vary.

McGraw Hill / Irwin

Work the Web

- Prospectuses are increasingly available online. To see some examples, visit:
  - http://www.fidelity.com

- To see a fund that *really* discloses information, try:
  - http://www.ipsfunds.com

  Check out the "plain language" risk disclosure!

McGraw Hill / Irwin

Mutual Fund Costs and Fees

Why Pay Loads and Fees?

- ◆ You may want a fund run by a particular manager, and all such funds are load funds.

- ◆ You want a specialized type of fund. Loads and fees for such funds tend to be higher as there is little competition among them.

Short-Term Funds

 Money market mutual fund
A mutual fund specializing in money market instruments.

- ◆ Short-term funds are collectively known as money market mutual funds, or MMMFs.

- ◆ MMMFs always maintain a $1 net asset value to make them resemble bank accounts.

- ◆ Depending on the type of securities purchased, MMMFs can be either taxable or tax-exempt.

Short-Term Funds

- Most banks offer what are called "money market" deposit accounts, or MMDAs, which are much like MMMFs.
- The distinction is that a bank money market account is a bank deposit and offers FDIC protection.

Work the Web

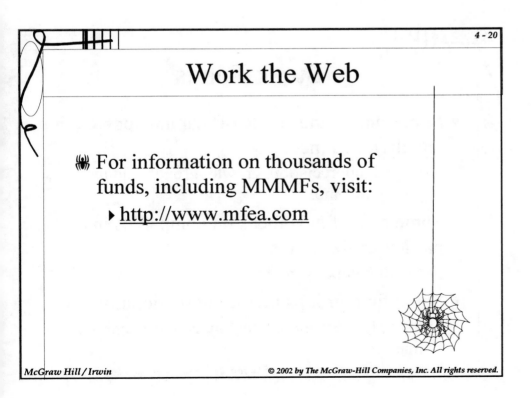

- For information on thousands of funds, including MMMFs, visit:
  - ▸ http://www.mfea.com

Long-Term Funds

- ◆ A fund's objective is the major determinant of the fund type.
- ◆ Historically, mutual funds were classified as stock, bond, or income funds. However, it is becoming increasingly difficult to do so.

Stock, bond, or income?

Stock Funds

- ◆ Some stock funds trade off capital appreciation and dividend income.
    - → Capital appreciation, growth, growth and income, equity income.
- ◆ Some stock funds focus on companies in a particular size range.
    - → Small company, midcap.
- ◆ Some fund groups invest internationally.
    - → Global, international, region, country, emerging markets.

Stock Funds

- Sector funds specialize in specific sectors of the economy.
- Other fund types include index funds, social conscience funds, and tax-managed funds.

Bond Funds

- Bond funds may be distinguished by their

  ① maturity range , ② credit quality,

  ③ taxability, ④ bond type, and ⑤ issuing country.
- Bond fund types include short-term and intermediate-term funds, general funds, high-yield funds, mortgage funds, world funds, insured funds, single-state municipal funds.

Stock and Bond Funds

- ◆ Funds that do not invest exclusively in either stocks or bonds are often called "blended" or "hybrid" funds.
- ◆ Examples include balanced funds, asset allocation funds, convertible funds, income funds.

Mutual Fund Objectives: Recent Developments

- ◆ In recent years, there has been a trend toward classifying a mutual fund's objective based on its actual holdings.
- ◆ For example, the *Wall Street Journal* classifies most general purpose funds based on the market "cap" of the stocks they hold, and also on whether the fund tends to invest in "growth" or "value" stocks (or both).

MUTUAL-FUND OBJECTIVES

Categories compiled by The Wall Street Journal, based on classifications by Lipper Inc.

STOCK FUNDS

Emerging Markets (EM): Funds that invest in emerging-market equity securities, where the "emerging market" is defined by a country's GNP per capita and other economic measures.

Equity Income (EI): Funds that seek high current income and growth of income through investment in equities.

European Region (EU): Funds that invest in markets or operations concentrated in the European region.

Global Stock (GL): Funds that invest in securities traded outside of the U.S. and may own U.S. securities as well.

Gold Oriented (AU): Funds that invest in gold mines, gold-oriented mining finance houses, gold coins or bullion.

Health/Biotech (HB): Funds that invest in companies related to health care, medicine and biotechnology.

International Stock (IL) (non-U.S.): Canadian; International; International Small Cap.

Latin American (LT): Funds that invest in markets or operations concentrated in the Latin American region.

Large-Cap Growth (LG): Funds that invest in large companies with long-term earnings that are expected to grow significantly faster than the earnings of stocks in major indexes. Funds normally have above-average price-to-earnings ratios, price-to-book ratios and three-year earnings growth.

Large-Cap Core (LC): Funds that invest in large companies, with wide latitude in the type of shares they buy. On average, the price-to-earnings ratios, price-to-book ratios, and three-year earnings growth are in line with those of the U.S. diversified large-cap funds' universe average.

Large-Cap Value (LV): Funds that invest in large companies that are considered undervalued relative to major stock indexes based on price-to-earnings ratios, price-to-book ratios or other factors.

Midcap Growth (MG): Funds that invest in midsize companies with long-term earnings that are expected to grow significantly faster than the earnings of stocks in major indexes. Funds normally have above-average price-to-earnings ratios, price-to-book ratios and three-year earnings growth.

Midcap Core (MC): Funds that invest in midsize companies, with wide latitude in the type of shares they buy. On average, the price-to-earnings ratios, price-to-book ratios, and three-year earnings growth are in line with those of the U.S. diversified midcap funds' universe average.

Midcap Value (MV): Funds that invest in midsize companies that are considered undervalued relative to major stock indexes based on price-to-earnings ratios, price-to-book ratios or other factors.

Multicap Growth (XG): Funds that invest in companies of various sizes, with long-term earnings that are expected to grow significantly faster than the earnings of stocks in major indexes. Funds normally have above-average price-to-earnings ratios, price-to-book ratios, and three-year earnings growth.

Multicap Core (XC): Funds that invest in companies of various sizes with average price-to-earnings ratios, price-to-book ratios and earnings growth.

Multicap Value (XV): Funds that invest in companies of various size, normally those that are considered undervalued relative to major stock indexes based on price-to-earnings ratios, price-to-book ratios or other factors.

Natural Resources (NR): Funds that invest in natural-resource stocks.

Pacific Region (PR): Funds that invest in China Region; Japan; Pacific Ex-Japan; Pacific Region.

Science & Technology (TK): Funds that invest in science and technology stocks. Includes Telecommunication funds.

Sector (SE): Funds that invest in financial services; real estate; specialty & miscellaneous.

S&P 500 Index (SP): Funds that are passively managed, and are designed to replicate the performance of the Standard & Poor's 500-stock index on a reinvested basis.

Small-Cap Growth (SG): Funds that invest in small companies with long-term earnings that are expected to grow significantly faster than the earnings of stocks in major indexes. Funds normally have above-average price-to-earnings ratios, price-to-book ratios, and three-year earnings growth.

Small-Cap Core (SC): Funds that invest in small companies, with wide latitude in the type of shares they buy. On average, the price-to-earnings ratios, price-to-book ratios, and three-year earnings growth are in line with those of the U.S. diversified small-cap funds' universe average.

Small-Cap Value (SV): Funds that invest in small companies that are considered undervalued relative to major stock indexes based on price-to-earnings ratios, price-to-book ratios or other factors.

Specialty Equity (SQ): Funds that invest in all market capitalization ranges, with no restrictions for any one range. May have strategies that are distinctly different from other diversified stock funds.

Utility (UT): Funds that invest in utility stocks.

TAXABLE BOND FUNDS

Short-Term Bond (SB): Ultra-short Obligation; Short Investment Grade Debt; Short-Intermediate Investment Grade Debt.

Short-Term U.S. (SU): Short U.S. Treasury; Short U.S. Government; Short-Intermediate U.S. Government debt.

Intermediate Bond (IB): Funds that invest in investment-grade debt issues (rated in the top four grades) with dollar-weighted average maturities of five to 10 years.

Intermediate U.S. (IG): Intermediate U.S. Government; Intermediate U.S. Treasury.

Long-Term Bond (AB): Funds that invest in corporate and government debt issues in the top grades.

Long-Term U.S. (LU): General U.S. Government; General U.S. Treasury; Target Maturity.

General U.S. Taxable (GT): Funds that invest in general bonds.

High-Yield Taxable (HC): Funds that aim for high current yields from fixed-income securities and tend to invest in lower-grade debt.

Mortgage (MT): Adjustable Rate Mortgage; GNMA; U.S. Mortgage.

World Bond (WB): Emerging Markets Debt; Global Income; International Income; Short World Multi-Market Income.

MUNICIPAL DEBT FUNDS

Short-Term Muni (SM): California Short-Intermediate Muni Debt; Other States Short-Intermediate Muni Debt; Short-Intermediate Muni Debt; Short Muni Debt.

Intermediate Muni (IM): Intermediate-term Muni Debt including single states.

General Muni (GM): Funds investing in muni-debt issues in the top four credit ratings.

Single-State Municipal (SS): Funds that invest in debt of individual states.

High-Yield Municipal (HM): Funds that invest in lower rated muni debt.

Insured Muni (NM): California Insured Muni Debt; Florida Insured Muni Debt; Insured Muni Debt; New York Insured Muni Debt.

STOCK & BOND FUNDS

Balanced (BL): Primary objective is to conserve principal, by maintaining a balanced portfolio of both stocks and bonds.

Stock/Bond Blend (MP): Multipurpose funds such as Balanced Target Maturity; Convertible Securities; Flexible Income; Flexible Portfolio; Global Flexible and Income funds, that invest in both stocks and bonds.

Mutual Fund Objectives: Recent Developments

- A mutual fund "style" box is a way of visually representing a fund's investment focus by placing the fund into one of nine boxes:

Style

	Value	Blend	Growth
Large			
Medium			
Small			

Size

Work the Web

- One of the best mutual fund sites is:
  - http://www.morningstar.com

  Try picking some funds using their "Fund Selector."

- To learn more about "social conscience" funds, visit:
  - http://www.socialinvest.org
  - http://www.domini.com

Mutual Fund Performance

- Mutual fund performance is very closely tracked by a number of organizations.

MUTUAL-FUND PERFORMANCE YARDSTICKS

Data are through Oct. 31. Bond data are preliminary.

HOW LIPPER INDEXES STACK UP

INVESTMENT OBJECTIVE	OCTOBER	YEAR-TO-DATE	TOTAL RETURN 1 YEAR	ANNUALIZED 3 YEARS	5 YEARS
GENERAL STOCK FUNDS					
Large-Cap Core	-1.16%	0.34%	9.64%	18.92%	19.95%
Large-Cap Growth	-5.29	-5.65	8.34	21.16	22.21
Large-Cap Value	0.8	2.4	5.92	11.9	17.21
Midcap Core	3.55	10.77	14.62	15.64	18.11
Midcap Growth	-8.09	-1.09	34.54	24.97	20.73
Midcap Value	-0.73	7.52	19.73	6.29	13.02
Multicap Core	-1.13	3.4	14.64	15.19	18.99
Multicap Growth	-5.81	2	26.81	23.65	22.69
Multicap Value	2.38	7.45	9.65	8.16	14.54
Small-Cap Core	-3.01	8.25	27.65	7.32	14.13
Small-Cap Growth	-7.5	1.59	37.48	16.82	17.99
Small-Cap Value	-0.91	11.15	19.04	2.26	11.29
Equity Income	2.1	6.06	6.78	9.3	14.62
S&P 500 Fund	-0.45	-2.02	5.8	17.78	21.37
SECTOR FUNDS					
Science & Technology	-10.97%	-5.06%	34.97%	41.28%	29.24%
Health/Biotech	-1.24	40.55	53.98	29.53	24.29
Financial Services	0.56	20.22	12.97	10.05	19.86
Natural Resources	-5.22	17.9	24.91	4.87	14.74
Utility	-2.62	4.87	14.83	18.23	16.54
Real Estate	-4.25	16.14	18.66	-1.3	N/A

INVESTMENT OBJECTIVE	OCTOBER	YEAR-TO-DATE	TOTAL RETURN 1 YEAR	ANNUALIZED 3 YEARS	5 YEARS
WORLD STOCK FUNDS					
International	-3.4%	-14.16%	3.45%	18.02%	11.21%
Emerging Market	-7.47	-26.67	-4.28	4.44	1.86
European	-3.04	4.25	15.64	15.91	17.7
Global	-2.44	-5.61	11.92	13.61	14.71
Pacific (excl. Japan)	-8.96	-28.96	-7.77	0.56	-5.14
Pacific	8.45	30.94	15.84	2.9	-1.44
MIXED EQUITY					
Balanced	0.09%	3.67%	7.88%	10.36%	13.12%
Global Flexible	-1.94	-1.43	8.89	9.97	12.04
FIXED INCOME					
General Bond	0.24%	5.3%	5.8%	4.12%	6.38%
General U.S. Government	0.8	7.72	8.69	4.66	5.32
General U.S. Treasury	1.3	11.7	9.41	5.36	5.87
Global Income	-1	-0.93	-0.97	0.92	3.92
GNMA	0.63	7.38	6.93	5.2	6
High Yield Bond	-3.42	-6	-3.2	0.1	5.12

BENCHMARKS FOR MUTUAL-FUND INVESTORS

INVESTMENT OBJECTIVE	OCTOBER	YEAR-TO-DATE	TOTAL RETURN 1 YEAR	ANNUALIZED 3 YEARS	5 YEARS
DJIA (w/divs.)	3.07%	3.44%	3.78%	15.69%	20.34%
S&P 500 (w/divs.)	-0.42%	-1.81%	6.09%	17.6%	21.67%

N.A.: Not applicable

Source: Lipper

NAV$ 10/31	FUND NAME	INV OBJ	OCT	1 YR	TOTAL RETURN & RANK †ANNUALIZED 3 YR†	5 YR†	10 YR†	MAX INIT CHRG	EXP RATIO
	Fidelity Invest								
18.95	A Mgr	MP	-0.8	+14.1 A	+13.4 A	+14.8 B	+14.7 B	0.00	0.75
52.06	AggrGr r	XG	-11.0	+19.1 E	+38.6 A	+27.5 B	NS ..	0.00	0.99
15.08	AggrInt	IL	-9.0	-4.7 E	+9.6 C	+10.3 C	NS ..	0.00	1.21
14.75	AMgrAggr	MP	-3.7	+42.0 A	NS ..	NS ..	NS ..	0.00	NA
20.06	AMgrGr	MP	-1.3	+9.4 B	+13.2 B	+16.4 A	NS ..	0.00	0.83
12.09	AMgrIn	MP	-0.8	+6.1 D	+7.3 D	+8.6 E	NS ..	0.00	0.69
15.57	Balanc	BL	+1.1	+8.1 C	+12.7 A	+14.2 B	+13.3 B	0.00	0.67
58.54	BluCh	LC	-1.7	+12.7 B	+20.6 A	+20.4 C	+22.8 A	0.00	0.88
22.27	Canad r	IL	-5.4	+40.2 A	+10.3 C	+12.7 B	+10.4 B	3.00	1.22
25.81	CapAp	XC	-7.2	+8.1 D	+14.9 C	+17.1 D	+17.2 C	0.00	0.67
14.96	ChinaReg	PR	-7.4	+6.8 A	+12.3 A	NS ..	NS ..	3.00	1.34
8.36	CpInc r	HC	-3.1	-1.7 B	+5.4 A	+7.8 A	+13.2 A	0.00	0.83
425.26	CngS	LV	+2.1	+7.6 C	+15.4 B	+18.0 C	+17.3 B	0.00	0.61
56.93	Contra	XG	-2.5	+10.2 E	+17.7 E	+19.9 D	+22.7 C	3.00	0.65
13.63	ContraII	XG	-0.4	+33.4 C	NS ..	NS ..	NS ..	3.00	0.91
27.08	CnvSc	MP	-2.1	+42.7 A	+24.4 A	+21.3 A	+20.4 A	0.00	0.85
21.40	DestI	LC	-3.1	-9.8 E	+7.4 E	+13.7 E	+19.5 B	8.24	0.31
16.07	DestII	LC	-0.4	+14.7 B	+19.2 B	+20.7 C	+23.6 A	8.24	0.48
21.18	DestINew p	LC	-3.3	-10.7 E	NS ..	NS ..	NS ..	8.24	NA
15.86	DestIINew p	LC	-0.5	+13.4 B	NS ..	NS ..	NS ..	8.24	NA
31.15	DisEq	XC	-1.5	+11.7 C	+17.3 B	+18.6 C	+19.8 B	0.00	0.65
31.64	DivGth	LV	+3.4	+18.4 A	+21.1 A	+24.8 A	NS ..	0.00	0.77
22.98	DivIntl	IL	-3.7	+12.2 A	+16.0 A	+17.2 A	NS ..	0.00	1.21
8.71	EmrMkt r	EM	-6.8	-7.1 D	-4.8 C	-9.4 E	NS ..	3.00	1.45
55.25	Eq Inc	EI	+2.9	+7.2 C	+11.1 B	+17.0 A	+18.0 A	0.00	0.69
28.88	EQII	EI	+2.7	+8.2 B	+13.5 A	+17.4 A	+19.6 A	0.00	0.66
34.88	Europ r	EU	-4.7	+8.5 C	+12.0 D	+15.8 B	+12.7 C	0.00	0.96

Mutual Fund Performance

- ◆ While looking at historical returns, the riskiness of the various fund categories should also be considered.
- ◆ Whether historical performance is useful in predicting future performance is a subject of ongoing debate.
- ◆ Some of the poorest-performing funds are those with very high costs.

Closed-End Funds & Exchange Traded Funds

CLOSED-END FUNDS

Closed-end funds sell a limited number of shares and invest the proceeds in securities. Unlike open-end funds, closed-ends generally do not buy their shares back from investors who wish to cash in their holdings. Instead, fund shares trade on a stock exchange.

Wednesday, June 27, 2001

YTD % CHG	52 WEEKS HI	LO	STOCK (SYM)	DIV	YLD %	VOL 100S	CLOSE	NET CHG
−17.7	15.13	9.29	IndiaFd **IFN**	j	...	714	9.93	+0.15
−26.6	12.81	8	IndiaGrFd **IGF**	.47e	5.7	103	8.26	+0.08
+ 2.4	3.50	1.27 ▲	IndonesiaFd **IF**		...	8	1.60	−0.12
+ 2.6	13.40	11.94	InsrdMuniFd **PIF**	.72	5.5	176	13.15	+0.11
+ 4.7	15.31	13.13	InvGrdMuni **PPM**	.90a	6.0	35	14.98	+0.05
−24.7	15	8	Italy Fd **ITA**	7.67e	95.3	49	8.05	−0.10
+ 2.2	7.75	5.50 ▲	JapanEquity **JEQ**	j	...	268	6.07	−0.01
+18.3	9.63	5.50	Japan OTC **JOF**	.82e	12.1	270	6.80	...
+ 9.0	8.88	6.69 ▲	JF China **JFC**		...	38	7.70	+0.07
−16.4	11.08	6.53 ▲	JF India **JFI**	1.47	19.7	67	7.47	+0.02
+22.7	4.19	2.20	KoreaEqty **KEF**		...	12	2.99	−0.02
+12.8	13.04	8.31	KoreaFd **KF**	.19e	1.8	469	10.31	−0.04
+10.9	7.56	4.31	KoreanInvFd **KIF**		...	20	6.24	...
+ 7.4	11.63	8.88	LatAmDiscv **LDF**	.04e	.4	78	10.20	−0.15
+ 2.9	16.06	11.31 ▲	LatAmEq **LAQ**	.08e	.6	125	13.25	−0.08
+ 3.9	13.57	11.31 ▲	LibtyASE **USA**	1.37e	10.7	537	12.86	−0.02
+ 0.7	12.56	7.95 ▲	LibtyASG **ASG**	1.19e	12.5	133	9.50	−0.10
+ 3.4	19.19	13.53 ▲	LncInNtlSec **LNV**	.80u	5.2	67	15.25	+0.20
+11.6	12.40	10.50 ▲	LncInNtlInco **LND**	.86a	7.2	13	12	...
+ 0.8	9.40	8.19	MFS Charter **MCR**	.65m	7.5	461	8.69	+0.02
− 0.3	6.80	6	MFS GvMkTr **MGF**	.41m	6.3	238	6.48	+0.01
+ 2.0	6.97	6.19	MFS Intermd **MIN**	.48	7.1	1762	6.76	−0.01
+ 3.1	6.77	5.75	MFS MultInco **MMT**	.52m	8.2	617	6.38	...
+13.5	8.50	7	MFS MuniTr **MFM**	.53	6.4	621	8.30	+0.09
+12.4	16.30	13.06	MFS SpcVal **MFV**	1.65a	10.5	122	15.74	−0.31
− 8.8	5.38	3.10	MalaysaFd **MF**	j	...	61	3.42	−0.03
− 3.4	9.56	7.44 ▲	MgdtInc **MHY**	.92	11.3	795	8.15	+0.11
+ 3.8	10.56	5.81	MghtHiYldPl **HYF**	1.08	15.3	497	7.07	+0.05

Closed-End Funds & Exchange Traded Funds

- Most closed-end funds sell at a discount relative to their net asset values, and the discount is sometimes substantial. The typical discount also fluctuates over time

- Despite a great deal of research, the closed-end fund discount phenomenon remains largely unexplained.

Closed-End Funds & Exchange Traded Funds

- An exchange traded fund, or ETF, is basically an index fund, except that it trades like a closed-end fund (without the discount phenomenon).

- An area where ETFs seem to have an edge over the more traditional index funds is the more specialized indexes.

Chapter Review

- ◆ Investment Companies and Fund Types
  - → Open-End versus Closed-End Funds
  - → Net Asset Value

- ◆ Mutual Fund Operations
  - → Mutual Fund Organization and Creation
  - → Taxation of Investment Companies
  - → The Fund Prospectus and Annual Report

Chapter Review

- ◆ Mutual Fund Costs and Fees
  - → Types of Expenses and Fees
  - → Expense Reporting
  - → Why Pay Loads and Fees?

- ◆ Short-Term Funds
  - → Money Market Mutual Funds
  - → Money Market Deposit Accounts

Chapter Review

- ◆ Long-Term Funds
  - → Stock Funds
  - → Taxable and Municipal Bond Funds
  - → Stock and Bond Funds
  - → Mutual Fund Objectives: Recent Developments
- ◆ Mutual Fund Performance
  - → Mutual Fund Performance Information
  - → How Useful are Fund Performance Ratings?

Chapter Review

- ◆ Closed-End Funds and Exchange Traded Funds
  - → Closed-End Funds Performance Information
  - → The Closed-End Fund Discount Mystery
  - → Exchange Traded Funds

5

Chapter

The Stock Market

Fundamentals
of Investments
Valuation & Management
second edition

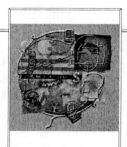

Charles J. Corrado   Bradford D. Jordan

The Stock Market

Goal

Our goal in this chapter is to get a "big picture" overview of who owns stocks, how a stock exchange works, and how to read and understand the stock market information reported in the financial press.

The Primary & Secondary Stock Markets

 Primary market
The market in which new securities are originally sold to investors.

 Secondary market
The market in which previously issued securities trade among investors.

The Primary Market for Common Stock

 Initial public offering (IPO)
An initial public offer occurs when a company offers stock for sale to the public for the first time.

The Primary Market for Common Stock

Several steps are involved in an IPO.

- Company appoints *investment banking firm* to arrange financing.

- Investment banker designs the stock issue and arranges for *fixed commitment* or *best effort underwriting*.

- Company prepares a *prospectus* (usually with outside help) and submits it to the *Securities and Exchange Commission* (SEC) for approval. Investment banker circulates preliminary prospectus (*red herring*).

The Primary Market for Common Stock

- Upon obtaining SEC approval, company finalizes prospectus. Underwriters place announcements (*tombstones*) in newspapers and begin selling shares.

The Primary Market for Common Stock

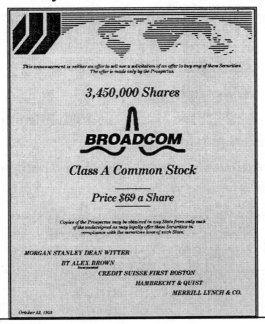

Work the Web

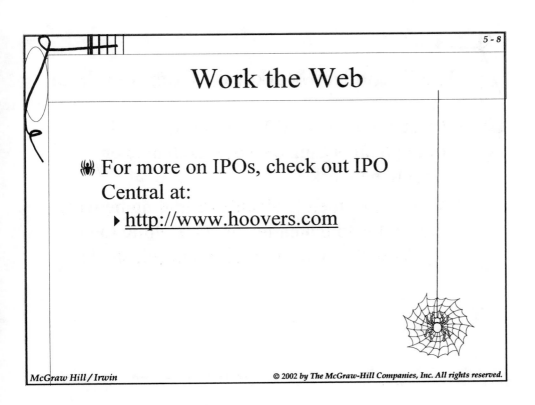

🕷 For more on IPOs, check out IPO Central at:
  ‣ http://www.hoovers.com

The Secondary Market for Common Stock

- ◆ An investor may trade:
  - ① Directly with other investors.
  - ② Indirectly through a broker who arranges transactions for others.
  - ③ Directly with a dealer who buys and sells securities from inventory.
- ◆ The price a dealer is willing to pay is called the *bid price*, while the price at which a dealer will sell is called the *ask price*. The difference between the prices is called the *spread*.

The Secondary Market for Common Stock

- ◆ Most common stock trading is directed through an organized stock exchange or trading network.
- ◆ Whether a stock exchange or trading network, the goal is to match investors wishing to buy stocks with investors wishing to sell stocks.

The New York Stock Exchange

- The New York Stock Exchange (NYSE), popularly known as the Big Board, celebrated its bicentennial in 1992.
- It has occupied its current building on Wall Street since the turn of the century, and today it is a not-for-profit New York State corporation.

NYSE Membership

- The NYSE has 1,366 exchange members, who are said to own "seats" on the exchange. Collectively, they own the exchange, although it is managed by a professional staff.
- The seats are regularly bought and sold. In 2000, seats were selling for $2 million. They can be leased too. Both prospective buyers and leaseholders are first closely scrutinized.
- Seat holders can buy and sell securities on the exchange floor without paying commissions.

Types of Members

- Over 500 NYSE members are *commission brokers*. They execute customer orders to buy and sell stocks.

- Almost 500 NYSE members are *specialists*, or *market makers*. They are obligated to maintain a fair and orderly market for the securities assigned to them.

Types of Members

- When commission brokers are too busy, they may delegate some orders to *floor brokers*, or two-dollar brokers, for execution.
  - → Floor brokers have become less important because of the efficient *SuperDOT system* (<u>d</u>esignated <u>o</u>rder <u>t</u>urnaround), which allows orders to be transmitted electronically directly to the specialist.

- A small number of NYSE members are *floor traders*, who independently trade for their own accounts.

NYSE-Listed Stocks

- In late 2000, stocks from 3,025 companies were listed, representing 281 billion shares with a market value of $16 trillion.

- An initial listing fee, as well as annual listing fees, is charged based on the number of shares.

- To apply for listing, companies have to meet certain minimum requirements with respect to the number of shareholders, trading activity, the number and value of shares held in public hands, annual earnings, etc.

Work the Web

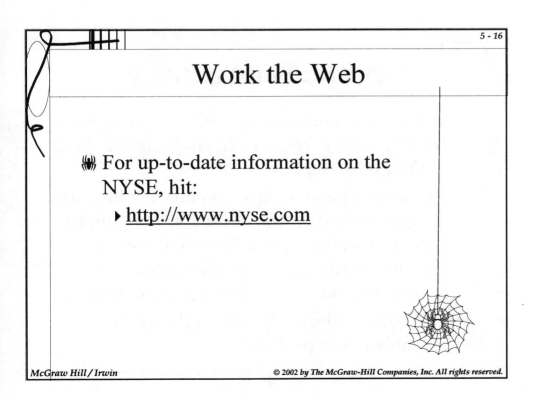

- For up-to-date information on the NYSE, hit:
  - http://www.nyse.com

Operation of the New York Stock Exchange

- ◆ The fundamental business of the NYSE is to attract and process *order flow*.
- ◆ In 2000, the average stock trading volume on the NYSE was just over 1 billion shares a day.
- ◆ About one-third of the volume is due to individual investors, while almost half is from institutional investors. The remainder represents NYSE-member trading, especially specialists acting as market makers.

NYSE Floor Activity

- ◆ There are a number of specialist's posts, each with a roughly figure-eight shape, on the floor of the exchange.
- ◆ At the telephone booths, commission brokers receive relayed customer orders, walk out to specialist's posts where the orders can be executed, and return to confirm order executions and receive new customer orders.
- ◆ The color of the coats worn indicate the person's job or position.

Stock Market Order Types

Type	Buy	Sell
Market order	Buy at best price available for immediate execution.	Sell at best price available for immediate execution.
Limit order	Buy at best price available, but not more than the preset limit price. Forgo purchase if limit is not met.	Sell at best price available, but not less than the preset limit price. Forgo sale if limit is not met.
Stop orders	*Start gain:* convert to a market order to buy when the stock price crosses the stop price from below.	*Stop gain:* convert to a market order to sell when the stock price crosses the stop price from below.
	Start loss: convert to a market order to buy when the stock price crosses the stop price from above.	*Stop loss:* convert to a market order to sell when the stock price crosses the stop price from above.

Stock Market Order Types

Type	Buy	Sell
Stop-limit orders	*Start-limit gain:* convert to a limit order to buy when the stock price crosses the stop price from below.	*Stop-limit gain:* convert to a limit order to sell when the stock price crosses the stop price from below.
	Start-limit loss: convert to a limit order to buy when the stock price crosses the stop price from above.	*Stop-limit loss:* convert to a limit order to sell when the stock price crosses the stop price from above.
Short-sale order	Borrow stock shares and then sell the borrowed shares with the hope of buying them back later at a lower price. According to the *NYSE uptick rule*, a short sale can only be executed if the last price change was an uptick.	

Nasdaq

- ◆ Introduced in 1971, the Nasdaq market is a computer network of securities dealers who disseminate timely security price quotes to Nasdaq subscribers.
- ◆ It is the second largest stock market in the U.S. in terms of total dollar volume of trading.
- ◆ The name "Nasdaq" is derived from the acronym NASDAQ, which stands for National Association of Securities Dealers Automated Quotations system.

Nasdaq

- ◆ There are two key differences between the NYSE and Nasdaq:
- ① Nasdaq is a computer network and has no physical location where trading takes place.
- ② Nasdaq has a multiple market maker system rather than a specialist system.
  - → Like NYSE specialists though, Nasdaq market makers use their inventory as a buffer to absorb buy and sell order imbalances.

Nasdaq

 Over-the-counter (OTC) market
Securities market in which trading is almost
exclusively done through dealers who buy
and sell for their own inventories.

- Nasdaq is often referred to as an OTC market.
- Note that the Nasdaq is actually made up of
two separate markets, the Nasdaq National
Market (NNM) and the Nasdaq SmallCap
Market.

Nasdaq Participants

- In 2000, there were about 500 competing
Nasdaq dealers (market makers), which
amounts to about a dozen or so per stock.
- In the late 1990s, the Nasdaq system was
opened to the *electronic communications
networks (ECNs)*.
    → ECNs are websites that allow individual investors
    to trade directly with one another.
    → ECN orders are transmitted to the Nasdaq and
    displayed along with market maker prices.

Work the Web

🕸 You can actually watch trading take
place on the web by visiting Island,
one of the biggest ECNs:

  ▸ http://www.island.com

The Nasdaq System

- ◆ The Nasdaq network operates with three levels of information access.
- ◆ Level 1 terminals display median quotes from all registered market markers for a particular security.
- ◆ Level 2 terminals display price quotes, in particular, *inside quotes*.
- ◆ Level 3 terminals allow Nasdaq dealers to enter or change their price quote information.

NYSE and Nasdaq Competitors

 Third market
Off-exchange market for securities listed on an organized exchange.

 Fourth market
Market for exchange-listed securities in which investors trade directly with one another, usually through a computer network.

 ◆ For dually listed stocks, regional exchanges also attract substantial trading volume.

Stock Market Information

◆ The most widely followed barometer of day-to-day stock market activity is the *Dow Jones Industrial Average (DJIA)*, or "*Dow*" for short.

◆ The DJIA is an index of the stock prices of 30 large companies representative of American industry.

THE DOW JONES AVERAGES

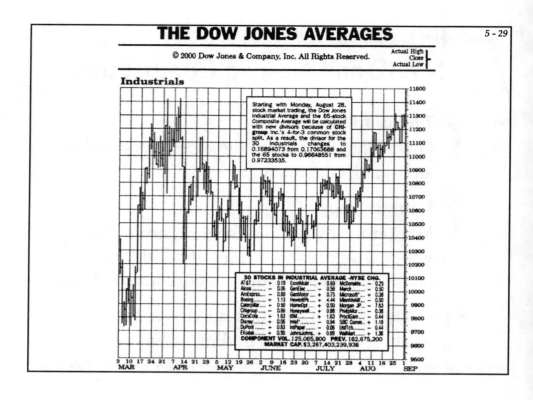

Work the Web

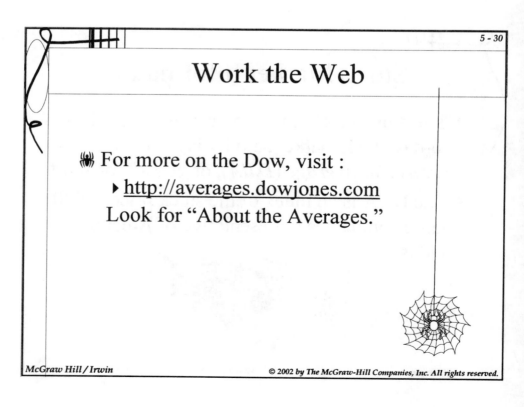

🕷 For more on the Dow, visit :

▸ http://averages.dowjones.com

Look for "About the Averages."

Stock Market Indexes

STOCK MARKET DATA BANK — 12/4/00

MAJOR INDEXES

†12-MO HIGH	LOW		DAILY HIGH	LOW	CLOSE	NET CHG	% CHG	†12-MO CHG	% CHG	FROM 12/31	% CHG
DOW JONES AVERAGES											
11722.98	9796.03	30 Industrials	10604.46	10319.31	10560.10	+ 186.56	+ 1.80	− 664.91	− 5.92	− 937.02	− 8.15
2960.50	2263.59	20 Transportation	2776.01	2733.63	x2767.77	+ 4.62	+ 0.17	− 137.75	− 4.74	− 209.43	− 7.03
401.47	269.20	15 Utilities	394.88	385.52	388.05	+ 2.67	+ 0.69	+ 106.74	+ 37.94	+ 104.69	+ 36.95
3305.46	2751.55	65 Composite	3201.11	3144.26	x3192.86	+ 38.74	+ 1.23	+ 45.62	+ 1.48	− 21.52	− 0.67
364.71	302.23	DJ US Total Mkt	306.99	301.74	305.06	+ 1.48	+ 0.49	− 23.50	− 7.15	− 36.51	− 10.69
STANDARD & POOR'S INDEXES											
1527.46	1314.95	500 Index	1332.06	1310.23	1324.97	+ 9.74	+ 0.74	− 98.36	− 6.91	− 144.28	− 9.82
1917.64	1554.92	Industrials	1582.32	1551.83	1572.32	+ 16.29	+ 1.05	− 196.75	− 11.12	− 269.60	− 14.64
341.15	215.62	Utilities	327.79	319.74	322.84	+ 3.10	+ 0.97	+ 97.72	+ 43.41	+ 95.62	+ 42.08
548.60	411.75	400 MidCap	490.95	484.33	488.72	− 1.80	− 0.37	+ 58.97	+ 13.72	+ 44.05	+ 9.91
225.12	183.00	600 SmallCap	201.68	199.47	199.90	− 1.25	− 0.62	+ 12.86	+ 6.88	+ 2.11	+ 1.07
324.40	280.79	1500 Index	284.76	280.29	283.20	+ 1.75	+ 0.62	− 15.79	− 5.28	− 25.69	− 8.32
NASDAQ STOCK MARKET											
5048.62	2597.93	Composite	2671.18	2567.18	2615.75	− 29.54	− 1.12	− 930.26	− 26.23	−1453.56	− 35.72
4704.73	2506.54	Nasdaq 100	2514.85	2475.63	2554.40	+ 4.66	+ 0.18	− 636.69	− 19.95	−1153.43	− 31.11
2841.00	1430.94	Industrials	1475.20	1434.05	1452.37	− 13.57	− 0.93	− 589.50	− 28.87	− 786.60	− 35.13
1990.01	1602.08	Insurance	1995.44	1974.55	1990.01	+ 0.29	+ 0.01	+ 59.06	+ 3.06	+ 93.73	+ 4.94
1789.09	1340.36	Banks	1764.22	1749.48	1758.95	− 8.67	− 0.49	+ 14.68	+ 0.84	+ 67.66	+ 4.00
2964.66	1469.82	Computer	1512.82	1435.89	1469.82	− 20.42	− 1.37	− 521.32	− 26.19	− 855.58	− 36.79
1230.06	463.36	Telecommunications	493.85	476.83	486.27	+ 1.86	+ 0.38	− 370.59	− 43.25	− 529.13	− 52.11
NEW YORK STOCK EXCHANGE											
677.58	576.42	Composite	638.11	629.56	637.41	+ 5.92	+ 0.94	− 4.25	− 0.66	− 12.89	− 1.98
851.94	739.53	Industrials	793.82	780.18	792.86	+ 10.78	+ 1.38	− 16.42	− 2.03	− 35.35	− 4.27
519.96	429.83	Utilities	440.84	434.49	438.75	+ 3.78	+ 0.87	− 77.15	− 14.95	− 72.40	− 14.16
477.51	353.51	Transportation	430.77	425.63	430.32	+ 0.79	+ 0.18	− 42.42	− 8.97	− 36.38	− 7.80
634.16	442.71	Finance	592.55	586.25	590.35	− 2.20	− 0.37	+ 70.10	+ 13.47	+ 73.74	+ 14.27
OTHERS											
1036.40	827.78	Amex Composite	858.20	851.83	857.08	+ 3.70	+ 0.43	+ 27.26	+ 3.29	− 19.89	− 2.27
813.71	692.40	Russell 1000	702.47	690.33	698.08	+ 3.92	+ 0.56	− 46.14	− 6.20	− 69.89	− 9.10
606.12	445.94	Russell 2000	456.89	450.39	450.39	− 6.45	− 1.41	− 15.36	− 3.30	− 54.36	− 10.77
844.78	714.47	Russell 3000	725.14	713.06	720.41	+ 3.12	+ 0.43	− 45.78	− 5.98	− 72.90	− 9.19
439.78	376.35	Value-Line	383.91	380.43	381.92	− 0.59	− 0.15	− 40.03	− 9.49	− 49.12	− 11.40
14751.64	11976.24	Wilshire 5000	....		12084.23	+ 46.79	+ 0.39	− 1135.6	− 8.59	−1728.44	− 12.51

McGraw Hill/Irwin   †-Based on comparable trading day in preceding year.

Stock Market Indexes

- Indexes can be distinguished in four ways:
  ① the market covered,
  ② the types of stocks included,
  ③ how many stocks are included, and
  ④ how the index is calculated (*price-weighted*, e.g. DJIA, versus *value-weighted*, e.g. S&P 500)

- Stocks that do not trade every day can cause *index staleness*.

Stock Market Indexes

- Note that for a price-weighted index, the problem of stock splits can be addressed by adjusting the index divisor.

$$\text{Index level} = \frac{\text{Sum of stock prices}}{\text{Index divisor}}$$

- As of August 28, 2000, the DJIA divisor was .16894073!

Chapter Review

- The Primary and Secondary Stock Markets
  - → The Primary Market for Common Stock
  - → The Secondary Market for Common Stock
  - → Dealers and Brokers
- The New York Stock Exchange
  - → NYSE Membership
  - → Types of Members
  - → NYSE-Listed Stocks

Chapter Review

- ◆ Operation of the New York Stock Exchange
  - → NYSE Floor Activity
  - → Special Order Types
- ◆ Nasdaq
  - → Nasdaq Operations
  - → Nasdaq Participants
  - → The Nasdaq System
- ◆ NYSE and Nasdaq Competitors

Chapter Review

- ◆ Stock Market Information
  - → The Dow Jones Industrial Average
  - → Stock Market Indexes
  - → More on Price-Weighted Indexes
  - → The Dow Jones Divisors

6

Chapter

Common Stock Valuation

Fundamentals
of Investments
Valuation & Management
second edition

Charles J. Corrado   Bradford D. Jordan

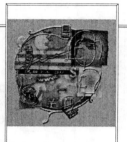

McGraw Hill / Irwin

Common Stock Valuation

Goal   Our goal in this chapter is to examine the methods commonly used by financial analysts to assess the economic value of common stocks.

- These methods are grouped into two categories:
  ① dividend discount models
  ② price ratio models

McGraw Hill / Irwin

Security Analysis: Be Careful Out There

Fundamental analysis
Examination of a firm's accounting statements and other financial and economic information to assess the economic value of a company's stock.

- The basic idea is to identify "undervalued" stocks to buy and "overvalued" stocks to sell.

- In practice however, such stocks may in fact be correctly priced for reasons not immediately apparent to the analyst.

The Dividend Discount Model

Dividend discount model (DDM)
Method of estimating the value of a share of stock as the present value of all expected future dividend payments.

$$V(0) = \frac{D(1)}{(1+k)} + \frac{D(2)}{(1+k)^2} + \frac{D(3)}{(1+k)^3} + \cdots + \frac{D(T)}{(1+k)^T}$$

where $V(0)$ = the present value of the future dividend stream
$D(t)$ = the dividend to be paid t years from now
k = the appropriate risk-adjusted discount rate

The Dividend Discount Model

- ◆ Assuming that the dividends will grow at a constant growth rate g,

$$D(t+1) = D(t) \times (1+g)$$

- ◆ Then

$$V(0) = \frac{D(0) \times (1+g)}{k-g}\left[1 - \left(\frac{1+g}{1+k}\right)^T\right] \qquad g \neq k$$

$$V(0) = T \times D(0) \qquad\qquad g = k$$

- ◆ This is the *constant growth rate model*.

The Dividend Discount Model

Example: Constant Growth Rate Model

- ◆ Suppose the dividend growth rate is 10%, the discount rate is 8%, there are 20 years of dividends to be paid, and the current dividend is $10. What is the value of the stock based on the constant growth rate model?

- ✦ $V(0) = \frac{\$10 \times (1.10)}{.08 - .10}\left[1 - \left(\frac{1.10}{1.08}\right)^{20}\right] = \$243.86$

- ✧ Thus the price of the stock should be $243.86.

The Dividend Discount Model

- Assuming that the dividends will grow *forever* at a constant growth rate *g*,

$$V(0) = \frac{D(0) \times (1+g)}{k-g} = \frac{D(1)}{k-g} \quad g < k$$

- This is the *constant perpetual growth model.*

The Dividend Discount Model

Example: Constant Perpetual Growth Model

- Consider the electric utility industry. In late 2000, the utility company Detroit Edison (DTE) paid a $2.06 dividend. Using D(0)=$2.06, k =8%, and g=2%, calculate a present value estimate for DTE. Compare this with the late-2000 DTE stock price of $36.13.

- $V(0) = \dfrac{\$2.06 \times (1.02)}{.08 - .02} = \$35.02$

- Our estimated price is a little lower than the $36.13 stock price.

The Dividend Discount Model

- ◆ The growth rate in dividends (g) can be estimated in a number of ways.
  - ① Using the company's historical average growth rate.
  - ② Using an industry median or average growth rate.
  - ③ Using the *sustainable growth rate*.

The Dividend Discount Model

Sustainable ~~growth rate~~ = ROE × Retention ratio

Return on equity (ROE) = Net income / Equity

Retention ratio = 1 – Payout ratio

The Dividend Discount Model

Example: The Sustainable Growth Rate

- DTE has a ROE of 12.5%, earnings per share (EPS) of $3.34, and a per share dividend ($D(0)$) of $2.06. Assuming $k = 8\%$, what is the value of DTE's stock?
  - ⟡ Payout ratio = $2.06/$3.34 = .617
    So, retention ratio = $1 - .617 = .383$ or 38.3%
  - ⟡ Sustainable growth rate = $12.5\% \times .383 = 4.79\%$
  - ⟡ $V(0) = \dfrac{\$2.06 \times (1.0479)}{.08 - .0479} = \$67.25 >> \$36.13$
  - ⟡ DTE's stock is perhaps undervalued, or more likely, its growth rate has been overestimated.

The Two-Stage Dividend Growth Model

- A two-stage dividend growth model assumes that a firm will initially grow at a rate g_1 for T years, and thereafter grow at a rate $g_2 < k$ during a perpetual second stage of growth.

$$V(0) = \frac{D(0)(1+g_1)}{k-g_1}\left[1 - \left(\frac{1+g_1}{1+k}\right)^T\right] + \left(\frac{1+g_1}{1+k}\right)^T \frac{D(0)(1+g_2)}{k-g_2}$$

Discount Rates for Dividend Discount Models

- ◆ The discount rate for a stock can be estimated using the *capital asset pricing model (CAPM)*.

- ◆ $\text{Discount rate} = \text{time value of money} + \text{risk premium}$

$$= \text{T-bill rate} + (\text{stock beta} \times \text{stock market risk premium})$$

T-bill rate = return on 90-day U.S. T-bills

stock beta = risk relative to an average stock

stock market risk premium = risk premium for an average stock

---

Observations on Dividend Discount Models

Constant Perpetual Growth Model

✓ Simple to compute.

✗ Not usable for firms that do not pay dividends.

✗ Not usable when $g > k$.

✗ Is sensitive to the choice of g and k.

✗ k and g may be difficult to estimate accurately.

✗ Constant perpetual growth is often an unrealistic assumption.

Observations on Dividend Discount Models

Two-Stage Dividend Growth Model

✓ More realistic in that it accounts for two stages of growth.

✓ Usable when $g > k$ in the first stage.

✗ Not usable for firms that do not pay dividends.

✗ Is sensitive to the choice of g and k.

✗ k and g may be difficult to estimate accurately.

Price Ratio Analysis

◆ *Price-earnings ratio (P/E ratio)*

→ Current stock price divided by annual earnings per share (EPS).

◆ *Earnings yield*

→ Inverse of the P/E ratio: earnings divided by price (E/P).

◆ High-P/E stocks are often referred to as *growth stocks*, while low-P/E stocks are often referred to as *value stocks*.

Price Ratio Analysis

- *Price-cash flow ratio (P/CF ratio)*
  - → Current stock price divided by current cash flow per share.
  - → In this context, cash flow is usually taken to be net income plus *depreciation*.
- Most analysts agree that in examining a company's financial performance, cash flow can be more informative than net income.
- Earnings and cash flows that are far from each other may be a signal of poor quality earnings.

Price Ratio Analysis

- *Price-sales ratio (P/S ratio)*
  - → Current stock price divided by annual sales per share.
  - → A high P/S ratio suggests high sales growth, while a low P/S ratio suggests sluggish sales growth.
- *Price-book ratio (P/B ratio)*
  - → Market value of a company's common stock divided by its book (accounting) value of equity.
  - → A ratio bigger than 1.0 indicates that the firm is creating value for its stockholders.

Price Ratio Analysis

Intel Corp (INTC) - Earnings (P/E) Analysis

Current EPS	$1.35
5-year average P/E ratio	30.4
EPS growth rate	16.5%

$$\frac{\text{expected}}{\text{stock price}} = \frac{\text{historical}}{\text{P/E ratio}} \times \text{projected EPS}$$

$$= \quad 30.4 \quad \times (\$1.35 \times 1.165)$$

$$= \underline{\$47.81}$$

* Late-2000 stock price = $89.88

Price Ratio Analysis

Intel Corp (INTC) - Cash Flow (P/CF) Analysis

Current CFPS	$1.97
5-year average P/CF ratio	21.6
CFPS growth rate	15.3%

$$\frac{\text{expected}}{\text{stock price}} = \frac{\text{historical}}{\text{P/CF ratio}} \times \text{projected CFPS}$$

$$= \quad 21.6 \quad \times (\$1.97 \times 1.153)$$

$$= \underline{\$49.06}$$

* Late-2000 stock price = $89.88

Price Ratio Analysis

Intel Corp (INTC) - Sales (P/S) Analysis

Current SPS	$4.56
5-year average P/S ratio	6.7
SPS growth rate	13.3%

$$\frac{\text{expected}}{\text{stock price}} = \frac{\text{historical}}{\text{P/S ratio}} \times \text{projected SPS}$$

$$= \quad 6.7 \quad \times (\$4.56 \times 1.133)$$

$$= \underline{\$34.62}$$

* Late-2000 stock price = $89.88

An Analysis of the McGraw-Hill Company

McGRAW-HILL NYSE-MHP

| RECENT PRICE | 59 | P/E RATIO | 24.6 | Trailing: 26.3 Median: 18.0 | RELATIVE P/E RATIO | 1.74 | DIV'D YLD | 1.6% | VALUE LINE | 1881 |

High:	21.5	15.3	16.2	18.8	19.3	21.9	24.6	37.7	51.7	63.1	62.1
Low:	13.4	10.0	12.4	13.3	13.8	15.6	15.9	22.4	34.3	47.1	41.9

TIMELINESS 3 Lowered 3/24/00

SAFETY 1 Raised 6/4/93

TECHNICAL 3 Raised 12/24/99

BETA .85 (1.00 = Market)

2003-05 PROJECTIONS
	Price	Gain	Ann'l Total Return
High	105	(+80%)	17%
Low	85	(+45%)	11%

Insider Decisions
	O	N	D	J	F	M	A	M	J
to Buy	0	1	0	0	0	0	0	0	0
Options	2	1	2	1	0	0	0	1	0
to Sell	0	1	2	1	0	0	0	1	0

Institutional Decisions
	3Q1998	4Q1999	1Q2000
to Buy	156	154	180
to Sell	173	187	182
Hld'd(000)	149418	148417	145129

Percent shares traded 12.0 / 8.0 / 4.0

LEGENDS
- 13.0 x "Cash Flow" p sh
- Relative Price Strength
- 2-for-1 split 4/96
- 2-for-1 split 3/99
- Options: Yes
- Shaded area indicates recession

Target Price Range 2003 2004 2005

% TOT. RETURN 7/00
	THIS STOCK	VL ARITH. INDEX
1 yr.	17.8	3.2
3 yr.	63.6	28.3
5 yr.	243.2	94.9

1984	1985	1986	1987	1988	1989	1990	1991	1992	1993	1994	1995	1996	1997	1998	1999	2000	2001	© VALUE LINE PUB., INC.	03-05
6.96	7.40	7.81	9.08	9.36	9.19	9.91	9.90	10.43	11.11	13.90	14.66	15.45	17.83	18.92	20.40	23.35	26.20	Sales per sh A	34.90
.85	.95	1.02	1.15	1.20	1.20	1.22	1.00	1.04	1.15	2.18	2.29	2.46	2.95	3.25	3.63	4.25	4.85	"Cash Flow" per sh	8.75
.72	.73	.76	.78	.86	.85	.88	.76	.78	.86	1.03	1.14	1.25	1.46	1.71	2.02	2.40	2.75	Earnings per sh B	3.95
.31	.34	.38	.42	.46	.50	.54	.55	.55	.57	.58	.60	.66	.72	.78	.86	.94	1.02	Div'ds Decl'd per sh C■	1.28
.25	.24	.21	.27	.23	.30	.49	.26	.28	.25	.39	.29	.32	.40	.91	.55	.55	.45	Cap'l Spending per sh	.45
3.46	3.85	4.26	4.28	4.75	4.52	4.88	5.09	4.62	4.16	4.50	5.17	6.84	7.24	7.87	8.64	9.45	10.40	Book Value per sh D	14.85
201.31	201.60	202.00	192.89	194.23	194.74	195.71	196.18	196.54	197.65	198.69	200.29	199.06	198.20	197.11	195.71	193.20	191.70	Common Shs Outst'g E	187.20
14.4	15.7	18.5	21.1	17.4	20.4	14.8	18.5	19.1	18.2	16.9	16.7	17.7	20.6	23.6	25.8	Bold figures are Value Line estimates		Avg Ann'l P/E Ratio	34.0
1.34	1.27	1.25	1.41	1.44	1.54	1.10	1.19	1.16	1.08	1.11	1.12	1.11	1.19	1.23	1.53			Relative P/E Ratio	1.80
3.0%	3.1%	2.7%	2.6%	3.1%	2.9%	4.1%	3.9%	3.7%	3.6%	3.4%	3.2%	3.0%	2.4%	1.9%	1.6%			Avg Ann'l Div'd Yield	1.3%

CAPITAL STRUCTURE as of 6/30/00
Total Debt $694.3 mill. **Due in 5 Yrs** $694.3 mill.
LT Debt $353.1 mill. **LT Interest** $23.0 mill.
(LT int. earned: 26.0x; total int. coverage: 18.2x)
(17% of Cap'l)

Leases, Uncapitalized Annual rentals $89.0 mill.
Pension Liability None

Pfd Stock None
Common Stock 194,700,000 shs. (83% of Cap'l)
outstanding as of 7/14/00

MARKET CAP: $11.5 billion (Large Cap)

	1938.6	1943.0	2050.5	2195.5	2760.9	2935.3	3074.7	3534.1	3729.1	3992.0	4515	5020	Sales ($mill)	6530
	20.2%	16.4%	16.4%	15.8%	21.9%	21.8%	21.5%	22.0%	22.8%	24.7%	25.5%	25.5%	Operating Margin	26.5%
	66.8	48.9	51.3	54.9	230.0	231.4	238.6	293.5	299.2	308.4	360	405	Depreciation ($mill)	520
	172.5	148.0	153.2	172.2	203.1	227.1	250.1	290.7	341.9	401.6	465	530	Net Profit ($mill)	745
	43.0%	42.7%	42.7%	41.8%	41.2%	41.2%	38.3%	38.3%	39.0%	39.0%	38.5%	38.5%	Income Tax Rate	38.5%
	8.9%	7.6%	7.5%	7.8%	7.4%	7.7%	8.1%	8.2%	9.2%	10.1%	10.3%	10.6%	Net Profit Margin	11.4%
	116.4	123.6	70.3	62.9	116.1	193.3	190.9	258.2	137.3	28.2	210	315	Working Cap'l ($mill)	550
	507.5	437.3	358.7	757.6	657.5	557.4	556.9	607.0	452.1	354.8	400	380	Long-Term Debt ($mill)	350
	954.3	999.0	908.8	823.0	913.1	1035.1	1361.1	1434.7	1551.8	1691.5	1825	1995	Shr. Equity ($mill)	2745
	13.4%	11.8%	13.2%	11.8%	14.4%	15.9%	14.2%	15.4%	18.1%	20.6%	22.0%	23.5%	Return on Total Cap'l	25.0%
	18.1%	14.8%	16.9%	20.9%	22.2%	21.9%	18.4%	20.3%	22.0%	23.7%	25.5%	26.5%	Return on Shr. Equity	27.0%
	7.0%	4.1%	4.8%	7.3%	9.7%	10.4%	8.7%	10.3%	12.1%	13.7%	15.5%	17.0%	Retained to Com Eq	18.5%
	61%	72%	71%	65%	56%	53%	53%	49%	45%	42%	39%	37%	All Div'ds to Net Prof	32%

CURRENT POSITION ($MILL.) 1998 1999 6/30/00
Cash Assets 10.5 6.5 8.7

CURRENT POSITION ($MILL.)
	1998	1999	6/30/00
Cash Assets	10.5	6.5	8.7
Receivables	950.3	1052.6	970.4
Inventory (FIFO)	264.7	295.3	410.6
Other	183.3	199.3	207.2
Current Assets	1428.8	1553.7	1596.9
Accts Payable	102.3	340.2	258.5
Debt Due	75.5	181.6	341.2
Other	1113.7	1003.7	934.2
Current Liab.	1291.5	1525.5	1533.9

ANNUAL RATES
of change (per sh)	Past 10 Yrs.	Past 5 Yrs.	Est'd '97-'99 to '03-'05
Sales	7.5%	10.0%	10.5%
"Cash Flow"	10.5%	17.5%	13.0%
Earnings	7.5%	14.0%	15.0%
Dividends	5.5%	6.5%	8.0%
Book Value	6.0%	12.0%	11.0%

QUARTERLY SALES ($ mill.)
Calendar	Mar.31	Jun.30	Sep.30	Dec.31	Full Year
1997	652.9	836.7	1143	901.5	3534.1
1998	703.4	861.1	1206	938.6	3729.1
1999	716.9	923.1	1318	1034	3992.0
2000	802.5	1019	1510	1183.5	4515
2001	890.0	1160	1675	1295	5020

EARNINGS PER SHARE B
Calendar	Mar.31	Jun.30	Sep.30	Dec.31	Full Year
1997	.08	.33	.72	.33	1.46
1998	.10	.39	.85	.37	1.71
1999	.12	.45	.96	.49	2.02
2000	.24	.55	1.10	.51	2.40
2001	.29	.60	1.26	.60	2.75

QUARTERLY DIVIDENDS PAID C■
Calendar	Mar.31	Jun.30	Sep.30	Dec.31	Full Year
1996	.165	.165	.165	.165	.66
1997	.18	.18	.18	.18	.72
1998	.195	.195	.195	.195	.78
1999	.215	.215	.215	.215	.86
2000	.235	.235			

BUSINESS: The McGraw-Hill Companies, Inc. is a multimedia information provider. Publishes textbooks, technical and popular books, periodicals (*Business Week, Aviation Week, ENR, et al*). Entered Macmillan/McGraw-Hill School Publish. joint venture in '89; purchased remaining 50% in 10/93. Markets info. svcs. for the financial and construc. fields (*Standard & Poor's, J.J. Kenny, F.W.* Dodge, *Data Resources, Platt's*). Owns 4 TV stations. Labor costs: est'd 32% of sales. 1999 deprec. rate: 31%. Has 16,376 emplys.; 7,370 stkhldrs. Offcrs. & Dirctrs. own 1.3% of shares (3/00 Proxy). Chairman, President and CEO: Harold (Terry) McGraw III. Inc.: New York. Address: 1221 Avenue of the Americas, New York, NY 10020. Tel.: 212-512-2000. Internet: www.mcgraw-hill.com.

McGraw-Hill recently announced its intention to acquire Tribune's education division, in order to strengthen its industry-leading K-12 product line. Tribune Education, a publisher of supplementary and higher education texts, as well as professional and consumer materials, had 1999 pro forma revenues of $384 million. MHP will pay $635 million, subject to post-closing adjustments for the division. Tribune and MHP will split the profits evenly, but MHP will keep the assets. The deal will be funded with commercial paper, which will bring the company's long-term debt up to about $1 billion. The deal should be only mildly dilutive (about 5¢ per share) in 2000, and accretive thereafter. It would also be complementary for McGraw-Hill, and although the Justice Department has asked for more information on the acquisition, we do not foresee any problems closing the deal in the current quarter. Meanwhile...

The company's other businesses are performing well. The Financial Services segment is holding up, even as new-issue volume continues to decrease. Non-transaction services are keeping the ship afloat until pent-up demand, caused by fears that the Fed will continue to raise interest rates, is released. The Information and Media Services division is being paced by *Business Week*. Ad pages were up significantly in the first half of the year, and 125% so far in the third quarter. We see nothing to slow these divisions in the near future either.

High-quality McGraw-Hill shares offer decent risk-adjusted total-return potential for the 3- to 5-year pull. A strong adoption schedule, the projected cost efficiencies of the Tribune purchase, and the continued strength of *Business Week* should help McGraw-Hill realize double-digit earnings growth over the next 3 to 5 years. The neutrally ranked stock is a quality selection for solid, consistent returns.
Daniel Davidowitz *August 25, 2000*

Sales (and Operating Margins*) by Business Line
	1998	1999	2000	2001
Ed./Prof Publ.	1629.3 (12.5%)	1734.5 (15.3%)	1905 (17.9%)	2790 (17.0%)
Financial Svcs.	1152.7 (31.6%)	1224.6 (30.2%)	1405 (31.3%)	1495 (31.3%)
Info./Media Svc.	956.1 (12.0%)	1032.5 (17.4%)	1405 (19.0%)	1735 (19.3%)
Segment Total	3729.1 (18.9%)	3992.0 (20.6%)	4515 (21.3%)	5020 (22.9%)
*After depreciation; before corporate and interest expenses.

(A) Includes Macmillan/McGraw-Hill Publishing Co. from 10/93. (B) Diluted earnings, beginning 1997. Excl. nonrecurring gains, (losses): '97, 4¢; '98, 10¢; '89, (61¢); '93, (82¢); '96, $1.23; '98, (5¢); '99, (12¢); Q1'00, 5¢. Next earnings report due late Oct. (C) Next div'd meeting about Oct. 19. Goes ex about Nov. 25. Approximate dividend payment dates: 12th of March, June, Sept. Dec. ■ Div'd reinvestment plan available. (D) Includes intangibles. In '99: $1253 mill., $6.40/share. (E) In millions, adjusted for stock splits.

Company's Financial Strength A+
Stock's Price Stability 95
Price Growth Persistence 85
Earnings Predictability 100

Getting the Most from the Value Line Page

P/E ratio—the stock's recent price divided by the latest six months' earnings per share plus earnings estimated for the next six months.

Trailing P/E—the recent price divided by the sum of earnings per share during the past 12 months.

Median P/E—the mean of the four middle values of the average annual price-earnings ratios over the past ten years.

The LEGENDS box contains the "Cash Flow" multiple as well as the amounts and dates of recent stock splits and dividends. Also shows if options are traded on the stock.

Monthly price ranges of the stock—plotted on a ratio (logarithmic) grid to show percentage changes in true proportion.

The "Cash Flow" line—a graphic presentation of cash flow per share, multiplied by a number selected so that the line correlates with a stock's monthly price range.

Relative P/E ratio—the stock's P/E divided by the median P/E for all stocks under Value Line review.

Dividend yield—cash dividends estimated to be declared in the next 12 months divided by the recent price.

Here is the core of Value Line's advice—the rank for Timeliness; the rank for Safety; the Technical rank. And next to each is normally the date each last changed. Beta shows the stock's sensitivity to fluctuations in the market as a whole.

Projected stock price returns to 2003-05, both absolute (gain/loss without dividends) and total (annual, including dividends).

The record of insider decisions—decisions by officers and directors to buy or sell as reported to the SEC.

The number of large institutions—including banks, insurance companies, mutual funds—buying or selling during the past three quarters and the total number of shares owned.

The capital structure as of recent date showing the percentage of capital in long-term debt and shareholders' equity. Also, Market Capitalization.

The stock's highest and lowest prices of the year.

The 3- to 5-year Target Price Range, estimated. These are the same ranges shown numerically in the "2003-05 Projections" box on the left side of the price chart.

The % Total Return shows price appreciation (plus dividends) of the stock for the past 1, 3, and 5 years and also for the stock market, as measured by the Value Line Arithmetic Index.

The number of shares traded monthly as a percentage of the total outstanding.

Statistical array that reveals significant long-term trends. Note that the statistics for the current and future years are estimated. The estimates are revised when necessary in the weekly Summary & Index.

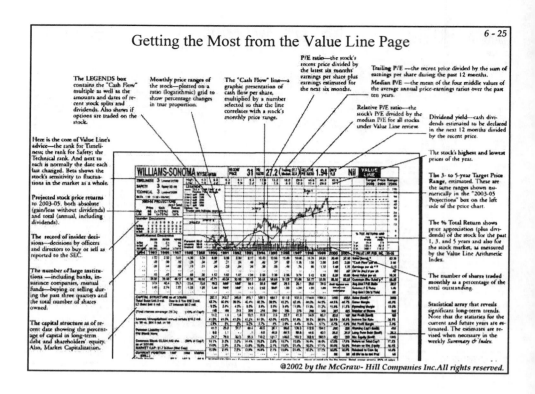

Getting the Most from the Value Line Page

Current position—current assets and current liabilities, the components of working capital.

Annual rates of change (on a per-share basis). Actual past, estimated future.

Sales and earnings are shown for each quarter, with earnings on a per share basis.

Quarterly dividends paid are actual payments. The total of dividends paid in four quarters may not equal the figure shown in the annual series on dividends declared. (Sometimes a dividend declared at the end of the year will be paid in the first quarter of the following year).

Footnotes explain a number of things, such as the way earnings are reported, and the net effect of nonrecurring items.

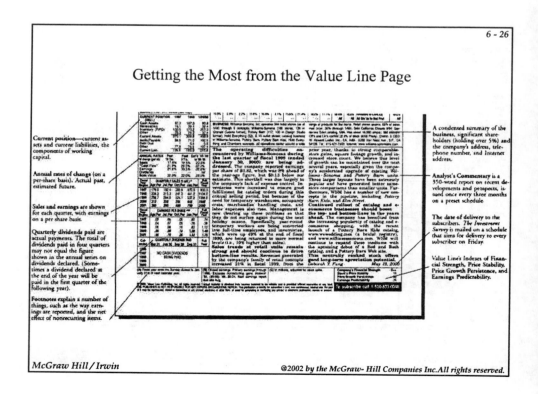

A condensed summary of the business, significant shareholders (holding over 5%) and the company's address, telephone number, and Internet address.

Analyst's Commentary is a 350-word report on recent developments and prospects, issued once every three months on a preset schedule.

The date of delivery to the subscribers. The Investment Survey is mailed on a schedule that aims for delivery to every subscriber on Friday.

Value Line's Indexes of Financial Strength, Price Stability, Price Growth Persistence, and Earnings Predictability.

McGraw Hill / Irwin

An Analysis of the McGraw-Hill Company

- ◆ Based on the CAPM,
  $k = 6\% + (.85 \times 9\%) = 13.65\%$
- ◆ Retention ratio $= 1 - \$1.02/\$2.75 = 62.9\%$

  sustainable $g = .629 \times 25.5\% = 16.04\%$
- ◆ Since $g > k$, the constant growth rate model cannot be used.

An Analysis of the McGraw-Hill Company

Price Ratio Calculations for McGraw-Hill Company (MHP)						
	1995	1996	1997	1998	1999	Average
EPS	$1.14	$1.25	$1.46	$1.71	$2.02	$1.52
P/E	16.70	17.70	20.60	23.60	26.80	21.08
CFPS	$2.29	$2.46	$2.95	$3.25	$3.63	$2.92
P/CFPS	8.31	8.99	10.19	12.42	14.91	10.96
SPS	$14.66	$15.45	$17.83	$18.92	$20.40	$17.45
P/SPS	1.30	1.43	1.69	2.13	2.65	1.84

Quick calculations used: P/CF = P/E $\times$ EPS/CFPS

P/S = P/E $\times$ EPS/SPS

An Analysis of the McGraw-Hill Company

Price Ratio Analysis for McGraw-Hill (MHP)
2000 Stock Price: $59

	Earnings (P/E)	Cash Flow (P/CF)	Sales (P/S)
Current value per share	$2.45	$4.25	$22.35
Five-year average price ratio	21.08	10.96	1.84
Growth rate	15.0%	13.0%	10.5%
Expected stock price	$59.39	$52.64	$45.44

Work the Web

- Check out:
  - New York Society of Security Analysts
    http://www.nyssa.com
  - American Association of Individual Investors
    http://www.aaii.com
  - Association for Investment Management and Research
    http://www.aimr.com

Chapter Review

- ◆ Security Analysis: Be Careful Out There
- ◆ The Dividend Discount Model
  - → Constant Dividend Growth Rate Model
  - → Constant Perpetual Growth
  - → Applications of the Constant Perpetual Growth Model
  - → The Sustainable Growth Rate

Chapter Review

- ◆ The Two-Stage Dividend Growth Model
  - → Discount Rates for Dividend Discount Models
  - → Observations on Dividend Discount Models
- ◆ Price Ratio Analysis
  - → Price-Earnings Ratios
  - → Price-Cash Flow Ratios
  - → Price-Sales Ratios
  - → Price-Book Ratios
  - → Applications of Price Ratio Analysis

Chapter Review

- ◆ An Analysis of the McGraw-Hill Company

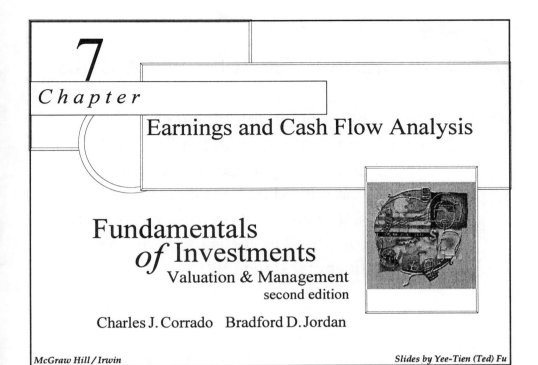

7
Chapter

Earnings and Cash Flow Analysis

Fundamentals *of* Investments
Valuation & Management
second edition

Charles J. Corrado   Bradford D. Jordan

McGraw Hill / Irwin

Slides by Yee-Tien (Ted) Fu

Cash Flow is a Company's Lifeblood.

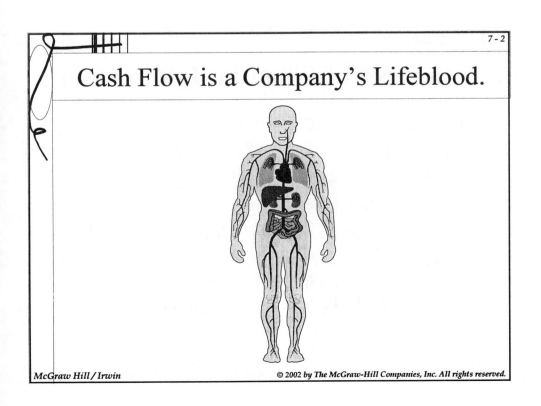

Earnings and Cash Flow Analysis

Goal

Our goal in this chapter is to acquaint you with the financial accounting concepts necessary to understand basic financial statements and perform earnings and cash flow analysis using these financial statements.

Sources of Financial Information

- ◆ Company annual reports
- ◆ Internet
  - → The New York Stock Exchange at http://www.nyse.com
- ◆ Securities and Exchange Commission (SEC)
  - → Electronic Data gathering and Retrieval (EDGAR) archives (including 10Ks and 10Qs) accessible through the Internet (http://www.sec.gov)

Sources of Financial Information

- SEC *Regulation FD* (*Fair Disclosure*) requires companies making a public disclosure of material nonpublic information to do so fairly without preferential recipients.
  - → Most companies satisfy Regulation FD by distributing important announcements via e-mail alerts to those who register for the service.

Financial Statements

 Balance sheet
Accounting statement that provides a snapshot view of a company's assets and liabilities on a particular date.

 Income statement
Summary statement of a firm's revenues and expenses over a specific accounting period, usually a quarter or a year.

Financial Statements

 Cash flow statement
Analysis of a firm's sources and uses of cash over the accounting period, summarizing operating, investing, and financing cash flows.

Work the Web

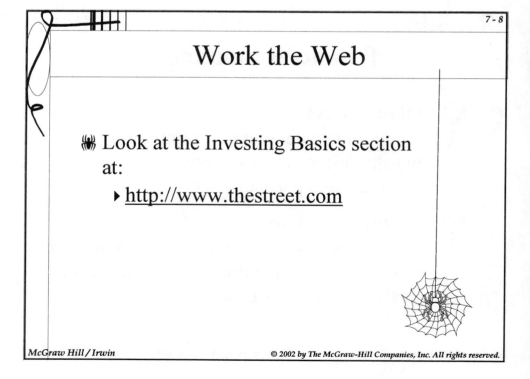 Look at the Investing Basics section at:
  ‣ http://www.thestreet.com

The Balance Sheet

- *Asset* - Anything a company owns that has value.
- *Liability* - A firm's financial obligation.
- *Equity* - An ownership interest in the company.
- Fundamental accounting identity:

> Assets = Liabilities + Equity

The Balance Sheet

TABLE 7.1

Borg Corporation
Balance Sheets, 2536 and 2535

	Year 2536	Year 2535
Current assets		
Cash	$ 2,000	$ 1,356
Accounts receivable	1,200	1,200
Prepaid expenses	500	500
Materials and supplies	300	300
Inventory	6,000	6,000
Total current assets	$ 10,000	$ 9,356
Fixed assets		
Plant facilities	$ 35,000	$35,000
Production equipment	20,000	20,000
Administrative facilities	15,000	15,000
Patents	10,000	10,000
Accumulated depreciation	(20,000)	(17,000)
Total fixed assets	$ 60,000	$63,000
Investments		
Cardassian Mining		
7% Preferred stock	$ 10,000	$10,000
Klingon Enterprises		
Common stock	10,000	
Goodwill	5,000	
Total investments	$ 25,000	$10,000
Other assets	5,000	5,000
Total assets	$100,000	$87,356
Current liabilities		
Short-term debt	$ 10,000	$10,000
Accounts payable	2,000	2,000
Leasing obligations	3,000	3,000
Total current liabilities	$ 15,000	$15,000
Long-term debt	$ 30,000	$20,000
Other liabilities	5,000	5,000
Total liabilities	$ 50,000	$40,000
Stockholder equity		
Paid-in capital	$ 10,000	$10,000
Retained earnings	40,000	37,356
Total stockholder equity	$ 50,000	$47,356
Total liabilities and equity	$100,000	$87,356
Shares outstanding	2,000	2,000
Year-end stock price	$40	$36

The Balance Sheet

Borg Corporation Condensed 2536 Balance Sheet			
Cash	$ 2,000	Current liabilities	$ 15,000
Operating assets	8,000	Long-term debt	30,000
Fixed assets	60,000	Other liabilities	5,000
Investments	25,000		
Other assets	5,000	Stockholder equity	50,000
Total assets	$100,000	Total liabilities and equity	$100,000

The Income Statement

- *Income* - The difference between a company's revenues and expenses, used to pay dividends to stockholders or kept as retained earnings within the company to finance future growth.

Net income = Revenues – Expenses

= Dividends + Retained earnings

The Income Statement

Borg Corporation Condensed Income Statement		
Net sales	$90,000	$90,000
Cost of goods sold	(70,000)	−70,000
Gross profit	$20,000	$20,000
Operating expenses	(13,000)	−13,000
Operating income	$ 7,000	$ 7,000
Investment income	700	+700
Interest expense	(2,000)	−2,000
Pretax income	$ 5,700	$ 5,700
Income taxes[a]	(2,056)	−2,056
Net income	$ 3,644	$ 3,644
Dividends	(1,000)	−1,000
Retained earnings	$ 2,644	$ 2,644

[a]A tax rate of 40 percent is applied to the total of operating income less interest expense plus the taxable 20 percent portion of preferred stock dividends (recorded as investment income): $7,000 − $2000 + 20% × $700 = $5,140 and 40% × $5,140 = $2,056.

The Cash Flow Statement

- *Cash flow* - Income realized in cash form, whether from operations, investments, or financing activities.

The Cash Flow Statement

Borg Corporation Condensed Cash Flow Statement		
Net income	$ 3,644	$ 3,644
Depreciation	3,000	+3,000
Operating cash flow	$ 6,644	$ 6,644
Investment cash flow[a]	(15,000)	−15,000
Financing cash flow[b]	9,000	+9,000
Net cash increase	$ 644	$ 644

[a]December 2536 purchase of 50 percent interest in Klingon Enterprises for $15,000 (including $5,000 goodwill).

[b]Issue of $10,000 par value 8 percent coupon bonds, less a $1,000 dividend payout.

Performance Ratios and Price Ratios

- Gross margin $= \dfrac{\text{Gross profit}}{\text{Net sales}}$

- Operating margin $= \dfrac{\text{Operating income}}{\text{Net sales}}$

- Return on assets (ROA) $= \dfrac{\text{Net income}}{\text{Total assets}}$

- Return on equity (ROE) $= \dfrac{\text{Net income}}{\text{Stockholder equity}}$

Performance Ratios and Price Ratios

- $$\text{Book value per share (BVPS)} = \frac{\text{Stockholder equity}}{\text{Shares outstanding}}$$

- $$\text{Earnings per share (EPS)} = \frac{\text{Net income}}{\text{Shares outstanding}}$$

- $$\text{Cash flow per share (CFPS)} = \frac{\textit{Operating} \text{ cash flow}}{\text{Shares outstanding}}$$

Performance Ratios and Price Ratios

- $$\text{Price-book (P/B)} = \frac{\text{Stock price}}{\text{BVPS}}$$

- $$\text{Price-earnings (P/E)} = \frac{\text{Stock price}}{\text{EPS}}$$

- $$\text{Price-cash flow (P/CF)} = \frac{\text{Stock price}}{\text{CFPS}}$$

Work the Web

 Check out the security analysis sections at:

▸ http://www.uoutperform.com

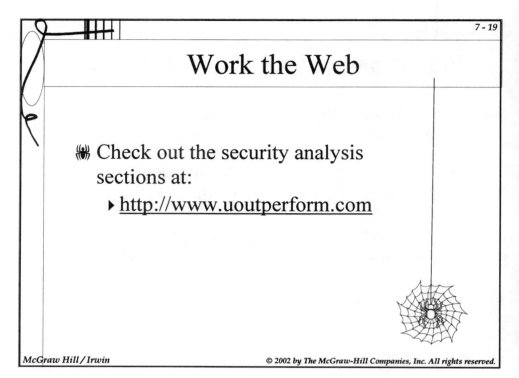

Financial Statement Forecasting

Pro forma financial statements
Statements prepared using certain assumptions about future income, cash flow, and other items. Pro forma literally means according to prescribed form.

The Pro Forma Income Statement

Borg Corporation
Pro Forma Income Statements

	Optimistic	Pessimistic
Net sales	$120,000	$100,000
Cost of goods sold	(90,000)	(80,000)
Gross profit	$ 30,000	$ 20,000
Operating expenses	(17,000)	(17,000)
Operating income	$ 13,000	$ 3,000
Investment income[a]	2,200	700
Interest expense[b]	(2,800)	(2,800)
Pretax income	$ 12,400	$ 900
Income taxes[c]	(4,136)	(136)
Net income	$ 8,264	$ 764
Dividends[d]	$ 1,000	$ 1,000
Retained earnings	$ 7,264	$ (236)

[a]Preferred stock dividends of $700 plus $1,500 noncash investment income from Ferengi Traders under optimistic sales results and $0 under pessimistic sales results, i.e., $700 + $1,500 = $2,200.

[b]Prior-year interest expense of $2,000 plus payment of 8 percent coupons on the December 2536 debt issue of $10,000, i.e. $2,000 + 8% × $10,000 = $2,800.

[c]Tax rate of 40% applied to the sum of operating income less interest expense plus the 20 percent taxable portion of preferred stock dividends, i.e., ($13,000 − $2,800 + 20% × $700) × 40% = $4,136.

[d]Assumes no change in dividends from prior year.

McGraw Hill/Irwin

The Pro Forma Cash Flow Statement

Borg Corporation
Pro Forma Cash Flow Statements

	Optimistic	Pessimistic
Net income	$ 8,264	$ 764
Depreciation/amortization[a]	3,200	3,200
Increase in operating assets[b]	(2,000)	(3,000)
Noncash investment income	(1,500)	0
Operating cash flow	$ 7,964	$ 964
Investment cash flow[c]	$ 0	$ 0
Financing cash flow[d]	$(1,000)	$(1,000)
Net cash increase	$ 6,964	$ (36)

[a]Assumes the same $3,000 depreciation as in the prior year and annual goodwill amortization of $200 based on a 25-year amortization schedule.

[b]Assumes an increase in operating assets of $2,000 under optimistic sales and $3,000 under pessimistic sales.

[c]Assumes no new investments.

[d]Assumes no change in dividend payouts.

McGraw Hill/Irwin

Borg Corporation Pro Forma Balance Sheets		
	Optimistic	Pessimistic
Cash[a]	$ 8,964	$ 1,964
Operating assets[b]	10,000	11,000
Fixed assets[c]	57,000	57,000
Investments[d]	26,300	24,800
Other assets	5,000	5,000
Total assets	$107,264	$99,764
Current liabilities	$ 15,000	$15,000
Long-term debt	30,000	30,000
Other liabilities	5,000	5,000
Stockholder equity[e]	57,264	49,764
Total liabilities and equity	$107,264	$99,764

[a]Prior-year cash of $2,000 plus $6,964 (optimistic) and −$36 (pessimistic) net cash increase from the pro forma cash flow statement.

[b]Prior-year operating assets of $8,000 plus an additional $2,000 under optimistic sales and $3,000 under pessimistic sales.

[c]Prior-year fixed assets of $60,000 less the assumed $3,000 depreciation.

[d]Prior-year investments of $25,000 plus noncash investment income of $1,500 under optimistic sales only less $200 goodwill amortization.

[e]Prior-year equity of $50,000 plus $7,264 (optimistic) and −$236 (pessimistic) retained earnings from the pro forma income statement.

Projected Profitability and Price Ratios

Borg Corporation

	Original	Optimistic	Pessimistic
Gross margin	22.22%	25%	20%
Operating margin	7.78%	10.83%	3%
ROA	3.64%	7.70%	.77%
ROE	7.29%	14.43%	1.54%
BVPS	$25	$28.63	$24.88
EPS	$1.82	$4.13	$.38
CFPS	$3.32	$3.98	$.48

Projected Profitability and Price Ratios

Borg Corporation

	Projected Stock Prices	
	Optimistic	Pessimistic
BVPS × P/B	$45.81	$39.81
EPS × P/E	$90.86	$8.36
CFPS × P/CF	$47.76	$5.76

Work the Web

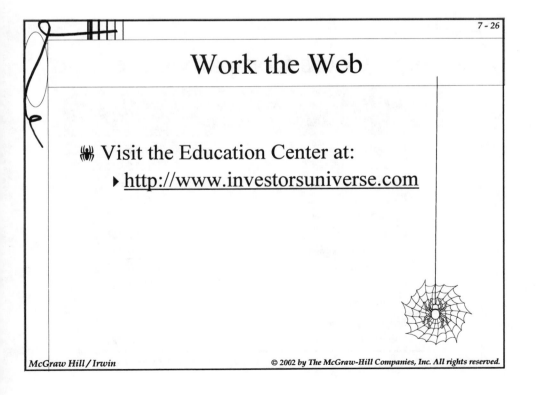

🕷 Visit the Education Center at:
  ▸ http://www.investorsuniverse.com

Adolph Coors Company Case Study

Adolph Coors Company 1999 Balance Sheet ($ in 000)	
Cash and cash equivalents	$ 163,808
Operating assets	449,013
Property, plant, equipment	714,001
Goodwill	31,292
Other assets	188,262
Total assets	$1,546,376
Current liabilities	$ 392,684
Long-term debt	105,000
Other liabilities	207,153
Total liabilities	$ 704,837
Paid-in capital	$ 15,476
Retained earnings	826,063
Total shareholder equity	$ 841,539
Total liabilities and equity	$1,546,376

McGraw Hill / Irwin

Adolph Coors Company Case Study

Adolph Coors Company 1999 Income Statement ($ in 000)	
Net sales	$2,056,646
Cost of goods sold	(1,215,965)
Gross profit	$ 840,681
Operating expenses	(698,698)
Operating income	$ 141,983
Other income	1,755
Net interest expense	6,929
Pretax income	$ 150,667
Income tax	(58,383)
Net income	$ 92,284
Earnings per share	$2.51
Shares outstanding (000)	36,729

McGraw Hill / Irwin

Adolph Coors Company
1999 Cash Flow Statement
($ in 000)

Net income	$ 92,284
Depreciation	123,770
Earnings in joint ventures	(32,189)
Loss on sale of properties	2,471
Change in deferred taxes	20,635
Changes in operating assets	(75,195)
Changes in current liabilities	38,012
Operating cash flow	$ 169,788
Net additions to properties	$(130,556)
Changes in other assets	39,793
Investing cash flow	$ (90,763)
Issuance/redemption of long-term debt	$ (40,000)
Issuance/purchase of stock	(10,994)
Dividends paid	(23,745)
Other financing	(1,692)
Financing cash flow	$ (76,431)
Net cash increase	$ 2,594
Net cash increase after foreign currency translation adjustment	$ 1,176

Adolph Coors Company Case Study

Adolph Coors Company
Pro Forma 2000 Income Statements
($ in 000, except earnings per share)

Sales Growth (%)	+10%	−10%
Net sales	$2,262,311	$1,850,981
Cost of goods sold[a]	(1,337,562)	(1,094,369)
Gross profit	$ 924,749	$ 756,613
Operating expenses*	(698,698)	(698,698)
Operating income	$ 226,051	$ 57,915
Other income	1,755	1,755
Net interest expense	6,929	6,929
Pretax income	$ 234,735	$ 66,599
Income tax[b]	(90,960)	(25,807)
Net income	$ 143,775	$ 40,792
Dividends	$ 23,745	$ 23,745
Retained earnings	$ 120,030	$ 17,047
Earnings per share	$3.91	$1.11
Shares outstanding	36,729	36,729

[a]Assumes a constant 1999 gross margin, which implies that cost of goods sold changes by the same ±10% as net sales.

[b]Assumes a constant 1999 average tax rate of 38.75 percent.

*Italics indicate items with constant 1999 values.

McGraw Hill / Irwin

© 2002 by The McGraw-Hill Companies, Inc. All rights reserved.

Adolph Coors Company Case Study

Adolph Coors Company Pro Forma 2000 Cash Flow Statements ($ in 000)		
Sales Growth (%)	+10%	−10%
Net income	$143,775	$ 40,792
Depreciation/amortization*	123,770	123,770
Changes in operating assets	(75,195)	(75,195)
Changes in current liabilities	38,012	38,012
Operating cash flow	$230,362	$127,379
Investing cash flow[a]	0	0
Financing cash flow[b]	(23,745)	(23,745)
Net cash increase	$206,617	$103,634

[a]Assumes zero investment cash flows.

[b]Assumes a zero change in shares outstanding, long-term debt, and other financing, but constant 1999 dividends of $23,745.

*Italics indicate items with constant 1999 values.

McGraw Hill / Irwin

Adolph Coors Company Pro Forma 2000 Balance Sheet ($ in 000)		
Sales Growth (%)	+10%	−10%
Cash	$ 370,425	$ 267,442
Operating assets[a]	524,208	524,208
Property, plant, equipment[b]	593,360	593,360
Goodwill	28,163	28,163
Other assets*	188,262	188,262
Total assets	$1,704,418	$1,601,435
Current liabilities[c]	$ 430,696	$ 430,696
Long-term debt	105,000	105,000
Other liabilities	207,153	207,153
Total liabilities	$ 742,849	$ 742,849
Paid-in capital	$ 15,476	$ 15,476
Retained earnings	946,093	843,110
Total shareholder equity	$ 961,569	$ 858,586
Total liabilities and equity	$1,704,418	$1,601,435

[a]1999 Operating assets of $449,013 plus an increase of $75,195.

[b]Depreciation and amortization of $123,770 is allocated as $3,129 of amortization (10 percent of 1999 goodwill) and $120,641 of depreciation.

[c]1999 Current liabilities of $392,684 plus $38,012.

*Italics indicate items with constant 1999 values.

Adolph Coors Company Case Study

	Original	+ 10%	− 10%
Gross margin	40.88%	40.88%	40.88%
Operating margin	6.90%	9.99%	3.13%
ROA	5.97%	8.44%	2.95%
ROE	10.97%	14.95%	4.75%
BVPS	$22.91	$26.18	$23.38
EPS	$2.51	$3.91	$1.11
CFPS	$4.62	$6.27	$3.47

Adolph Coors Company Case Study

	Projected Stock Prices	
	+ 10%	− 10%
BVPS × P/B	$58.27	$52.03
EPS × P/E	$79.46	$22.54
CFPS × P/CF	$69.19	$38.26

Chapter Review

- ◆ Sources of Financial Information

- ◆ Financial Statements
  - → The Balance Sheet
  - → The Income Statement
  - → The Cash Flow Statement
  - → Performance Ratios and Price Ratios

Chapter Review

- ◆ Financial Statement Forecasting
  - → The Pro Forma Income Statement
  - → The Pro Forma Cash Flow Statement
  - → The Pro Forma Balance Sheet
  - → Projected Profitability and Price Ratios

- ◆ Adolph Coors Company Case Study

8
Chapter

Stock Price Behavior and Market Efficiency

Fundamentals
of Investments
Valuation & Management
second edition

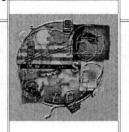

Charles J. Corrado   Bradford D. Jordan

McGraw Hill / Irwin
Slides by Yee-Tien (Ted) Fu

One of the Funny Things about the Stock Market

One of the funny things about the stock market is that every time one man buys, another sells, and both think they are astute..

– William Feather

McGraw Hill / Irwin

Stock Price Behavior and Market Efficiency

Goal Our goal in this chapter is to discuss bull markets, bear markets, as well as other market phenomena and psychology. We will also consider if anyone can consistently "beat the market."

Technical Analysis

 Technical analysis
Techniques for predicting market direction based on (1) historical price and volume behavior, and (2) investor sentiment.

◆ Technical analysts essentially search for bullish (positive) and bearish (negative) signals about stock prices or market direction.

Dow Theory

- ◆ The Dow theory is a method of interpreting and signaling changes in the stock market direction based on the monitoring of the Dow Jones Industrial and Transportation Averages.

- ◆ The Dow theory identifies three forces:
  - ① a primary direction or trend,
  - ② a secondary reaction or trend, and
  - ③ daily fluctuations.

Dow Theory

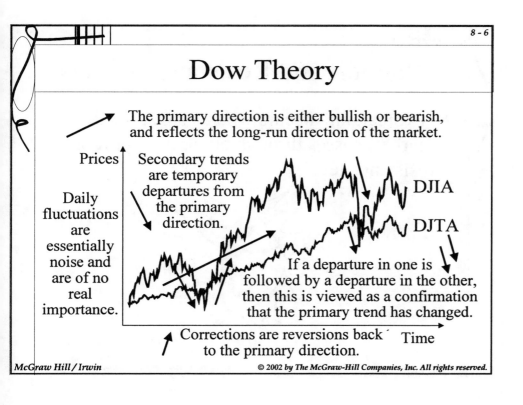

The primary direction is either bullish or bearish, and reflects the long-run direction of the market.

Prices

Secondary trends are temporary departures from the primary direction.

Daily fluctuations are essentially noise and are of no real importance.

DJIA

DJTA

If a departure in one is followed by a departure in the other, then this is viewed as a confirmation that the primary trend has changed.

Corrections are reversions back to the primary direction.

Time

Support and Resistance Levels

- A *support level* is a price or level below which a stock or the market as a whole is unlikely to go, while a *resistance level* is a price or level above which a stock or the market as a whole is unlikely to rise.

- Resistance and support areas are usually viewed as psychological barriers - bargain hunters help "support" the lower level, while profit takers "resist" the upper level.

Support and Resistance Levels

- A "breakout" occurs when a stock (or the market) passes through either a support or a resistance level.

Technical Indicators

STOCK MARKET DATA BANK	12/18/00		
DIARIES			
NYSE	MON	FRI	WK AGO
Issues traded	3,344	3,316	3,315
Advances	1,888	1,385	1,669
Declines	1,084	1,680	1,180
Unchanged	360	411	466
New highs	224	126	239
New lows	96	181	52
Adv vol (000)	709,792	465,213	739,502
Decl vol (000)	408,363	1,051,612	413,520
Total vol (000)	1,145,667	1,549,869	1,202,571
Closing tick	+686	+226	+468
Closing arms (trin)	1.09	1.93	.77
zBlock trades	25,189	25,422	25,652
NASDAQ			
Issues traded	4,703	4,599	4,637
Advances	1,606	1,381	2,309
Declines	2,440	2,511	1,673
Unchanged	657	707	655
New highs	59	26	90
New lows	206	255	122
Adv vol (000)	738,438	774,521	1,629,705
Decl vol (000)	1,290,249	1,753,356	697,823
Total vol (000)	2,057,304	2,541,547	2,412,520
Block trades	n.a.	34,920	30,321
AMEX			
Issues traded	808	789	810
Advances	297	226	355
Declines	354	385	281
Unchanged	157	178	174
New highs	12	10	21
New lows	77	61	37
Adv vol (000)	53,756	7,189	59,612
Decl vol (000)	11,976	60,957	4,364
Closed vol (000)	68,540	72,741	66,784
Comp vol (000)	103,405	112,540	98,963
Block trades	n.a.	1,732	1,456

Technical Indicators

Notes:

- The "advance/decline line" shows, for some period, the cumulative difference between advancing and declining issues.

- "Closing tick" is the difference between the number of shares that closed on an uptick and those that closed on a downtick.

- "Closing arms" or "trin" (<u>tr</u>ading <u>in</u>dex) is the ratio of average trading volume in declining issues to average trading volume in advancing issues.

- "zBlock trades" are trades in excess of 10,000 shares.

Charting

♦ *Relative strength charts* measure the performance of one investment relative to another.

Month	Stock A (4 shares)	Stock B (2 shares)	Relative Strength
1	$100	$100	1.00
2	96	96	1.00
3	88	90	0.98
4	88	80	1.10
5	80	78	1.03
6	76	76	1.00

McGraw Hill / Irwin

Charting

♦ *Moving average charts* are average daily prices or index levels, calculated using a fixed number of previous days' prices or levels, updated each day.

♦ Since the price fluctuations are smoothed out, such charts are used to identify short- and long-term trends, often along the lines suggested by Dow theory.

McGraw Hill / Irwin

Charting

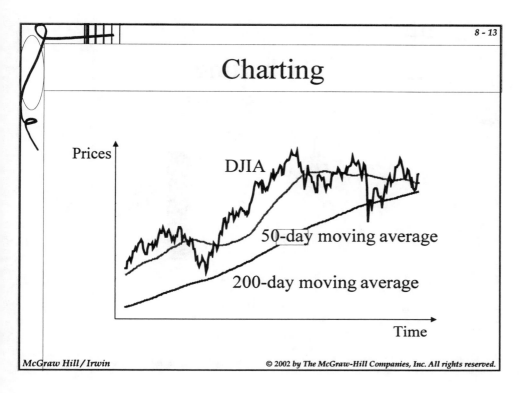

Prices

DJIA

50-day moving average

200-day moving average

Time

Charting

- A *hi-lo-close chart* is a bar chart showing, for each day, the high price, low price, and closing price.

- A *candlestick chart* is an extended version of the hi-lo-close chart. It plots the high, low, open, and closing prices, and also shows whether the closing price was above or below the opening price.

Charting

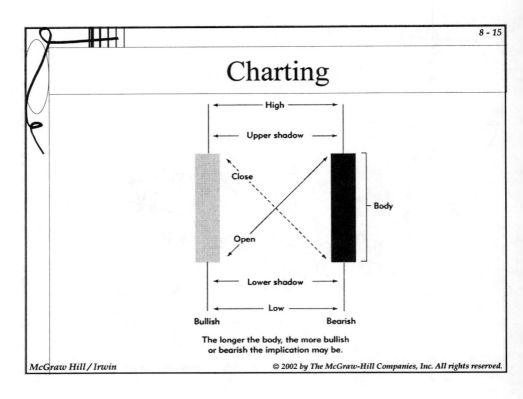

The longer the body, the more bullish
or bearish the implication may be.

Charting

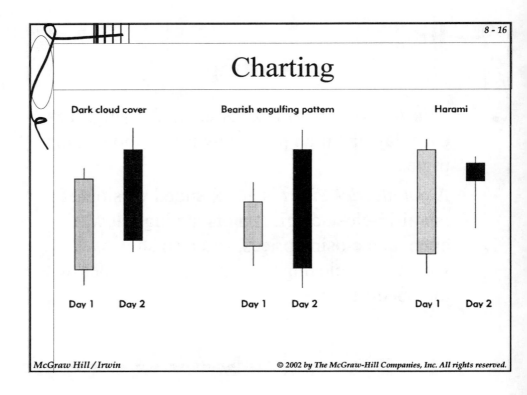

Charting

- *Point-and-figure charts* are a way of showing only major price moves and their direction.
- A "major" upmove is marked with an "X," while a "major" downmove is marked with an "O." A new column starts every time there is a change in direction.

Charting

Stock Price Information

Date	Price		Date	Price		Date	Price	
July 2	$50		July 13	$55		July 25	55	
July 3	51		July 16	56		July 26	56	X
July 5	52	X	July 17	54	O	July 27	58	X
July 6	51		July 18	54		July 30	60	X
July 9	54	X	July 19	54		July 31	54	O
July 10	54		July 20	53		August 1	55	
July 11	56	X	July 23	52	O	August 2	52	O
July 12	55		July 24	54	X	August 3	50	O

Point-and-Figure Chart

60			X	
58			X	
56	X		X	
54	X	O	X	O
52	X	O		O
50				O

Charting

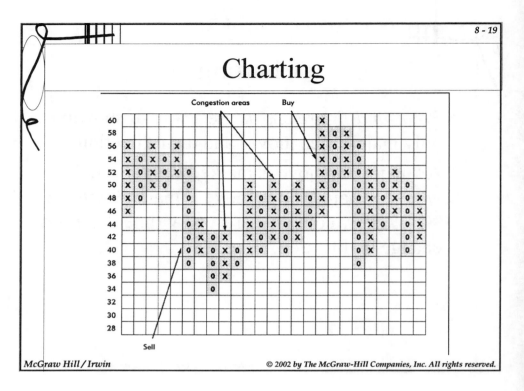

Chart Formations

- Once a chart is drawn, technical analysts examine it for various formations or pattern types in an attempt to predict stock price or market direction.

- One example is the *head-and-shoulders formation.*
  - → *When the stock price "pierces the neckline" after the right shoulder is finished, it's time to sell.*

Chart Formations

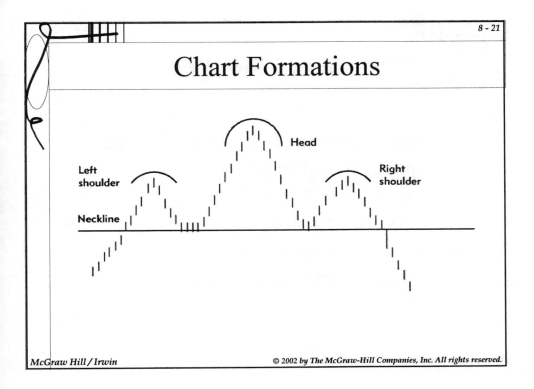

Other Technical Indicators

- The "odd-lot" indicator looks at whether odd-lot purchases are up or down.
- Followers of the "hemline" indicator claim that hemlines tend to rise in good times.
- The Super Bowl indicator forecasts the direction of the market based on whether the National Football Conference or the American Football Conference wins. A win by the National Football Conference is bullish.

Work the Web

 Learn more about technical analysis at:
  ▸ http://stockcharts.com
  Select "Chart School." Then try
    "Tools & Charts."

 You may also want to look at:
  ▸ http://www.bigcharts.com

Market Efficiency

Market efficiency
Relation between stock prices and information available to investors indicating whether it is possible to "beat the market." If a market is efficient, it is not possible, except by luck.

Efficient market hypothesis (EMH)
Theory asserting that, as a practical matter, the major financial markets reflect all relevant information at a given time.

What Does "Beat the Market" Mean?

- The *excess return* on an investment is the return in excess of that earned by other investments having the same risk.

- *"Beating the market"* means consistently earning a positive excess return.

Forms of Market Efficiency

 Weak-form efficient market
A market in which past prices and volume figures are of no use in beating the market.

 Semistrong-form efficient market
A market in which publicly available information is of no use in beating the market.

 Strong-form efficient market
A market in which information of any kind, public or private, is of no use in beating the market.

Why would a Market be Efficient?

- ◆ The driving force toward market efficiency is simply competition and the profit motive.
- ◆ Even relatively small performance enhancements can be worth tremendous amounts of money (when multiplied by the dollar amount involved), thereby creating the incentive to unearth relevant information and use it.

Are Financial Markets Efficient?

- ◆ Market efficiency is very difficult to test.
- ◆ There are four basic reasons for this:
  - ① The risk-adjustment problem.
  - ② The relevant information problem.
  - ③ The dumb luck problem.
  - ④ The data snooping problem.

Are Financial Markets Efficient?

◆ Nevertheless, three generalities about market efficiency can be made:

① Short-term stock price and market movements appear to be difficult to predict with any accuracy.

② The market reacts quickly and sharply to new information, and various studies find little or no evidence that such reactions can be profitably exploited.

③ If the stock market can be beaten, the way to do so is not obvious.

Some Implications of Market Efficiency

If markets are efficient ...

◆ ... security selection becomes less important, as the securities will be fairly priced.

◆ ... little role exists for professional money managers.

◆ ... it makes little sense to time the market.

Stock Price Behavior and Market Efficiency

◆ The *day-of-the-week effect* refers to the tendency for Monday to have a negative average return.

Average Daily S&P 500 Returns by Day of the Week
July 1962 - December 1994
Dividends Not Included

Weekday:	Mon	Tue	Wed	Thu	Fri
Avg return:	−.078%	.035%	.098%	.026%	.063%

Stock Price Behavior and Market Efficiency

◆ The *January effect* refers to the tendency for small stocks to have large returns in January.

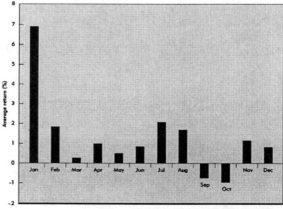

Stock Price Behavior and Market Efficiency

- On October 19, 1987 (Black Monday), the Dow plummeted 500 points to 1,700, leaving investors with about $500 billion in losses. The market lost over 20% of its value on a record volume of 600 million shares traded.

- NYSE circuit breakers are rules that kick in to slow or stop trading when the DJIA declines by more than a preset amount in a trading session.

Stock Price Behavior and Market Efficiency

- In 36 years (from 1963 to mid-1998), the S&P 500 index outperformed the general equity mutual funds (GEFs) 22 times.

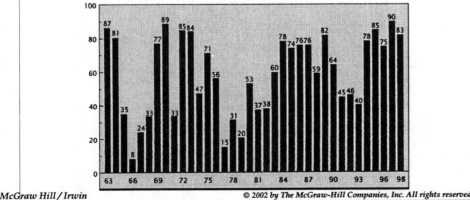

Chapter Review

- ◆ Technical Analysis
  - → Dow Theory
  - → Support and Resistance Levels
  - → Technical Indicators
  - → Charting
    - • Relative Strength Charts
    - • Moving Average Charts
    - • Hi-Lo-Close and Candlestick Charts
    - • Point-and-Figure Charts
  - → Chart Formations
  - → Other Technical Indicators

Chapter Review

- ◆ Market Efficiency
  - → What Does "Beat the Market" Mean?
  - → Forms of Market Efficiency
  - → Why would a Market be Efficient?
  - → Are Financial Markets Efficient?
  - → Some Implications of Market Efficiency

Chapter Review

- ◆ Stock Price Behavior and Market Efficiency
    - → The Day-of-the-Week Effect
    - → The Amazing January Effect
    - → The October 1987 Crash
    - → Performance of Professional Money Managers

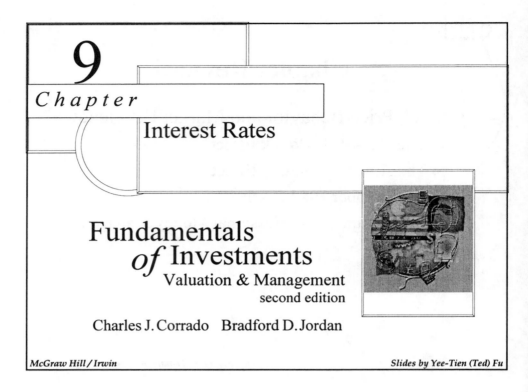

9

Chapter

Interest Rates

Fundamentals
of Investments
Valuation & Management
second edition

Charles J. Corrado   Bradford D. Jordan

Time is Money

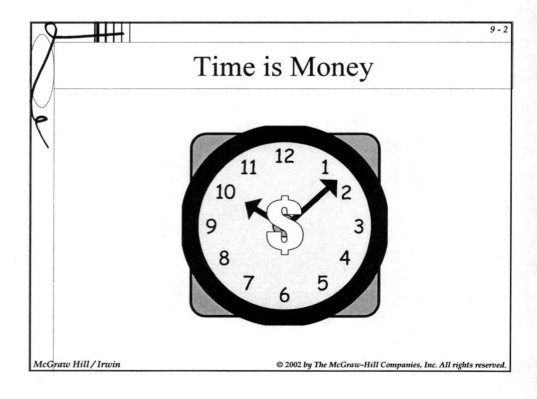

Interest Rates

Goal

Our goal in this chapter is to discuss the many different interest rates that are commonly reported in the financial press, as well as their basic determinants and separable components.

Interest Rate History

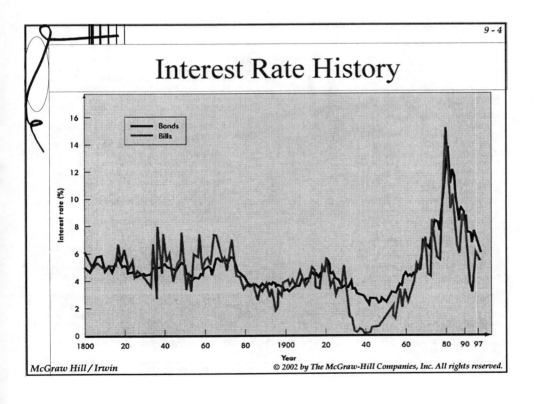

Work the Web

 For a look at interest rates from 3000 B.C., visit the historical research section at:

▸ http://www.pei-intl.com

MONEY RATES

Wednesday, January 17, 2001

The key U.S. and foreign annual interest rates below are a guide to general levels but don't always represent actual transactions.

PRIME RATE: 9.00% (effective 01/04/01). The base on corporate loans posted by at least 75% of the nation's 30 largest banks.

DISCOUNT RATE: 5.50% (effective 01/04/01). The charge on loans to depository institutions by the Federal Reserve Banks.

FEDERAL FUNDS: 6% high, 5 3/4 % low, 5 3/4% near closing bid, 5 7/8% offered. Reserves traded among commercial banks for overnight use in amounts of $1 million or more. Source: Prebon Yamane (U.S.A.) Inc. FOMC fed funds target rate 6.00% effective 01/03/01.

CALL MONEY: 7.75% (effective 01/04/01). The charge on loans to brokers on stock exchange collateral. Source: Reuters.

COMMERCIAL PAPER: placed directly by General Electric Capital Corp.: 5.79% 30 to 37 days; 5.71% 38 to 49 days; 5.65% 50 to 64 days; 5.54% 65 to 85 days; 5.50% 86 to 104 days; 5.44% 105 to 126 days; 5.35% 127 to 155 days; 5.30% 156 to 202 days; 5.25% 203 to 220 days.

EURO COMMERCIAL PAPER: placed directly by General Electric Capital Corp.: 4.78% 30 days; 4.77% two months; 4.76% three months; 4.73% four months; 4.70% five months; 4.67% six months.

DEALER COMMERCIAL PAPER: High-grade unsecured notes sold through dealers by major corporations: 5.80% 30 days; 5.70% 60 days; 5.60% 90 days.

CERTIFICATES OF DEPOSIT: Typical rates in the secondary market: 5.87% one month; 5.67% three months; 5.52% six months.

BANKERS ACCEPTANCES: 5.89% 30 days; 5.78% 60 days; 5.69% 90 days 5.63% 120 days; 5.58% 150 days; 5.53% 180 days. Offered rates of negotiable, bank-backed business credit instruments typically financing an import order. Source: Reuters

LONDON LATE EURODOLLARS: 5.8% - 5.75% one month; 5.81% - 5.69% two months; 5.75% - 5.63% three months; 5.69% - 5.56% four months; 5.63% - 5.50% five months; 5.56% - 5.44% six months.

LONDON INTERBANK OFFERED RATES (LIBOR): 5.89875% one month; 5.73875% three months; 5.59500% six months; 5.5025% one year. British Banker's Association average of interbank offered rates for dollar deposits in the London market based on quotations at 16 major banks. Effective rate for contracts entered into two days from date appearing at top of this column.

EURO LIBOR: 4.81000% one month; 4.79188% three months; 4.70250% six months; 4.60313% one year. British Banker's Association average of interbank offered rates for Euro deposits in the London market based on quotations at 16 major banks. Effective rate for contracts entered into two days from date appearing at top of this column.

EURO INTERBANK OFFERED RATES (EURIBOR): 4.812% one month; 4.795% three months; 4.708% six months; 4.606% one year. European Banking Federation-sponsored rate among 57 Euro zone banks.

FOREIGN PRIME RATES: Canada 7.50%; Germany 4.75% ; Japan 1.50%; Switzerland 5.625%; Britain 6.00%. These rate indications aren't directly comparable; lending practices vary widely by location.

TREASURY BILLS: Results of the Monday, January 15, 2001, auction of short-term U.S. government bills, sold at a discount from face value in units of $1,000 to $1 million: 5.220% 13 weeks; 5.055% 26 weeks.

OVERNIGHT REPURCHASE RATE: 5.46% Dealer financing rate for overnight sale and repurchase of Treasury securities. Source: Reuters.

FREDDIE MAC: Posted yields on 30-year mortgage commitments. Delivery within 30 days 7.00%, 60 days 7.05%, standard conventional fixed-rate mortgages: 5.375%, 2% rate capped one-year adjustable rate mortgages. Source: Reuters.

FANNIE MAE: Posted yields on 30 year mortgage commitments (priced at par) for delivery within 30 days 7.27%, 60 days 7.35%, standard conventional fixed-rate mortgages; 6.45%, 6/2 rate capped one-year adjustable rate mortgages. Source: Reuters.

MERRILL LYNCH READY ASSETS TRUST: 5.88%. Annualized average rate of return after expenses for the past 30 days; not a forecast of future returns.

CONSUMER PRICES INDEX: December, 174.0, up 3.4% from a year ago. Bureau of Labor Statistics.

Money Market Rates

- *Prime rate* - The basic interest rate on short-term loans that the largest commercial banks charge to their most creditworthy corporate customers.

- *Bellwether rate* - Interest rate that serves as a leader or as a leading indicator of future trends, e.g. inflation.

- *Federal funds rate* - Interest rate that banks charge each other for overnight loans of $1 million or more.

Money Market Rates

- *Discount rate* - The interest rate that the Fed offers to commercial banks for overnight reserve loans.

- *Call money rate* - The interest rate brokerage firms pay for call money loans from banks. This rate is used as the basis for customer rates on margin loans.

- *Commercial paper* - Short-term, unsecured debt issued by the largest corporations.

Money Market Rates

- *Certificate of deposit (CD)* - Large-denomination deposits of $100,000 or more at commercial banks for a specified term.
- *Banker's acceptance* - A postdated check on which a bank has guaranteed payment. Commonly used to finance international trade transactions.
- *London Eurodollars* - Certificates of deposit denominated in U.S. dollars at commercial banks in London.

Money Market Rates

- *London Interbank Offered Rate (LIBOR)* - Interest rate that international banks charge one another for overnight Eurodollar loans.
- *U.S. Treasury bill (T-bill)* - A short-term U.S. government debt instrument issued by the U.S. Treasury.

Work the Web

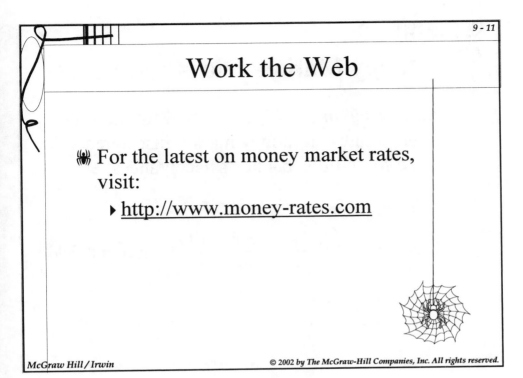

 For the latest on money market rates, visit:

> http://www.money-rates.com

Money Market Prices and Rates

Pure discount security
An interest-bearing asset that makes a single payment of face value at maturity with no payments before maturity.

♦ There are several different ways market participants quote interest rates.

Money Market Prices and Rates

◆ *Bank discount basis* - A method for quoting interest rates on money market instruments. Used for T-bills, banker's acceptances, etc.

$$\text{Current price} =$$
$$\text{Face Value} \times \left(1 - \frac{\text{Days to maturity}}{360} \times \text{Discount yield}\right)$$

Money Market Prices and Rates

	TREASURY BILLS				
MATURITY	DAYS TO MAT.	BID	ASKED	CHG.	ASKED YLD.
Jan 25 '01	7	5.44	5.36	+0.03	5.44
Feb 01 '01	14	5.48	5.40	+0.03	5.49
Feb 08 '01	21	5.27	5.19	+0.03	5.28
Feb 15 '01	28	5.25	5.17	+0.02	5.26
Feb 22 '01	35	5.25	5.21	+0.03	5.31
Mar 01 '01	42	5.23	5.19	+0.02	5.29
Mar 08 '01	49	5.21	5.17	+0.02	5.28
Mar 15 '01	56	5.19	5.15	+0.02	5.26
Mar 22 '01	63	5.20	5.18	+0.01	5.30
Mar 29 '01	70	5.20	5.18	+0.01	5.31
Apr 05 '01	77	5.22	5.20	+0.01	5.33
Apr 12 '01	84	5.22	5.20	....	5.34
Apr 19 '01	91	5.21	5.20	....	5.34
Apr 26 '01	98	5.15	5.13	+0.01	5.27
May 03 '01	105	5.13	5.11	+0.01	5.26
May 10 '01	112	5.11	5.09	+0.01	5.24
May 17 '01	119	5.10	5.08	+0.01	5.24
May 24 '01	126	5.13	5.11	+0.01	5.28
May 31 '01	133	5.11	5.09	....	5.26
Jun 07 '01	140	5.06	5.04	....	5.21
Jun 14 '01	147	5.06	5.04	....	5.22
Jun 21 '01	154	5.06	5.04	....	5.22
Jun 28 '01	161	5.05	5.03	....	5.22
Jul 05 '01	168	5.06	5.04	....	5.23
Jul 12 '01	175	5.05	5.03	−0.02	5.23
Jul 19 '01	182	5.04	5.03	....	5.23
Aug 30 '01	224	4.96	4.94	−0.02	5.14
Nov 29 '01	315	4.71	4.70	−0.05	4.92

Work the Web

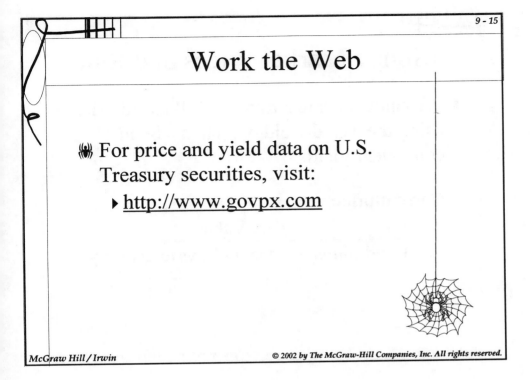

🕸 For price and yield data on U.S. Treasury securities, visit:

    ▸ http://www.govpx.com

Money Market Prices and Rates

• A bank discount yield can be converted to a bond equivalent yield.

$$\text{Bond equivalent yield} = \frac{365 \times \text{Discount yield}}{360 - \text{Days to maturity} \times \text{Discount yield}}$$

Note that this formula is correct only for maturities of six months or less. Moreover, if February 29 occurs within the next 12 months, 366 days must be used.

Money Market Prices and Rates

- We can calculate a treasury bill asked price using the asked yield, which is a bond equivalent yield.

$$\text{Current price} = \frac{\text{Face Value}}{1 + \text{Bond equivalent yield} \times \text{Days to maturity}/365}$$

Money Market Prices and Rates

- *"Simple" interest basis* - Another method for quoting interest rates. Calculated just like *annual percentage rates (APRs)*. Used for CDs, etc.
- The bond equivalent yield on a T-bill with less than six months to maturity is also an APR.
- An APR understates the true interest rate, which is usually called the *effective annual rate (EAR)*.

Money Market Prices and Rates

- In general, if we let m be the number of periods in a year, an APR can be converted to an EAR as follows:

$$1 + EAR = \left(1 + \frac{APR}{m}\right)^m$$

Money Market Prices and Rates

Example: Prices and Rates

- Suppose a T-bill with 170 days to maturity has a asked discount of 3.22%.
- For $1 million in face value, asked price =

$$\$1,000,000 \times \left(1 - \frac{170}{360} \times .0322\right) = \$984,794$$

- So, on this 170-day investment, you earn $15,206 in interest on an investment of $984,794, or 1.544%.
- 365/170 = 2.147. So APR = 2.147×1.544% = 3.315%

Money Market Prices and Rates

Example: Prices and Rates ...*continued*

✧ Bond equivalent yield $= \dfrac{365 \times .0322}{360 - 170 \times .0322} = 3.315\%$

$\qquad\qquad\qquad\qquad = APR$

✧ $1 + EAR = \left(1 + \dfrac{.03315}{2.147}\right)^{2.147} = 1.03344$

So EAR $= 3.344\%$

Rates and Yields on Fixed-Income Securities

- ◆ Fixed-income securities include long-term debt contracts from a wide variety of issuers:
  - → the U.S. government,
  - → real estate purchases (mortgage debt),
  - → corporations, and
  - → municipal governments.

Rates and Yields on Fixed-Income Securities

- The *Treasury yield curve* is a plot of Treasury yields against maturities.

- It is fundamental to bond market analysis because it represents the interest rates for default-free lending across the maturity spectrum.

Rates and Yields on Fixed-Income Securities

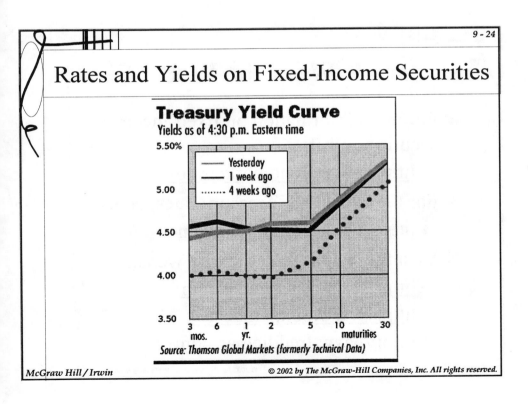

Rates and Yields on Fixed-Income Securities

YIELD COMPARISONS

Based on Merrill Lynch Bond Indexes, priced as of midafternoon Eastern time.

	11/17	11/16	52 Week — High	Low
Corp.-Govt. Master	5.47%	5.45%	6.24%	4.84%
Treasury 1-10yr	4.78	4.75	5.90	4.19
10+ yr	5.44	5.41	6.20	4.86
Agencies 1-10 yr	5.47	5.47	6.34	4.71
10 + yr	5.84	5.81	6.50	5.22
Corporate				
1-10 yr High Qlty	5.66	5.66	6.41	5.08
Med Qlty	6.31	6.30	6.67	5.59
10 + yr High Qlty	6.49	6.48	6.91	5.91
Med Qlty	7.08	7.06	7.22	6.46
Yankee bonds (1)	6.42	6.41	6.96	5.87
Current-coupon mortgages (2)				
GNMA 6.00%	6.27	6.27	6.83	5.79
FNMA 6.00%	6.34	6.34	6.86	5.87
FHLMC 6.00%	6.36	6.36	6.87	5.89
High-yield corporates	10.13	10.18	10.81	8.17
Tax-Exempt Bonds				
7-12-yr G.O. (AA)	4.36	4.36	4.86	4.07
12-22-yr G.O. (AA)	4.75	4.75	5.25	4.50
22 + yr revenue (A)	4.95	4.95	5.37	4.67

Note: High quality rated AAA-AA; medium quality A-BBB/Baa; high yield, BB/Ba-C.
(1) Dollar-denominated, SEC-registered bonds of foreign issuers sold in the U.S. (2) Reflects the 52-week high and low of mortgage-backed securities indexes rather than the individual securities shown.

McGraw Hill / Irwin

Work the Web

- For more information on fixed-income securities, visit:
  - http://www.bondmarkets.com
- For the latest U.S. Treasury rates, check:
  - http://www.bloomberg.com
- Visit these mortgage security websites:
  - http://www.fanniemae.com
  - http://www.ginniemae.gov
  - http://www.freddiemac.com

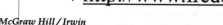

McGraw Hill / Irwin

The Term Structure of Interest Rates

- The *term structure of interest rates* is the relationship between time to maturity and the interest rates for default-free, pure discount instruments.
- The term structure is sometimes called the "*zero coupon yield curve*" to distinguish it from the Treasury yield curve, which is based on coupon bonds.

The Term Structure of Interest Rates

- The term structure can be seen by examining yields on U.S. Treasury STRIPS.
- STRIPS are pure discount instruments created by "stripping" the coupons and principal payments of U.S. Treasury notes and bonds into separate parts,which are then sold separately.
- The term STRIPS stands for Separate Trading of Registered Interest and Principal of Securities.

The Term Structure of Interest Rates

U.S. TREASURY STRIPS

MAT.	TYPE	BID	ASKED	CHG.	ASKED YLD.	MAT.	TYPE	BID	ASKED	CHG.	ASKED YLD.	MAT.	TYPE	BID	ASKED	CHG.	ASKED YLD.
May	13	ci	50:25	50:31	+ 11	5.55	Nov	23	ci	27:00	27:06	+ 16	5.79	May	04	ci	85:07	85:10	+ 7	4.84
Aug	13	ci	49:31	50:05	+ 12	5.57	Feb	24	ci	26:19	26:25	+ 17	5.79	May	04	np	84:26	84:29	+ 7	4.59
Nov	13	ci	49:06	49:12	+ 12	5.58	May	24	ci	26:08	26:14	+ 17	5.79	Jul	04	ci	84:28	84:30	+ 7	4.73
Feb	14	ci	48:12	48:18	+ 13	5.60	Aug	24	ci	25:29	26:02	+ 17	5.78	Aug	04	ci	84:14	84:17	+ 8	4.76
May	14	ci	47:19	47:25	+ 13	5.62	Nov	24	ci	25:18	25:23	+ 17	5.78	Aug	04	np	83:26	83:29	+ 7	4.97
Aug	14	ci	46:26	47:00	+ 13	5.64	Nov	24	bp	25:22	25:28	+ 18	5.76	Nov	04	ci	83:06	83:09	+ 8	4.85
Nov	14	ci	46:02	46:08	+ 13	5.66	Feb	25	ci	25:11	25:17	+ 16	5.75	Nov	04	bp	82:18	82:21	+ 8	5.05
Feb	15	ci	45:12	45:18	+ 14	5.67	Feb	25	bp	25:13	25:18	+ 17	5.75	Nov	04	np	82:25	82:28	+ 8	4.97
Feb	15	bp	45:08	45:14	+ 15	5.69	May	25	ci	25:03	25:09	+ 16	5.74	Jan	05	ci	82:09	82:12	+ 8	4.92
May	15	ci	44:21	44:27	+ 14	5.68	Aug	25	ci	24:26	25:00	+ 16	5.72	Feb	05	ci	81:28	81:31	+ 8	4.94
Aug	15	ci	43:30	44:03	+ 13	5.70	Aug	25	bp	24:23	24:29	+ 16	5.74	Feb	05	np	81:24	81:27	+ 8	4.98
Aug	15	bp	43:27	44:01	+ 15	5.71	Nov	25	ci	24:11	24:16	+ 16	5.75	May	05	ci	80:25	80:28	+ 9	4.98
Nov	15	ci	43:07	43:13	+ 13	5.71	Feb	26	ci	24:00	24:06	+ 16	5.74	May	05	bp	80:17	80:20	+ 9	5.05
Nov	15	bp	43:03	43:09	+ 15	5.73	Feb	26	bp	24:06	24:11	+ 16	5.71	May	05	np	80:28	81:00	+ 9	4.94
Feb	16	ci	42:19	42:25	+ 13	5.71	May	26	ci	23:22	23:28	+ 15	5.74	Aug	05	ci	79:28	79:31	+ 9	4.95
Feb	16	bp	42:14	42:20	+ 14	5.74	Aug	26	ci	23:14	23:19	+ 15	5.73	Aug	05	bp	79:14	79:18	+ 9	5.07
May	16	ci	41:30	42:04	+ 14	5.72	Aug	26	bp	23:13	23:19	+ 15	5.73	Aug	05	np	79:27	79:30	+ 9	4.96
May	16	bp	41:31	42:05	+ 16	5.72	Nov	26	ci	23:01	23:07	+ 15	5.74	Nov	05	ci	79:05	79:09	+ 9	4.88
Aug	16	ci	41:08	41:14	+ 14	5.74	Nov	26	bp	23:04	23:10	+ 16	5.72	Nov	05	np	78:29	79:01	+ 9	4.95
Nov	16	ci	40:19	40:25	+ 14	5.75	Feb	27	ci	22:22	22:28	+ 15	5.74	Jan	06	ci	78:05	78:09	+ 10	4.97
Nov	16	bp	40:23	40:29	+ 16	5.73	Feb	27	bp	22:28	23:02	+ 17	5.71	Feb	06	ci	77:24	77:28	+ 10	4.99
Feb	17	ci	39:31	40:05	+ 16	5.76	May	27	ci	22:15	22:21	+ 15	5.72	Feb	06	bp	77:19	77:23	+ 10	5.03
May	17	ci	39:13	39:19	+ 16	5.76	Aug	27	ci	22:08	22:14	+ 15	5.71	Feb	06	np	77:22	77:26	+ 10	5.01
May	17	bp	39:14	39:20	+ 16	5.75	Aug	27	bp	22:11	22:16	+ 16	5.69	May	06	ci	76:23	76:27	+ 10	5.02
Aug	17	ci	38:27	39:01	+ 16	5.76	Nov	27	ci	21:30	22:04	+ 15	5.70	May	06	np	76:21	76:25	+ 10	5.03
Aug	17	bp	38:28	39:02	+ 16	5.75	Nov	27	bp	22:03	22:08	+ 16	5.68	Jul	06	ci	76:13	76:17	+ 10	4.94
Nov	17	ci	38:11	38:17	+ 16	5.75	Feb	28	ci	21:23	21:28	+ 15	5.69	Jul	06	np	76:21	76:24	+ 10	4.88
Feb	18	ci	37:20	37:26	+ 15	5.78	May	28	ci	21:15	21:20	+ 15	5.68	Aug	06	ci	76:00	76:04	+ 10	4.96
May	18	ci	37:03	37:09	+ 15	5.78	Aug	28	ci	21:06	21:11	+ 14	5.68	Nov	06	ci	75:11	75:15	+ 11	4.89
May	18	bp	37:03	37:09	+ 15	5.78	Aug	28	bp	21:17	21:23	+ 15	5.62	Feb	07	ci	73:20	73:24	+ 9	5.08
Aug	18	ci	36:20	36:26	+ 15	5.77	Nov	28	ci	20:30	21:03	+ 15	5.67	Feb	07	np	73:15	73:19	+ 9	5.11
Nov	18	ci	36:01	36:07	+ 15	5.78	Nov	28	bp	21:12	21:17	+ 15	5.60	May	07	ci	72:21	72:25	+ 9	5.09
Nov	18	bp	36:01	36:07	+ 15	5.78	Feb	29	ci	21:02	21:08	+ 17	5.60	May	07	np	72:16	72:20	+ 9	5.12
Feb	19	ci	35:15	35:21	+ 15	5.79	Feb	29	bp	21:09	21:15	+ 17	5.56	Aug	07	ci	71:21	71:25	+ 10	5.11

McG

The Term Structure of Interest Rates

- An asked yield for a U.S. Treasury STRIP is an APR, calculated as two times the true semiannual rate.

$$\text{Present value} = \frac{\text{Future value}}{(1 + r)^N}$$

So

$$\text{STRIPS Price} = \frac{\text{Face value}}{\left(1 + \frac{\text{YTM}}{2}\right)^{2M}}$$

where M is the number of years to maturity

McGraw Hill / Irwin

Nominal versus Real Interest Rates

 Nominal interest rates
Interest rates as they are normally observed and quoted, with no adjustment for inflation.

 Real interest rates
Interest rates adjusted for the effect of inflation, calculated as the nominal rate less the rate of inflation.

$$\frac{\text{Real}}{\text{interest rate}} = \frac{\text{Nominal}}{\text{interest rate}} - \text{Inflation rate}$$

Nominal versus Real Interest Rates

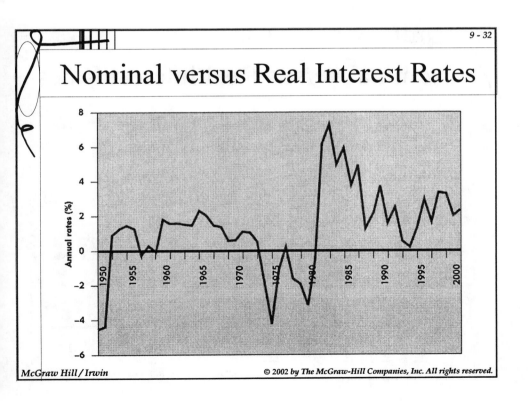

Nominal versus Real Interest Rates

- ◆ The *Fisher hypothesis* asserts that the general level of nominal interest rates follows the general level of inflation.

- ◆ According to the Fisher hypothesis, interest rates are on average higher than the rate of inflation.

Nominal versus Real Interest Rates

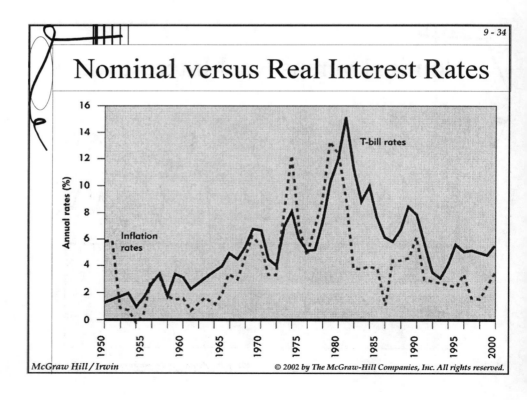

Traditional Theories of the Term Structure

 Expectations theory
The term structure of interest rates is a
reflection of financial market beliefs
regarding future interest rates.

 Maturity preference theory
Long-term interest rates contain a maturity
premium necessary to induce lenders into
making longer term loans.

Traditional Theories of the Term Structure

 Market segmentation theory
Debt markets are segmented by maturity,
with the result that interest rates for various
maturities are determined separately in each
segment.

Problems with Traditional Theories

Expectations theory
- → The term structure is almost always upward sloping, but interest rates have not always risen.
- → It is often the case that the term structure turns down at very long maturities.

Maturity preference theory
- → The U.S. government borrows much more heavily short term than long term.
- → Many of the biggest buyers of fixed-income securities, such as pension funds, have a strong preference for long maturities.

Problems with Traditional Theories

Market segmentation theory
- → The U.S. government borrows at all maturities.
- → Many institutional investors, such as mutual funds, are more than willing to move maturities to obtain more favorable rates.
- → There are bond trading operations that exist just to exploit even very small perceived premiums.

Modern Term Structure Theory

- Long-term bond prices are much more sensitive to interest rate changes than short-term bonds. This is called *interest rate risk*.

- So, the modern view of the term structure suggests that:

$$NI = RI + IP + RP$$

where NI = Nominal interest rate
RI = Real interest rate
IP = Inflation premium
RP = Interest rate risk premium

Liquidity and Default Risk

$$NI = RI + IP + RP + LP + DP$$

where NI = Nominal interest rate
RI = Real interest rate
IP = Inflation premium
RP = Interest rate risk premium
LP = Liquidity premium
DP = Default premium

Chapter Review

- ◆ Interest Rate History and Money Market Rates
  - → Interest Rate History
  - → Money Market Rates

- ◆ Money Market Prices and Rates
  - → Bank Discount Rate Quotes
  - → Treasury Bill Quotes
  - → Bank Discount Yields versus Bond Equivalent Yields
  - → Bond Equivalent Yields, APRs, and EARs

Chapter Review

- ◆ Rates and Yields on Fixed-Income Securities
  - → The Treasury Yield Curve
  - → Rates on Other Fixed-Income Investments

- ◆ The Term Structure of Interest Rates
  - → Treasury STRIPS
  - → Yields for U.S. Treasury STRIPS

- ◆ Nominal versus Real Interest Rates
  - → Real Interest Rates
  - → The Fisher Hypothesis

Chapter Review

- ◆ Traditional Theories of the Term Structure
    - → Expectations Theory
    - → Maturity Preference Theory
    - → Market Segmentation Theory
- ◆ Determinants of Nominal Interest Rates: A Modern Perspective
    - → Problems with Traditional Theories
    - → Modern Term Structure Theory
    - → Liquidity and Default Risk

10

Chapter

Bond Prices and Yields

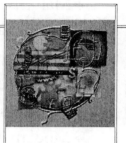

Fundamentals
of Investments
Valuation & Management
second edition

Charles J. Corrado   Bradford D. Jordan

McGraw Hill / Irwin

Slides by Yee-Tien (Ted) Fu

Bond Prices and Yields

Goal

Our goal in this chapter is to understand the relationship between bond prices and yields, and to examine some of the fundamental tools of bond risk analysis used by fixed-income portfolio managers.

Bond Basics

 Straight bond
An IOU that obligates the issuer to pay to the bondholder a fixed sum of money (called the principal, par value, or face value) at the bond's maturity, along with constant, periodic interest payments (called coupons) during the life of the bond.

- U.S. Treasury bonds are straight bonds.
- Special features may be attached, creating convertible bonds, "putable" bonds, etc.

Bond Basics

- Two basic yield measures for a bond are its *coupon rate* and *current yield*.

$$\text{Coupon rate} = \frac{\text{Annual coupon}}{\text{Par value}}$$

$$\text{Current yield} = \frac{\text{Annual coupon}}{\text{Bond price}}$$

Work the Web

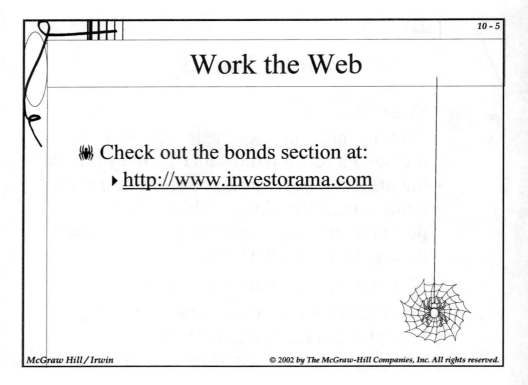

🕷 Check out the bonds section at:
  ‣ http://www.investorama.com

Straight Bond Prices and Yield to Maturity

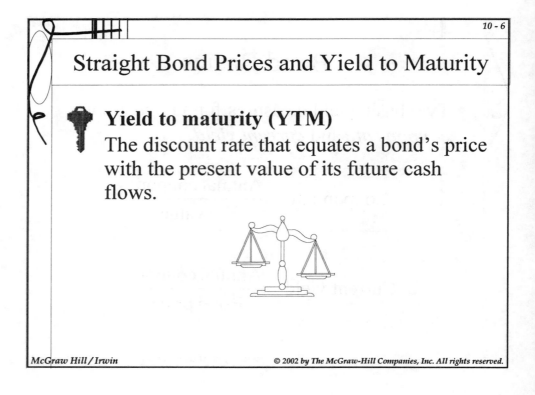

Yield to maturity (YTM)
The discount rate that equates a bond's price with the present value of its future cash flows.

Straight Bond Prices and Yield to Maturity

Bond price = present value of all the coupon payments
+ present value of the principal payment

$$\text{Bond price} = \frac{C}{YTM}\left[1 - \frac{1}{\left(1 + \frac{YTM}{2}\right)^{2M}}\right] + \frac{FV}{\left(1 + \frac{YTM}{2}\right)^{2M}}$$

where C = annual coupon, the sum of 2 semiannual
coupons
FV = face value
M = maturity in years

Premium and Discount Bonds

- ◆ Bonds are commonly distinguished according
  to the relative relationship between their
  selling price and their par value.

- ◆ *Premium bonds:* price > par value
                 YTM < coupon rate

- ◆ *Discount bonds:* price < par value
                 YTM > coupon rate

- ◆ *Par bonds:*   price = par value
                 YTM = coupon rate

Premium and Discount Bonds

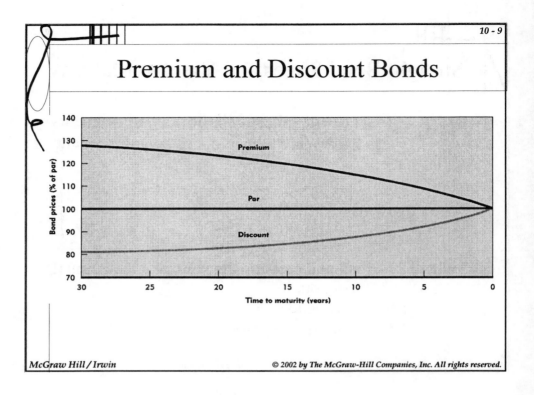

Premium and Discount Bonds

♦ In general, when the coupon rate and YTM are held constant …

for discount bonds: the longer the term to maturity, the greater the discount from par value, and

for premium bonds: the longer the term to maturity, the greater the premium over par value.

Relationships among Yield Measures

- Since the current yield is always between the coupon rate and the yield to maturity (unless the bond is selling at par) ...

  for premium bonds:
  coupon rate > current yield > YTM

  for discount bonds:
  coupon rate < current yield < YTM

  for par value bonds:
  coupon rate = current yield = YTM

Work the Web

- To obtain current information on Treasury bond prices and yields, try the search tool at:
  - http://www.bondsonline.com

Calculating Yields

- To calculate a bond's yield given its price, we use the straight bond formula and then try different yields until we come across the one that produces the given price.

$$\text{Bond price} = \frac{C}{\text{YTM}}\left[1 - \frac{1}{\left(1 + \frac{\text{YTM}}{2}\right)^{2M}}\right] + \frac{FV}{\left(1 + \frac{\text{YTM}}{2}\right)^{2M}}$$

- To speed up the calculation, financial calculators and spreadsheets may be used.

Yield to Call

- A *callable bond* allows the issuer to buy back the bond at a specified *call price* anytime after an initial *call protection period*, until the bond matures.

Yield to Call

- *Yield to call (YTC)* is a yield measure that assumes a bond issue will be called at its earliest possible call date.

$$\text{Callable bond price} = \frac{C}{YTC}\left[1 - \frac{1}{\left(1 + \frac{YTC}{2}\right)^{2T}}\right] + \frac{CP}{\left(1 + \frac{YTC}{2}\right)^{2T}}$$

where C = constant annual coupon
CP = call price of the bond
T = time in years to earliest possible call date
YTC = yield to call assuming semiannual coupons

McGraw Hill / Irwin

Interest Rate Risk

Interest rate risk
The possibility that changes in interest rates will result in losses in a bond's value.

- The yield actually earned or "realized" on a bond is called the *realized yield*, and this is almost never exactly equal to the *yield to maturity*, or *promised yield*.

McGraw Hill / Irwin

Interest Rate Risk and Maturity

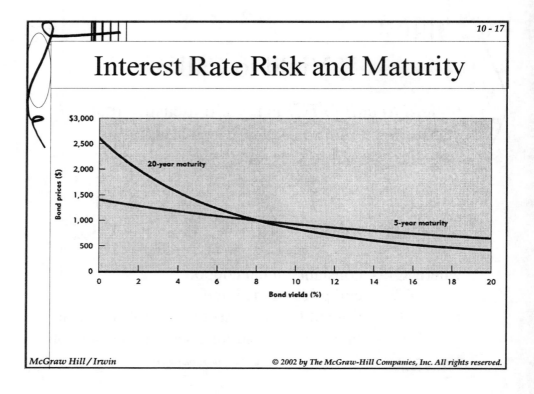

Malkiel's Theorems

① Bond prices and bond yields move in opposite directions. As a bond's yield increases, its price decreases. Conversely, as a bond's yield decreases, its price increases.

② For a given change in a bond's YTM, the longer the term to maturity of the bond, the greater will be the magnitude of the change in the bond's price.

Malkiel's Theorems

③ For a given change in a bond's YTM, the size of the change in the bond's price increases at a diminishing rate as the bond's term to maturity lengthens.

④ For a given change in a bond's YTM, the absolute magnitude of the resulting change in the bond's price is inversely related to the bond's coupon rate.

Malkiel's Theorems

⑤ For a given absolute change in a bond's YTM, the magnitude of the price increase caused by a decrease in yield is greater than the price decrease caused by an increase in yield.

Malkiel's Theorems

Bond Prices and Yields

	Time to Maturity		
Yields	5 Years	10 Years	20 Years
7%	$1,041.58	$1,071.06	$1,106.78
9%	960.44	934.96	907.99
Price difference	$ 81.14	$ 136.10	$ 198.79

Twenty-Year Bond Prices and Yields

	Coupon Rates		
Yields	6 Percent	8 Percent	10 Percent
6%	$1,000.00	$1,231.15	$1,462.30
8%	802.07	1,000.00	1,197.93
10%	656.82	828.41	1,000.00

Duration

Duration

A measure of a bond's sensitivity to changes in bond yields. The original measure is called *Macaulay duration*.

$$\%\Delta \text{ in bond price} \approx -\text{Duration} \times \frac{\Delta \text{ in YTM}}{\left(1 + \frac{YTM}{2}\right)}$$

→ Two bonds with the same duration, but not necessarily the same maturity, will have approximately the same price sensitivity to a (small) change in bond yields.

Duration

$$\text{Modified duration} = \frac{\text{Macaulay duration}}{\left(1 + \text{YTM}\middle/2\right)}$$

So,

$$\%\Delta \text{ in bond price} \approx -\text{Modified duration} \times \Delta \text{ in YTM}$$

Calculating Macaulay's Duration

- ✦ Macaulay's duration values are stated in years, and are often described as a bond's *effective maturity.*
- ✦ *For a zero coupon bond,* duration = maturity.
- ✦ *For a coupon bond,* duration = a weighted average of individual maturities of all the bond's separate cash flows, where the weights are proportionate to the present values of each cash flow.

Calculating Macaulay's Duration

Calculating Bond Duration

Years	Cash Flow	Discount Factor	Present Value	Years × Present Value ÷ Bond Price
0.5	$ 40	.96154	$ 38.4615	.0192 years
1	40	.92456	36.9822	.0370
1.5	40	.88900	35.5599	.0533
2	40	.85480	34.1922	.0684
2.5	40	.82193	32.8771	.0822
3	1040	.79031	821.9271	2.4658
			$1,000.00	2.7259 years
			Bond Price	Bond Duration

Calculating Macaulay's Duration

* In general, for a bond paying constant semiannual coupons,

$$\text{Duration} = \frac{1 + YTM/2}{YTM} - \frac{1 + YTM/2 + M(C - YTM)}{YTM + C\left[\left(1 + YTM/2\right)^{2M} - 1\right]}$$

where C = constant annual coupon rate

M = bond maturity in years

YTM = yield to maturity assuming semiannual coupons

Calculating Macaulay's Duration

- ◆ If a bond is selling for par value, the duration formula can be simplified:

$$\text{Par value bond duration} = \frac{1 + \dfrac{\text{YTM}}{2}}{\text{YTM}} \left[1 - \frac{1}{\left(1 + \dfrac{\text{YTM}}{2}\right)^{2M}} \right]$$

Properties of Duration

① All else the same, the longer a bond's maturity, the longer is its duration.

② All else the same, a bond's duration increases at a decreasing rate as maturity lengthens.

③ All else the same, the higher a bond's coupon, the shorter is its duration.

④ All else the same, a higher yield to maturity implies a shorter duration, and a lower yield to maturity implies a longer duration.

Properties of Duration

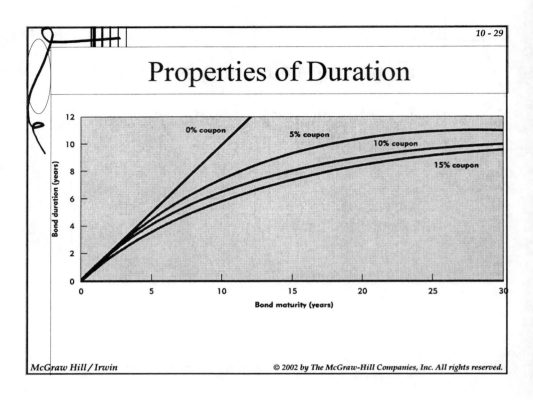

Dedicated Portfolios

Dedicated portfolio
A bond portfolio created to prepare for a future cash outlay, e.g. pension funds.
The date the payment is due is commonly called the portfolio's *target date*.

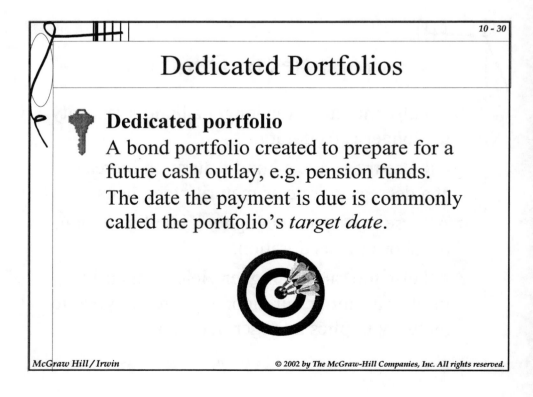

Work the Web

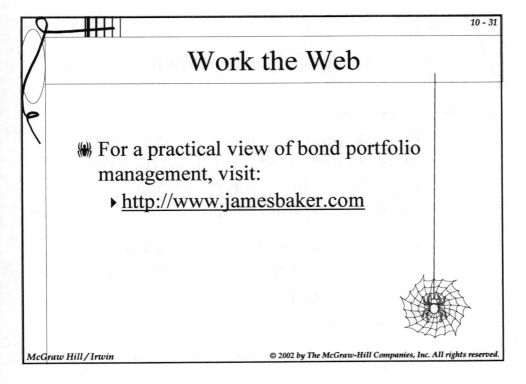

For a practical view of bond portfolio management, visit:

▸ http://www.jamesbaker.com

Reinvestment Risk

Reinvestment rate risk
The uncertainty about future or target date portfolio value that results from the need to reinvest bond coupons at yields not known in advance.

→ A simple solution is to purchase zero coupon bonds. In practice however, U.S. Treasury STRIPS are the only zero coupon bonds issued in sufficiently large quantities, and they have lower yields than even the highest quality corporate bonds.

Price Risk versus Reinvestment Rate Risk

 Price risk
The risk that bond prices will decrease.
Arises in dedicated portfolios when the
target date value of a bond or bond portfolio
is not known with certainty.

♦ Interest rate increases act to decrease bond
prices (price risk) but increase the future value
of reinvested coupons (reinvestment rate risk),
and vice versa.

Immunization

 Immunization
Constructing a portfolio to minimize the
uncertainty surrounding its target date value.

♦ It is possible to engineer a portfolio such that
price risk and reinvestment rate risk offset
each other more or less precisely.

Immunization by Duration Matching

- A dedicated portfolio can be immunized by *duration matching* - matching the duration of the portfolio to its target date.
- Then the impacts of price and reinvestment rate risk will almost exactly offset, and interest rate changes will have a minimal impact on the target date value of the portfolio.

Immunization by Duration Matching

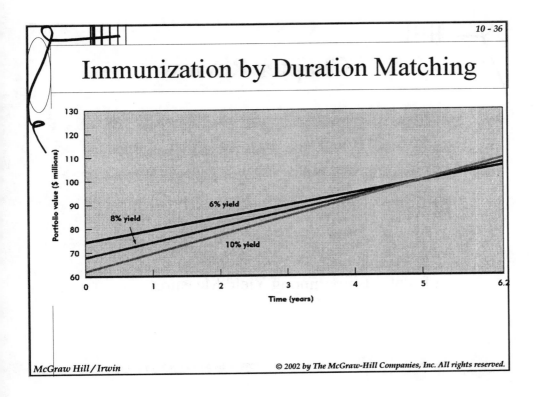

Dynamic Immunization

 Dynamic immunization
Periodic rebalancing of a dedicated bond portfolio to maintain a duration that matches the target maturity date.

- The advantage is that the reinvestment risk caused by continually changing bond yields is greatly reduced.

- The drawback is that each rebalancing incurs management and transaction costs.

Chapter Review

- Bond Basics
  - Straight Bonds
  - Coupon Rate and Current Yield

- Straight Bond Prices and Yield to Maturity
  - Straight Bond Prices
  - Premium and Discount Bonds
  - Relationships among Yield Measures

Chapter Review

- ◆ More on Yields
  - → Calculating Yields
  - → Yield to Call

- ◆ Interest Rate Risk and Malkiel's Theorems
  - → Promised Yield and Realized Yield
  - → Interest Rate Risk and Maturity
  - → Malkiel's Theorems

Chapter Review

- ◆ Duration
  - → Macaulay Duration
  - → Modified Duration
  - → Calculating Macaulay's Duration
  - → Properties of Duration

- ◆ Dedicated Portfolios and Reinvestment Risk
  - → Dedicated Portfolios
  - → Reinvestment Risk

Chapter Review

◆ Immunization
  → Price Risk versus Reinvestment Rate Risk
  → Immunization by Duration Matching
  → Dynamic Immunization

11

Chapter

Corporate Bonds

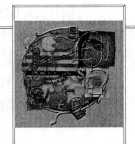

Fundamentals
of Investments
Valuation & Management
second edition

Charles J. Corrado   Bradford D. Jordan

McGraw Hill / Irwin

Slides by Yee-Tien (Ted) Fu

Corporate Bonds

Goal

Our goal in this chapter is to introduce the specialized knowledge that money managers who trade in corporate bonds possess.

McGraw Hill / Irwin

Corporate Bond Basics

 Corporate bond

A security issued by a corporation that represents a promise to pay to its bondholders a fixed sum of money (called the bond's *principal*, or par or face value) at a future maturity date, along with periodic payments of interest (called *coupons*).

Corporate Bond Basics

◆ Corporate bonds differ from common stock in three fundamental ways.

Corporate Bonds	Common Stock
Represent a creditor's claim on the corporation.	Represents an ownership claim on the corporation.
Promised cash flows (coupons and principal) are stated in advance.	Amount and timing of dividends may change at any time.
Mostly issued as callable bonds.	Almost never callable.

Corporate Bond Basics

- There are several trillion dollars of corporate bonds outstanding in the United States.
- More than half of these are owned by life insurance companies and pension funds.
  - → These institutions can eliminate much of their financial risk via *cash flow matching*.
  - → They can also diversify away most default risk by including a large number of different bond issues in their portfolios.

Corporate Bond Basics

Software Iz Us Five-Year Note Issue		
Issue amount	$20 million	Note issue total face value is $20 million
Issue date	12/15/99	Notes offered to the public in December 1999
Maturity date	12/31/04	Remaining principal due December 31, 2004
Face value	$1,000	Face value denomination is $1,000 per note
Coupon interest	$100 per annum	Annual coupons are $100 per note
Coupon dates	6/30, 12/31	Coupons are paid semiannually
Offering price	100	Offer price is 100 percent of face value
Yield to maturity	10%	Based on stated offer price
Call provision	Not callable	Notes may not be paid off before maturity
Security	None	Notes are unsecured
Rating	Not rated	Privately placed note issue

Corporate Bond Basics

♦ Bonds issued with a standard, relatively simple set of features are popularly called *plain vanilla bonds*.

Work the Web

🕸 For more information on corporate bonds, visit:
   ‣ http://www.investinginbonds.com
   ‣ http://www.bondresources.com

Types of Corporate Bonds

- *Debentures* - Unsecured bonds issued by a corporation.
- *Mortgage bond* - Debt secured with a property lien.
- *Collateral trust bond* - Debt secured with financial collateral.
- *Equipment trust certificate* - Shares in a trust with income from a lease contract.

These securities have not been registered under the Securities Act of 1933 and may not be offered or sold in the United States or to U.S. persons except to accordance with the results restrictions applicable thereto. These securities having been previously sold, this announcement appears as a matter of record only.

March 11, 1994

$243,000,000

NWA Trust No. 1

$177,000,000 8.26% Class A Senior Aircraft Notes
$66,000,000 9.36% Class B Subordinated Aircraft Notes

NORTHWEST AIRLINES

The 8.26% Class A Senior Aircraft Notes and the 9.36% Class B Subordinated Aircraft Notes are secured by, among other things, a security interest in certain aircraft sold by Northwest Airlines, Inc. ("Northwest") to an owner trust for a purchase price of $443 million and the lease relating to such Aircraft, including the right to receive amounts payable by Northwest under such lease. The Noteholders also have the benefit of a liquidity facility, initially provided by General Electric Capital Corporation, to support certain payments of interest on the Notes.

Lehman Brothers   BT Securities Corporation

Bond Indentures

 Bond indenture
A formal written agreement between the corporation and the bondholders that spells out in detail their rights and obligations with respect to the bond issue.

- In practice, very few bond investors read the original indenture. Instead, they may refer to an *indenture summary* provided in the *prospectus* of the bond issue.

Bond Indentures

- The Trust Indenture Act of 1939 requires that any bond issue subject to regulation by the Securities and Exchange Commission (SEC) must have a trustee appointed to represent the interests of the bondholders.
- The Act is available at the SEC website:
  → http://www.sec.gov

Bond Indentures

- ◆ Some of the important provisions frequently specified in bond indentures include:

  - → *Bond seniority provisions* - Different bond issues can usually be differentiated according to the seniority of their claims on the firm's assets. Bond seniority may be protected by a *negative pledge clause.*

  - → *Call provisions* - A call provision allows the issuer to buy back all or part of its outstanding bonds at a specified call price sometime before the bonds mature, hence facilitating *bond refunding.*

Bond Indentures

No matter how low market interest rates may fall, the maximum price of an unprotected callable bond is generally bounded above by its call price.

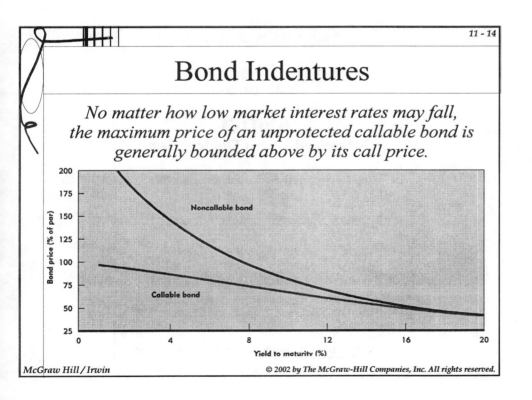

Bond Indentures

→ *Put provisions* - A bond with a put provision can be sold back to the issuer at a prespecified price (normally set at par value) on any of a sequence of prespecified dates. Such bonds are often called *extendible bonds*.

→ *Bond-to-stock conversion provisions* - Convertible bonds are bonds that holders can exchange for common stock according to a prespecified conversion ratio.

This announcement is neither an offer to sell, nor a solicitation of an offer to buy, any of these securities.
The offer is made only by the Prospectus and related Prospectus Supplement.

June 24, 1998

$517,500,000

AMD
Advanced Micro Devices, Inc.

6% Convertible Subordinated Notes due 2005

The 6% Convertible Subordinated Notes due 2005 (the "Notes") will be convertible at the option of the holder into shares of common stock, par value $.01 per share (the "Common Stock"). of Advanced Micro Devices, Inc. (the "Company") at any time at or prior to maturity, unless previously redeemed or repurchased, at a conversion price of $37.00 per share (equivalent to a conversion rate of 27.027 shares per $1,000 principal amount of Notes), subject to adjustment in certain events.

Price 100%

Copies of the Prospectus and related Prospectus Supplement may be obtained in any State from such of the undersigned as may legally offer these securities in compliance with the securities laws of such State.

Donaldson, Lufkin & Jenrette
Securities Corporation

Salomon Smith Barney

Bond Indentures

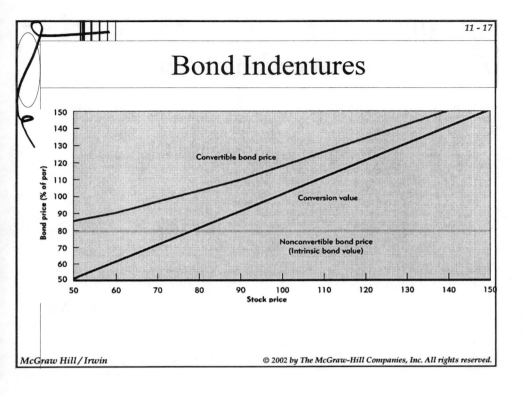

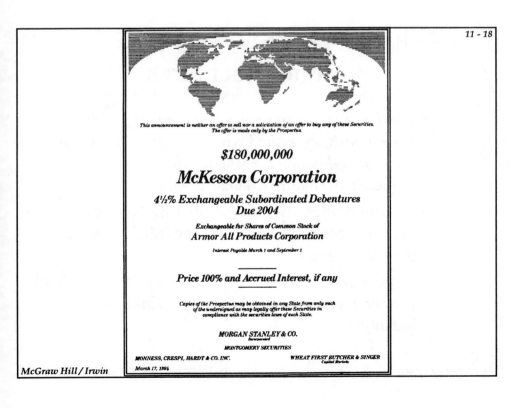

Work the Web

🕷 Find out more about convertible bonds at:
  ▸ http://www.convertbond.com

Bond Indentures

➔ *Bond maturity and principal payment provisions* - *Term bonds* are issued with a single maturity date, while *serial bonds* are issued with a regular sequence of maturity dates.

➔ *Sinking fund provisions* - A sinking fund is an account used to provide for scheduled redemptions of outstanding bonds.

➔ *Coupon payment provisions* - An exact schedule of coupon payment dates is specified in the bond indenture.

Protective Covenants

◆ A bond indenture is likely to contain a number of *protective covenants*, which are restrictions designed to protect bondholders.

→ *Negative covenant ("thou shalt not") example -* The firm cannot pay dividends to stockholders in excess of what is allowed by a formula based on the firm's earnings.

→ *Positive covenant ("thou shalt") example -* Proceeds from the sale of assets must be used either to acquire other assets of equal value or to redeem outstanding bonds.

Event Risk

Event risk
The possibility that the issuing corporation will experience a significant change in its bond credit quality.

→ *Example:* In October 1992, Marriott Corporation announced its intention to spin off part of the company. The spinoff, called Host Marriott, would acquire most of the parent company's debt and its poorly performing real estate holdings.

Bonds Without Indentures

 Private placement
A new bond issue sold to one or more parties in private transactions not available to the public.

- Private placements are exempt from registration requirements with the SEC, although they often have formal indentures.

- Debt issued without an indenture is basically a simple IOU of the corporation.

Preferred Stock

- Preferred stockholders have a claim to dividend payments that is senior to the claim of common stockholders. However, their claim is subordinate to the claims of bondholders and other creditors.

Preferred Stock

- ◆ Preferred stock has some of the features of both bonds and common stock.
- ◆ Typically, preferred stock issues
  - → do not grant voting rights to their holders,
  - → promise a stream of fixed dividend payments,
  - → have no specified maturity but are often callable,
  - → may have their dividends suspended without setting off a bankruptcy process (as long as common stock dividends are also suspended),
  - → cumulate unpaid preferred dividends, and
  - → may be convertible.

Adjustable-Rate Bonds & Preferred Stock

- ◆ Many bond, note, and preferred stock issues allow the issuer to adjust the annual coupon according to a rule or formula based on current market interest rates. These securities are called *adjustable-rate* or *floating-rate* securities.

Corporate Bond Credit Ratings

- When a corporation sells a new bond issue to investors, it usually subscribes to several bond rating agencies for a credit evaluation of the bond issue.
- Each contracted rating agency then provides a *credit rating* - an assessment of the credit quality of the bond issue based on the issuer's financial condition.

TABLE 11.2

Corporate Bond Credit Rating Symbols

Moody's	Rating Agency Duff and Phelps	Standard & Poor's	Credit Rating Description
		Investment-Grade Bond Ratings	
Aaa	1	AAA	Highest credit rating, maximum safety
Aa1	2	AA+	
Aa2	3	AA	High credit quality, investment-grade bonds
Aa3	4	AA–	
A1	5	A+	
A2	6	A	Upper-medium quality, investment-grade bonds
A3	7	A–	
Baa1	8	BBB+	
Baa2	9	BBB	Lower-medium quality, investment-grade bonds
Baa3	10	BBB–	
		Speculative-Grade Bond Ratings	
Ba1	11	BB+	Low credit quality, speculative-grade bonds
Ba2	12	BB	
Ba3	13	BB–	
B1	14	B+	Very low credit quality, speculative-grade bonds
B2	15	B	
B3	16	B–	
		Extremely Speculative-Grade Bond Ratings	
Caa	17	CCC+	Extremely low credit standing, high-risk bonds
		CCC	
		CCC–	
Ca		CC	Extremely speculative
C		C	
		D	Bonds in default

Corporate Bond Credit Ratings

Why are bond ratings important?

♦ Only a few institutional investors have the resources and expertise necessary to properly evaluate a bond's credit quality on their own.

♦ Many financial institutions have *prudent investment guidelines* stipulating that only securities with a certain level of investment safety may be included in their portfolios.

Work the Web

🕷 Visit these rating agencies:
  ▸ Duff and Phelps: http://www.dcrco.com
  ▸ Fitch: http://www.fitchibca.com
  ▸ Moody's: http://www.moodys.com
  ▸ Standard & Poor's: http://www.ratings.com
  ▸ McCarthy, Crisanti and Maffei: http://www.mcmwatch.com

Junk Bonds

High-yield bonds

Bonds with a speculative credit rating that is offset by a yield premium offered to compensate for higher credit risk.
Also called *junk bonds*.

- ◆ Junk bonds are attractive investments for many institutional investors with well-diversified portfolios.

HIGH-YIELD BONDS

Friday, January 12, 2001

	TOTAL DAILY RETURN	INDEX VALUE	AVERAGE PRICE CHANGE	YEAR TO DATE	VOL.
SSMB Index	+ 0.10	99.19	+ 0.07	+ 4.69	M

Volume Key: H = Heavy, M = Moderate, L = Light
Dec 31, 1998 = 100

Key Gainers

NAME	TYPE/ COUP.	MAT.	3 PM BID	PRICE CHANGE	PRINCIPAL RETURN	YLD.-y
Level 3	a/ 9.125	5/08	88¾	+ ¾	+ 0.83	11.44
Nextlink	a/ 10.750	11/08	92	+ 1	+ 1.08	12.37
Winstar Com	c/ 0.000	4/10	39	+ 2	+ 5.41	19.40

Key Losers
NONE

SSMB Components

NAME	TYPE/ RATING	COUP.	MAT.	3 PM BID	NET CHG.	YLD.-y
AK Steel	a/BB	9.125	12/06	94	unch	10.51
Allied Waste	b/B +	10.000	8/09	97¼	+ ¼	10.49
American Std	a/BB +	7.375	2/08	98	unch	7.75
Chancellor	b/BB +	8.125	12/07	102¾	unch	7.44
Charter	a/B +	8.625	4/09	92¼	unch	10.03

NAME	TYPE/ RATING	COUP.	MAT.	3 PM BID	NET CHG.	YLD.-y
Echostar	a/B	9.375	2/09	97	unch	9.92
Federal Mogu	e/B +	7.500	1/09	25	unch	z
Global Xing	a/BB	9.625	5/08	100¾	unch	9.44
HMH Prop	a/BB	7.875	8/08	97¼	unch	8.37
Intermedia	a/B	8.600	6/08	86	unch	11.46
Level 3	a/B	9.125	5/08	88¾	+ ¾	11.44
Lyondell Che	a/BB	9.875	5/07	100½	unch	9.75
Nextel Comm	c/B	0.000	9/07	81	unch	11.37
PSINet	a/CCC	11.000	8/09	27	unch	z
Packaging Co	b/BB-	9.625	4/09	105	unch	8.56
Revlon	a/CCC+	8.125	2/06	72	unch	16.53
Tenet	b/BB-	8.125	12/06	102½	unch	7.55
Trump AC	e/B-	11.250	5/06	67	unch	22.12
Vintage Pet.	b/BB-	8.625	2/09	102½	unch	8.01
Williams	a/B +	10.875	10/09	87½	− ½	13.34

Volume indicators are based solely on the traders' subjective judgement given the relative level of inquiry and trading activity on any given day.

Price quotes follow accrued interest conventions.

a-Senior. b-Senior Sub. c-Senior, Zero To Full. d-Senior, Split Cpn. e-Secured. y-yield is the lower of yield to maturity and yield to call. z-omitted for reset or bankrupt bonds, negative yields, or yields above 35%.

Source: Salomon Smith Barney

Bond Market Trading

- An active secondary market with a substantial volume of bond trading exists, thus satisfying most of the liquidity needs of investors.
- Corporate bond trading is characteristically an OTC activity. Nevertheless, bond trading on the New York Stock Exchange is watched by bond investors and traders throughout the world.

U.S. EXCHANGE BONDS

Friday, January 12, 2001
Quotations as of 2 p.m. Eastern Time

DOW JONES BOND AVERAGES

2000 HIGH	2000 LOW	2001 HIGH	2001 LOW		2001 CLOSE	2001 CHG.	2001 %YLD	2000 CLOSE	2000 CHG.
97.41	93.23	99.50	97.85	20 Bonds	99.50	+ 0.09	7.71	95.80	– 0.29
98.99	90.69	98.44	96.85	10 Utilities	97.92	– 0.09	7.45	94.28	– 0.13
99.86	95.53	101.16	98.86	10 Industrials	101.08	+ 0.27	7.97	97.32	– 0.46

VOLUME

Total New York	$9,005,000
Corporation Bonds	$8,888,000
Foreign Bonds	$117,000
Amex Bonds	$154,000

SALES SINCE JAN. 1

New York	
2001	$99,629,000
2000	$105,434,000
1999	$147,239,000
AMEX	
2001	$2,326,000
2000	$7,216,000
1999	$6,269,000

DIARIES

New York	DOMESTIC FRI.	DOMESTIC THU.	ALL ISSUES FRI.	ALL ISSUES THU.
Issues Traded	125	134	132	142
Advances	51	72	52	78
Declines	56	43	59	45
Unchanged	18	19	21	19
New highs	22	21	22	22
New lows	3	2	3	2

BONDS	CUR YLD.	VOL.	CLOSE	NET CHG.
BellsoT 6⅝33	7.4	111	90⅞	– ½
BellsoT 7⅝35	7.6	15	100	+ ¾
BethSt 8.45s05	15.4	87	55	– 8⅞
Bluegrn 8¼12	cv	3	60	– 2
Bordn 8⅜16	11.8	142	70¾	...
BoydGm 9¼03	9.5	4	96⅞	– 1⅝
BrnSh 9½06	10.3	25	92½	+ ⅝
Capstar 4¾04	cv	15	78	+ 3⅝
ChespkE 9⅛06	9.0	10	102	+ 1
ChiqBr 10s09	20.4	5	49	...
vjClardg 11¾02f	...	10	68	– 5
ClrkOil 9½04	10.8	24	88¼	– ⅝
Coastl 8⅛02	8.0	5	101½	– ¼
CoeurDA 7¼05	cv	3	31	...
Coeur 6⅜04	cv	70	32	+ 1½
Conseco 10½04	10.3	56	101½	+ ⅜
Conseco 10¼02	11.2	528	91¾	+ ¼
CrownC 7⅛02	8.6	315	82½	+ 2¼
CypSemi 4s05	cv	20	90	+ 6
DR Hrtn 10s06	9.7	10	103½	...
Dole 7s03	7.1	4	99	– ¼
Dole 7⅞13	7.9	75	100	...
DukeEn 6¼04	6.3	25	100	+ ⅜
DukeEn 7⅞24	7.7	75	101¾	– ¾
DukeEn 6¾25	7.2	130	93⅞	+ 1⅜

BONDS	CUR YLD.	VOL.	CLOSE	NET CHG.
KaufB 9⅝06	9.5	116	101⅞	+ 1⅜
KerrM 7½14	cv	57	100	– 3
Leucadia 7¾13	7.9	15	98¼	+ 1⅜
LglsLt 9s22	8.4	14	107	– ¼
Lucent 6.9s01	6.9	100	99¾	...
Lucent 7¼06	7.3	520	98⅞	– ⅛
Lucent 6½28	8.4	10	77⅜	– 4¾
Lucent 6.45s29	8.3	86	77½	+ ⅛
MSC Sf 7⅞04	cv	66	88	– 1
MailWell 5s02	cv	30	74	...
MarO 7s02	7.0	77	99¾	+ ⅜
Mascotch 03	cv	223	58¾	...
NStl 8¾06	25.4	30	33	+ ½
NETelTel 6⅝08	6.6	25	97	+ ¼
NETelTel 6⅞23	7.5	58	91½	– ½
NYTel 5⅞03	6.0	10	98⅛	+ ⅜
NYTel 7⅜11	7.5	5	98⅝	– 1⅝
NYTel 7s25	7.4	5	94¼	– ⅛
Noram 6s12	cv	18	88⅜	– ⅜
OreStl 11s03	15.2	190	72¼	...
PG&E 7.1s05	10.6	35	67⅛	– 28⅞
ParkerD 5½04	cv	5	85½	+ ¼
PepBoys zr11	...	10	57½	– ¼
PhilPt 9.18s21	8.8	15	104½	...
PhilPt 7.2s23	7.8	10	92¾	– 1¼
Polaroid 11½06	16.9	337	68	– ⅛
PotEl 5s02	cv	5	95⅝	– 1⅜
PSEG 5s37	7.8	5	64¼	– 2¾
Quanx 6.88s07	cv	176	84¾	– 1⅛
ReynTob 8⅝02	7.9	93	101	+ 1
ReynTob 7⅝03	7.7	60	99	– ⅜
ReynTob 9¼13	9.2	40	101	+ ⅞
Safwy 9.65s04	8.8	58	109⅝	+ ⅜
SearsAc 6¾05	7.0	20	96⅝	– 4⅛
SilicnGr 5¼04	cv	10	58	...
Solectrn zrN20	...	100	55½	+ 2
SoCG 5¾03	5.9	30	97½	+ ⅞

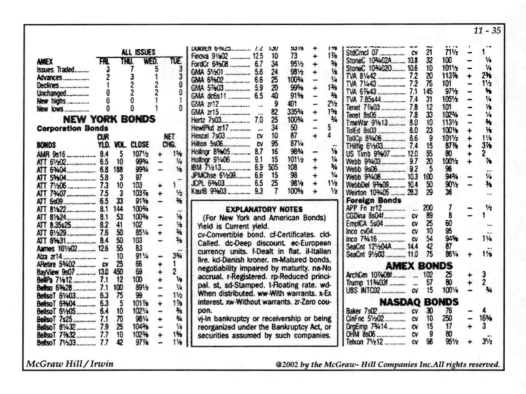

AMEX — ALL ISSUES

	FRI.	THU.	WED.	TUE.
Issues Traded	3	7	5	3
Advances	2	3	1	3
Declines	1	2	2	0
Unchanged	0	2	2	0
New highs	0	0	1	1
New lows	0	0	1	0

NEW YORK BONDS
Corporation Bonds

BONDS	CUR YLD.	VOL.	CLOSE	NET CHG.
AMR 9s16	8.4	5	107½	+ 1⅜
ATT 6½02	6.5	10	99¾	- ¼
ATT 6¾04	6.8	188	99¾	- ⅛
ATT 5⅜04	5.8	3	97	
ATT 7½06	7.3	10	103	+ 1
ATT 7¾07	7.5	3	103⅞	+ ½
ATT 6s09	6.5	33	91⅜	- ⅜
ATT 8½22	8.1	144	100¾	
ATT 8¼24	8.1	53	100⅜	- ⅛
ATT 8.35s25	8.2	41	102	- ⅛
ATT 6½29	7.6	50	85¼	+ ⅜
ATT 8⅝31	8.4	50	103	- ⅝
Aames 10½02	12.6	55	83	
Alza zr14	--	10	91¼	- 3¾
ARetire 5¾02	cv	25	66	+ 1
BayView 9s07	13.0	450	69	+ 2
BellPa 7⅛12	7.1	12	100	+ ⅛
Bellso 6⅞28	7.1	100	89½	- ⅛
BellsoT 6¼03	6.3	75	99	- 1½
BellsoT 6⅜04	6.3	5	101⅞	+ 1⅞
BellsoT 6½05	6.4	10	102¼	- ⅜
BellsoT 7s25	7.1	70	98¼	- ¾
BellsoT 8¼32	7.9	25	104⅜	- ¼
BellsoT 7⅞32	7.7	10	102⅜	+ 1⅞
BellsoT 7½33	7.7	42	97⅞	- 1⅛

BONDS	CUR YLD.	VOL.	CLOSE	NET CHG.
DukeEn 6¾25	7.2	130	93⅛	+ 1⅜
Finova 9½02	12.5	10	73	+ 1⅞
FordCr 6⅜08	6.7	34	95½	+ ⅜
GMA 5⅞01	5.6	24	98½	+ ⅛
GMA 6⅜02	6.6	25	100¾	- ¼
GMA 5⅞03	5.9	20	99⅝	+ 1⅜
GMA dc6s11	6.5	40	91⅜	- ⅜
GMA zr12	--	9	40⅛	- 2½
GMA zr15	--	82	335¾	+ 1⅝
Hertz 7s03	7.0	25	100¾	- ¾
HewlPkd zr17	--	34	50	- 5
Hexcel 7s03	cv	10	87	+ 4
Hilton 5s06	cv	95	87¼	
Hollngr 8⅝05	8.7	16	98¾	- ⅛
Hollngr 9¼06	9.1	15	101½	+ ¼
IBM 7½13	6.9	505	108	+ ¾
JPMChse 6½09	6.6	15	98	+ ¼
JCPL 6⅜03	6.5	25	98½	+ 1½
KaufB 9⅜03	9.3	7	100⅜	+ ½

BONDS	CUR YLD.	VOL.	CLOSE	NET CHG.
StdCmcl 07	cv	21	71½	- 1
StoneC 10¾02A	10.8	32	100	- ¼
StoneC 10¾020	10.6	10	101½	- ¼
TVA 8¼42	7.2	20	113⅞	+ 2⅜
TVA 7¼43	7.2	76	101	- 1½
TVA 6⅝43	7.1	145	97½	- ⅝
TVA 7.85s44	7.4	31	105½	- ¼
Tenet 7⅞03	7.8	12	101	- ⅛
Tenet 8s05	7.8	33	102¾	- ¼
TmeWar 9⅛13	8.0	10	113½	- ⅜
TollEd 8s03	8.0	23	100⅛	+ ⅛
TollCp 8¾06	8.6	9	101½	+ 1½
THilfig 6⅞03	7.4	15	87⅜	+ 3⅞
US Timb 9⅝07	12.0	55	80	+ 2
Webb 9¾03	9.7	20	100½	+ ⅞
Webb 9s06	9.2	5	98	
Webb 9⅜06	10.3	100	94¾	- ¼
WebbDel 9⅜09	10.4	50	90½	- ⅜
Weirton 10⅜05	28.3	29	38	

Foreign Bonds

BONDS	CUR YLD.	VOL.	CLOSE	NET CHG.
APP Fn zr12	--	200	7	- ½
CGDina 8s041	cv	89	8	- 1
EmptCA 5s04	cv	25	60	
Inco cv04	cv	10	95	
Inco 7¾16	cv	54	94⅜	- 1¼
SeaCnt 12½04A	14.4	42	87	
SeaCnt 9½03	11.0	75	86¼	+ 1⅛

AMEX BONDS

BONDS	CUR YLD.	VOL.	CLOSE	NET CHG.
ArchCm 10¾08f	--	102	25	+ 3
Trump 11¾03f	--	57	80	+ 2
UBS INTC02	cv	15	100¼	- ¾

NASDAQ BONDS

BONDS	CUR YLD.	VOL.	CLOSE	NET CHG.
Baker 7s02	cv	30	76	- 4
CinFnc 5½02	cv	10	250	- 16⅜
OrgEmp 7¾14	cv	15	17	+ 3
OHM 8s06	cv	9	80	
Tebxon 7½12	cv	98	95½	+ 3½

EXPLANATORY NOTES
(For New York and American Bonds)
Yield is Current yield.
cv-Convertible bond. cf-Certificates. cld-Called. dc-Deep discount. ec-European currency units. f-Dealt in flat. il-Italian lire. kd-Danish kroner. m-Matured bonds, negotiability impaired by maturity. na-No accrual. r-Registered. rp-Reduced principal. st, sd-Stamped. t-Floating rate. wd-When distributed. ww-With warrants. x-Ex interest. xw-Without warrants. zr-Zero coupon.
vj-In bankruptcy or receivership or being reorganized under the Bankruptcy Act, or securities assumed by such companies.

McGraw Hill / Irwin

Work the Web

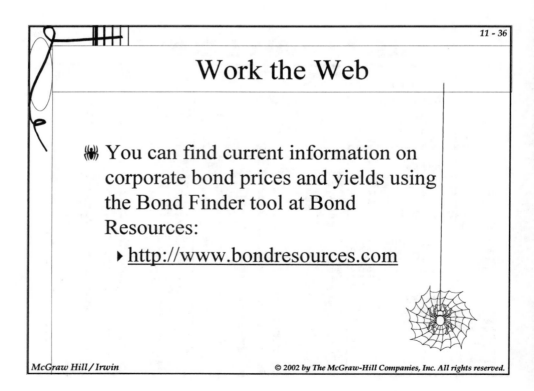

- You can find current information on corporate bond prices and yields using the Bond Finder tool at Bond Resources:
  - http://www.bondresources.com

McGraw Hill / Irwin

Chapter Review

- Corporate Bond Basics
- Types of Corporate Bonds

Chapter Review

- Bond Indentures
    - Bond Seniority Provisions
    - Call Provisions
    - Graphical Analysis of Callable Bond Prices
    - Put Provisions
    - Bond-to-Stock Conversion Provisions
    - Graphical Analysis of Convertible Bond Prices
    - Bond Maturity and Principal Payment Provisions
    - Sinking Fund Provisions
    - Coupon Payment Provisions

Chapter Review

- ◆ Protective Covenants
- ◆ Event Risk
- ◆ Bonds Without Indentures
- ◆ Preferred Stock
- ◆ Adjustable-Rate Bonds and Adjustable-Rate Preferred Stock
- ◆ Corporate Bond Credit Ratings
  - → Why Bond Ratings Are Important

Chapter Review

- ◆ Junk Bonds
- ◆ Bond Market Trading

12

Chapter

Government Bonds

Fundamentals
of Investments
Valuation & Management
second edition

Charles J. Corrado   Bradford D. Jordan

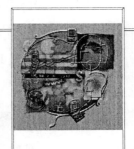

McGraw Hill / Irwin   *Slides by Yee-Tien (Ted) Fu*

Government Bonds

Goal

Our goal in this chapter is to examine the securities issued by federal, state, and local governments, which together represent more than $7 trillion of outstanding securities.

Government Bond Basics

- In 1999, the gross public debt of the U.S. government was more than $5 trillion, making it the largest single borrower in the world.

- The U.S. Treasury finances government debt by issuing marketable as well as non-marketable securities.

http://www.ustreas.gov

Government Bond Basics

- Marketable securities include T-bills, T-notes, and T-bonds, while non-marketable securities include U.S. Savings Bonds, Government Account Series, and State and Local Government Series.

- Another large market is the market for municipal government debt. There are more than 80,000 state and local governments in the U.S., and together they contribute about $2 trillion of outstanding debt.

Work the Web

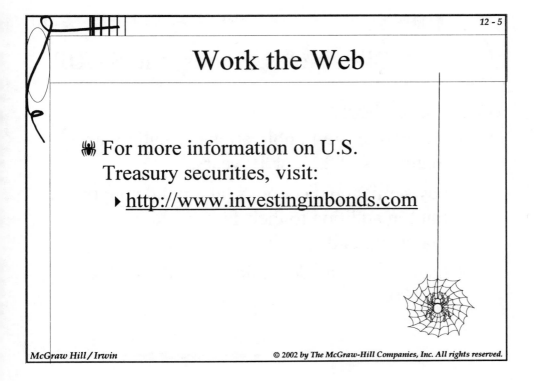

🕷 For more information on U.S.
Treasury securities, visit:

▸ http://www.investinginbonds.com

U.S. T-Bills, Notes, Bonds, and STRIPS

Treasury Bills

- are short-term obligations with maturities of 13, 26, or 52 weeks,
- pay only their *face value* (or redemption value) at maturity,
- have face value denominations as small as $1,000, and
- are sold on a *discount basis* (the discount represents the *imputed interest* on the bill).

U.S. T-Bills, Notes, Bonds, and STRIPS

Treasury Notes

- ◆ are medium-term obligations, usually with maturities of 2, 5, or 10 years,
- ◆ pay semiannual coupons (at a fixed coupon rate) in addition to their face value (at maturity), and
- ◆ have face value denominations as small as $1,000.

U.S. T-Bills, Notes, Bonds, and STRIPS

Treasury Bonds

- ◆ are long-term obligations with maturities of more than 10 years (usually 30 years),
- ◆ pay semiannual coupons (at a fixed coupon rate) in addition to their face value (at maturity), and
- ◆ have face value denominations as small as $1,000.

U.S. T-Bills, Notes, Bonds, and STRIPS

Treasury STRIPS (Separate Trading of Registered Interest and Principal of Securities)

◆ are derived from 10-year T-notes and 30-year T-bonds (e.g. a 30-year T-bond can be separated into 61 strips - 60 semiannual coupons + a single face value payment), and

◆ are effectively zero coupon bonds (zeroes), so the YTMs are the interest rates the investors will receive if the bonds are held until maturity.

U.S. T-Bills, Notes, Bonds, and STRIPS

Example: Calculating the price of a STRIPS

◆ What is the price of a STRIPS maturing in 20 years with a face value of $10,000 and a semiannual YTM of 7%?

✧ The STRIPS price is calculated as the present value of a single cash flow.

✧ STRIPS price $= \dfrac{\$10,000}{\left(1 + \dfrac{0.07}{2}\right)^{40}} = \$2,525.72$

TABLE 12.1	Zero Coupon Bond Prices, $10,000 Face Value			
			Bond Maturity	
Yield to Maturity	5 Years	10 Years	20 Years	30 Years
3.0%	$8,616.67	$7,424.70	$5,512.62	$4,092.96
3.5	8,407.29	7,068.25	4,996.01	3,531.30
4.0	8,203.48	6,729.71	4,528.90	3,047.82
4.5	8,005.10	6,408.16	4,106.46	2,631.49
5.0	7,811.98	6,102.71	3,724.31	2,272.84
5.5	7,623.98	5,812.51	3,378.52	1,963.77
6.0	7,440.94	5,536.76	3,065.57	1,697.33
6.5	7,262.72	5,274.71	2,782.26	1,467.56
7.0	7,089.19	5,025.66	2,525.72	1,269.34
7.5	6,920.20	4,788.92	2,293.38	1,098.28
8.0	6,755.64	4,563.87	2,082.89	950.60
8.5	6,595.37	4,349.89	1,892.16	823.07
9.0	6,439.28	4,146.43	1,719.29	712.89
9.5	6,287.23	3,952.93	1,562.57	617.67
10.0	6,139.13	3,768.89	1,420.46	535.36
10.5	5,994.86	3,593.83	1,291.56	464.17
11.0	5,854.31	3,427.29	1,174.63	402.58
11.5	5,717.37	3,268.83	1,068.53	349.28
12.0	5,583.95	3,118.05	972.22	303.14
12.5	5,453.94	2,974.55	884.79	263.19
13.0	5,327.26	2,837.97	805.41	228.57
13.5	5,203.81	2,707.96	733.31	198.58
14.0	5,083.49	2,584.19	667.80	172.57
14.5	4,966.23	2,466.35	608.29	150.02
15.0	4,851.94	2,354.13	554.19	130.46

U.S. T-Bills, Notes, Bonds, and STRIPS

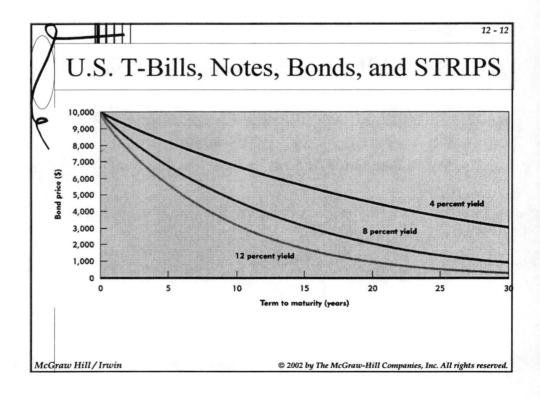

Treasury Bond and Note Prices

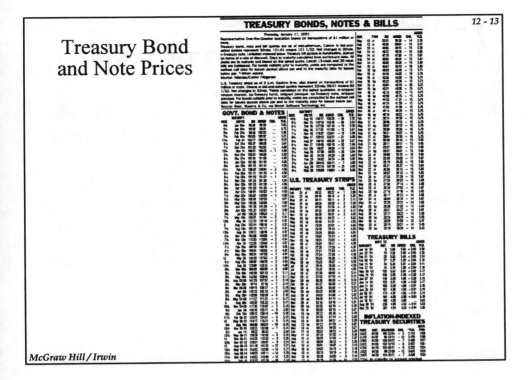

Treasury Bond and Note Prices

- When a callable T-bond has a price above par, the reported yield is a *yield to call (YTC)*. Since 1985 however, the Treasury has issued only noncallable bonds.

- T-bonds and notes pay semiannual coupons, so bond yields are stated on a semiannual basis.

- The relationship between the price of a note or bond and its YTM was discussed in Chapter 10 (Bond Prices and Yields).

Straight Bond Prices and Yield to Maturity

Bond price = present value of all the coupon payments
+ present value of the principal payment

$$\text{Bond price} = \frac{C}{YTM}\left[1 - \frac{1}{\left(1 + \frac{YTM}{2}\right)^{2M}}\right] + \frac{FV}{\left(1 + \frac{YTM}{2}\right)^{2M}}$$

where C = annual coupon, the sum of 2 semiannual
coupons
FV = face value
M = maturity in years

Treasury Bond and Note Prices

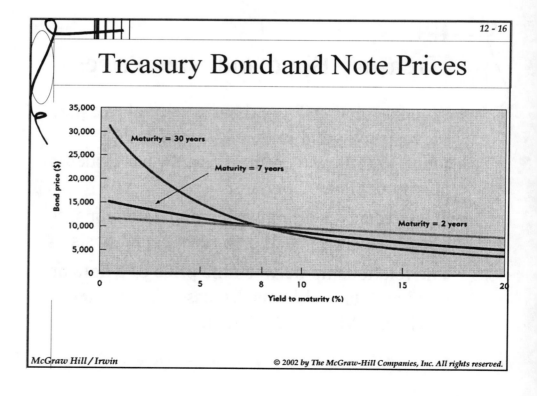

Inflation-Indexed Treasury Securities

- ◆ In recent years, the U.S. Treasury has issued securities that guarantee a fixed rate of return in excess of realized inflation rates.

- ◆ These inflation-indexed Treasury securities pay a fixed coupon rate on their current principal and adjust their principal semiannually according to the most recent inflation rate.

U.S. Treasury Auctions

- ◆ The Federal Reserve Bank conducts regularly scheduled auctions for T-bills, notes, and bonds.

U.S. Treasury Auctions

General Auction Pattern for U.S. Treasury Securities as of 2001			
Security	Purchase Minimum	Purchase in Multiples of	General Auction Schedule
4-week bill	$1,000	$1,000	Weekly
13-week bill	1,000	1,000	Weekly
26-week bill	1,000	1,000	Weekly
2-year note	1,000	1,000	Monthly
5-year note	1,000	1,000	February, May, August, November
10-year note	1,000	1,000	February, May, August, November
30-year bond	1,000	1,000	February, August

U.S. Treasury Auctions

- At each Treasury auction, the Federal Reserve accepts sealed bids of two types.

① Competitive bids specify a bid price/yield and a bid quantity. Such bids can only be submitted by Treasury securities dealers.

② Noncompetitive bids specify only a bid quantity, and may be submitted by individual investors. The price/yield is determined by the results of the competitive auction process.

U.S. Treasury Auctions

- ◆ All noncompetitive bids are accepted automatically and are subtracted from the total issue amount.
- ◆ Then a *stop-out bid* is determined. This is the price at which all competitive bids are sufficient to finance the remaining amount.
- ◆ Since 1998, all U.S. Treasury auctions have been single-price auctions in which all accepted bids pay the stop-out bid.

Work the Web

- 🕷 For recent information on Treasury auctions, visit:
  - ▸ http://www.publicdebt.treas.gov

U.S. Savings Bonds

- ◆ The U.S. Treasury offers an investment opportunity for individual investors in the form of savings bonds.

U.S. Savings Bonds

Series EE Savings Bonds

- ◆ have face value denominations ranging from $50 to $10,000,
- ◆ are sold at exactly half the face value,
- ◆ accrue interest semiannually (the interest rate is set at 90% of the yield on newly issued 5-year T-notes), and
- ◆ can be redeemed for the original price plus all prior accrued interest.

U.S. Savings Bonds

Series I Savings Bonds

- have face value denominations ranging from $50 to $10,000,

- are sold at face value,

- accrue interest semiannually (the interest rate is set at a fixed rate plus the recent inflation rate), and

- can be redeemed for the original price plus all prior accrued interest.

Work the Web

For the latest on Savings Bonds, visit:
  - http://www.savingsbonds.com

Federal Government Agency Securities

- Most U.S. government agencies consolidate their borrowing through the Federal Financing Bank, which obtains funds directly from the U.S. Treasury.

- However, several federal agencies are authorized to issue securities directly to the public. E.g. the Resolution Trust Funding Corporation, the World Bank, and the Tennessee Valley Authority.

Federal Government Agency Securities

- Bonds issued by U.S. government agencies share an almost equal credit quality with U.S. Treasury issues.

- They are attractive in that they offer higher yields than comparable U.S. Treasury securities.

- However, the market for agency debt is less active than the market for U.S. Treasury debt.
  → Compared to T-bonds, agency bonds have a wider bid-ask spread.

Federal Government Agency Securities

GOVERNMENT AGENCY & SIMILAR ISSUES

Wednesday, January 17, 2001

Over-the-Counter mid-afternoon quotations based on large transactions, usually $1 million or more. Colons in-bid-and asked quotes represent 32nds; 101:01 means 101 1/32. All yields are calculated to maturity, and based on the asked quote. *-callable issue, maturity date shown. For issues callable prior to maturity, yields are computed to the earliest call date for issues quoted above par, or 100, and to the maturity date for issues below par.

Source: Bear, Stearns & Co. via Street Software Technology Inc.

RATE	MAT.	BID	ASKED	YLD.		RATE	MAT.	BID	ASKED	YLD.
Fannie Mae Issues						5.25	1-06*	98:15	98:19	5.57
6.53	1-02	101:10	101:12	5.18		5.75	4-06	99:20	99:24	5.79
5.38	3-02	100:04	100:06	5.21		5.13	10-06	95:14	95:18	5.84
6.63	4-02	101:19	101:21	5.22		5.75	3-09	99:05	99:09	5.86
6.75	8-02	102:06	102:08	5.24		6.45	4-09*	98:18	98:22	5.66
6.38	10-02	101:26	101:30	5.20		7.63	9-09	103:14	103:16	7.06
5.25	1-03	99:30	100:01	5.24		5.63	9-09	104:20	104:24	5.91
5.75	4-03	100:30	101:01	5.25		7.00	3-10	107:12	107:15	5.93
4.75	11-03	98:13	98:16	5.32		6.88	9-10	106:22	106:26	5.94
5.13	2-04	99:05	99:08	5.39		6.75	9-29	106:26	106:30	5.23
5.88	4-04*	99:12	99:15	6.05		6.75	3-31	107:00	107:04	6.22
5.63	5-04	100:14	100:17	5.44						
6.50	8-04	103:10	103:13	5.44		**Federal Farm Credit Bank**				
7.10	10-04*	100:31	101:02	6.18		5.63	2-02	101:12	101:14	5.18
7.13	2-05	105:24	105:27	5.50		5.25	5-02	99:29	99:31	5.27
5.75	6-05	100:25	100:29	5.52		6.86	5-02	101:29	101:31	5.27
7.00	7-05	105:19	105:22	5.55		6.75	9-02	101:29	101:31	5.46
6.00	12-05	101:24	101:27	5.56		6.25	12-02	100:00	100:03	5.19
7.13	3-07	107:09	107:12	5.59						
6.63	10-07	105:00	105:03	5.70		**Federal Home Loan Bank**				
5.75	2-08	99:24	99:28	5.77		4.88	1-02	99:20	99:22	5.20
6.00	5-08	101:03	101:07	5.79		5.13	2-02	99:27	99:29	5.21
5.25	1-09	96:00	96:04	5.85		5.25	4-02	99:25	99:30	5.29
6.50	4-09*	98:28	99:00	6.86		5.75	5-02	101:18	101:20	5.42
6.40	5-09*	99:17	99:21	6.45		6.75	8-02	102:06	102:06	5.23
6.38	6-09	103:02	103:06	5.89		6.38	11-02	101:30	102:01	5.18
6.63	9-09	104:21	104:25	5.91		6.38	11-02	101:28	101:31	5.23
7.25	1-10	109:00	109:04	5.93		6.88	8-03	103:14	103:17	5.39
7.13	6-10	108:12	108:16	5.93		5.13	9-03	99:12	99:15	5.34
6.63	11-10	105:03	105:07	5.92		5.38	1-04	99:28	99:27	5.39
6.25	5-29	100:03	100:07	6.23		6.00	5-04	99:24	99:27	6.05
7.25	5-30	113:23	113:27	6.22		6.88	8-05	105:02	105:05	5.58
6.63	11-30	105:18	105:22	6.20		5.80	9-08	99:05	99:10	5.91
Freddie Mac						**GNMA Mtge. Issues**				
5.50	5-02	100:08	100:10	5.24		5.50	30Yr	95:06	95:08	6.29
6.63	8-02	102:00	102:02	5.24		6.00	30Yr	97:20	97:22	6.44
6.25	10-02	101:20	101:22	5.22		6.50	30Yr	98:12	98:14	6.55
5.75	7-03	100:28	100:31	5.32		7.00	30Yr	101:00	101:02	6.86
6.38	11-03	102:19	102:22	5.34		7.50	30Yr	102:08	102:10	7.06
5.00	1-04	98:28	98:31	5.38		8.00	30Yr	103:04	103:06	7.16
6.30	6-04*	100:04	100:07	5.63		8.50	30Yr	103:24	103:26	6.90
6.88	1-05	104:28	104:31	5.47		9.00	30Yr	104:02	104:04	6.96
7.00	7-05	105:19	105:22	5.55		9.50	30Yr	104:09	104:11	7.26

Work the Web

- For more information on agency securities, visit:
  - http://www.investinginbonds.com
- To see where your student loan funds come from, visit:
  - http://www.salliemae.com

Municipal Bonds

- Municipal notes and bonds, or *munis*, are intermediate- to long-term interest-bearing obligations of state and local governments, or agencies of those governments.

- Since their coupon interest is usually exempt from federal income tax, the market for municipal debt is commonly called the *tax-exempt market*.

Municipal Bonds

- The federal income tax exemption makes municipal bonds attractive to investors in the highest income tax brackets.

- However, yields on municipal debt are less than yields on corporate debt with similar features and credit quality.

- The risk of default is also real despite their usually-high credit ratings.

City of Bedford Falls General Obligation Bonds

Issue amount	$50 million	Bond issue represents a total face value amount of $50 million
Issue date	12/15/99	Bonds were offered to the public on December 15, 1999
Maturity date	12/31/29	All remaining principal must be paid at maturity on December 31, 2029
Par value	$5,000	Each bond has a face value of $5,000
Coupon rate	6%	Annual coupons of $300 per bond
Coupon dates	12/31, 6/30	Semiannual coupons of $150
Offering price	100	Offer price is 100% of par value
Yield to maturity	6%	Based on stated offer price
Call provision	Callable after 12/31/09	Bonds are call-protected for 10 years
Call price	100	Bonds are callable at par value
Trustee	Potters Bank of Bedford Falls	The trustee is appointed to represent the bondholders and administer the sinking fund
Sinking fund	$2.5 million annual par redemptions after 12/31/09	City must redeem at par value $2.5 million of the bond issue each year beginning in 2010

McGraw Hill / Irwin

Municipal Bond Features

- Municipal bonds
  - → are typically callable,
  - → pay semiannual coupons,
  - → have a par value denomination of $5,000,
  - → have prices that are stated as a percentage of par value (though municipal bond dealers commonly use yield quotes in their trading procedures),
  - → are commonly issued with a serial maturity structure (hence the term *serial bonds,* versus *term bonds*),

McGraw Hill / Irwin

Municipal Bond Features

- ◆ Municipal bonds
  - → may be putable, or have variable interest rates, or both (*variable-rate demand obligation, VRDO*), and
  - → may be strippable (hence creating *muni-strips*).

Municipal Bond Features

TAX-EXEMPT BONDS

Representative prices for several active tax-exempt revenue and refunding bonds, based on institutional trades. Changes rounded to the nearest one-eighth. Yield is to maturity. n-New. Source: The Bond Buyer.

ISSUE	COUPON	MAT	PRICE	CHG	BID YLD	ISSUE	COUPON	MAT	PRICE	CHG	BID YLD
Allghny Sanitary PA	5.500	12-01-30	104¹/₈	+ ¹/₈	5.05	Nev LasVeg Monorail	5.375	01-01-40	101	+ ¹/₈	5.23
Atlanta GA airport	5.600	01-01-30	104³/₄	+ ¹/₈	5.04	NYC Muni Wtr Fin	5.500	06-15-33	103³/₄	+ ¹/₈	5.04
CA State construct	5.500	10-01-30	105	+ ¹/₈	4.86	NYC Muni Wtr Fin	5.125	06-15-31	99	...	5.19
Chic IL gen oblig	5.500	01-01-35	102³/₄	+ ¹/₈	5.15	NYS Dorm Auth	5.250	07-01-30	101	+ ¹/₈	5.11
Chic skyway toll	5.500	01-01-31	103¹/₈	...	5.13	NYS Dorm Auth	5.500	05-15-30	103³/₈	+ ¹/₈	5.05
Ctrl CA Jt Pwrs	6.000	02-01-30	102	+ ¹/₈	5.76	NYS PwrAuth rev2000	5.250	11-15-40	100³/₄	+ ¹/₈	5.15
Dekalb GA wtr&swr	5.125	10-01-31	99³/₈	+ ¹/₈	5.17	OrangeCoFL tourist2000	5.500	10-01-31	103¹/₂	+ ¹/₈	5.01
Dekalb GA wtr&swr	5.375	10-01-35	102¹/₈	+ ¹/₈	5.11	Phila PA gen oblig	5.000	09-15-31	97¹/₈	+ ¹/₄	5.19
EmpireSt Dev Cp NY	5.250	01-01-30	101	+ ¹/₈	5.12	Phila PA gen oblig	5.250	09-15-25	100³/₄	...	5.15
Hamilton Co OH	5.250	12-01-32	101³/₈	+ ¹/₈	5.08	Phila SD PA gen obl	5.750	02-01-30	106¹/₄	...	4.96
HI Dept Bdgt&Fin	5.700	07-01-20	104³/₈	+ ¹/₈	5.15	PR Elec Pwr Auth	5.250	07-10-29	102¹/₄	+ ¹/₈	4.97
Houston TX airport	5.500	07-01-30	103¹/₈	+ ¹/₈	5.08	PR Ind Tour Edu Med	5.000	07-01-33	99¹/₄	+ ¹/₈	5.01
Houston TX airport	5.700	07-01-28	104⁷/₈	+ ¹/₈	5.05	PR Infra Fin Auth	5.500	10-01-40	105⁵/₈	+ ¹/₈	4.83
IL Hlth Facs Auth	6.125	11-15-22	102¹/₄	+ ¹/₈	5.83	PR Infra Fin Auth	5.500	10-01-32	105⁵/₈	+ ¹/₈	4.82
IN Hlth FacFinAuth	5.500	02-15-30	101¹/₈	...	5.29	SanDiego UnifSchDist	5.000	07-01-25	99⁷/₈	+ ¹/₈	5.01
IN Trans Fin Auth	5.375	12-01-25	101	...	5.24	SC Trans Infra Bk	5.500	10-01-30	103¹/₂	...	5.04
LA LocGovAuth 2000	6.550	09-01-25	99⁷/₈	+ ¹/₈	6.56	Tallahass FL HlthFacs	6.375	12-01-30	103¹/₄	+ ¹/₈	5.95
MA Bay TranspAuth	5.250	07-01-30	100⁷/₈	+ ¹/₈	5.14	Univ of CA rev bds	5.300	09-01-30	102¹/₂	+ ¹/₈	4.97
MA Wtr Poll Abate	5.500	08-01-30	103³/₄	+ ¹/₈	5.04	Westchstr HlthCareNY	6.000	11-01-30	102⁵/₈	...	5.63
MI St Hosp FinAuth	6.000	12-01-27	102³/₄	...	5.67	Westchstr HlthCareNY	5.875	11-01-25	102	+ ¹/₈	5.61

Types of Municipal Bonds

- ◆ Bonds issued by a municipality that are secured by the full faith and credit (general taxing powers) of the issuer are known as *general obligation bonds (GOs)*.

- ◆ Municipal bonds secured by revenues collected from a specific project or projects are called *revenue bonds*.
  - → Example: Airport and seaport development bonds that are secured by user fees and lease revenues.

Types of Municipal Bonds

- ◆ *Hybrid bonds* are municipal bonds secured by project revenues with some form of general obligation credit guarantees.
  - → A common form of hybrid is the *moral obligation bond*.

Municipal Bond Credit Ratings

Municipal Bond Credit Ratings			
Rating Agency			
Standard & Poor's	Moody's	Fitch	Credit Rating Description
Investment-Grade Bond Ratings			
AAA	Aaa	AAA	Highest credit quality
AA	Aa	AA	High credit quality
A	A	A	Good credit quality
BBB	Baa	BBB	Satisfactory credit quality
Speculative-Grade Bond Ratings			
BB	Ba	BB	Speculative credit quality
B	B	B	Highly speculative quality
CCC	Caa	CCC	Poor credit quality
CC	Ca	CC	Probable default
Extremely Speculative-Grade Bond Ratings			
C	C	C	Imminent default
D		DDD	In default
		DD, D	

McGraw Hill / Irwin

Municipal Bond Insurance

- Insured municipal bonds, besides being secured by the issuer's resources, are also backed by an insurance policy written by a commercial insurance company.

- With bond insurance, the credit quality of the bond issue is additionally determined by the financial strength of the insurance company.

McGraw Hill / Irwin

Work the Web

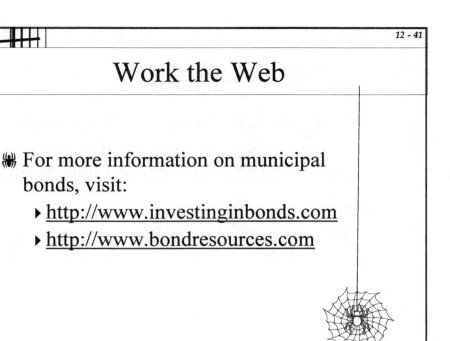

For more information on municipal
bonds, visit:
- http://www.investinginbonds.com
- http://www.bondresources.com

Equivalent Taxable Yield

- Which is better? A corporate bond paying an
  annual coupon interest of 8% or a municipal
  bond paying an annual coupon interest of 5%?

Method 1:

$$\frac{\text{Equivalent}}{\text{taxable yield}} = \frac{\text{Tax-exempt yield}}{1-\text{Marginal tax rate}}$$

Method 2:

$$\frac{\text{After-tax}}{\text{yield}} = \frac{\text{Taxable}}{\text{yield}} \times (1 - \text{Marginal tax rate})$$

Equivalent Taxable Yield

- Which is better? A corporate bond paying an annual coupon interest of 8% or a municipal bond paying an annual coupon interest of 5%?

Method 3:

$$\text{Critical marginal tax rate} = 1 - \frac{\text{Tax-exempt yield}}{\text{Taxable yield}}$$

Taxable Municipal Bonds

- The Tax Reform Act of 1986 imposed notable restrictions on the types of municipal bonds that qualify for federal tax exemption of interest payments.

- In particular, the act expanded the definition of *private activity bonds*, which are taxable municipal bonds used to finance facilities used by private businesses.
  → The yields on such bonds are often similar to the yields on corporate bonds.

Chapter Review

- ◆ Government Bond Basics
- ◆ U.S. Treasury Bills, Notes, Bonds, and STRIPS
  - → Treasury Bond and Note Prices
  - → Inflation-Indexed Treasury Securities
- ◆ U.S. Treasury Auctions
- ◆ U.S. Savings Bonds
  - → Series EE Savings Bonds
  - → Series I Savings Bonds

Chapter Review

- ◆ Federal Government Agency Securities
- ◆ Municipal Bonds
  - → Municipal Bond Features
  - → Types of Municipal Bonds
  - → Municipal Bond Credit Ratings
  - → Municipal Bond Insurance
- ◆ Equivalent Taxable Yield
- ◆ Taxable Municipal Bonds

13
Chapter

Mortgage-Backed Securities

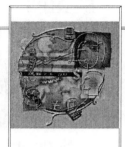

Fundamentals
of Investments
Valuation & Management
second edition

Charles J. Corrado   Bradford D. Jordan

McGraw Hill / Irwin

Slides by Yee-Tien (Ted) Fu

Mortgage-Backed Securities

Goal

Our goal in this chapter is to examine the investment characteristics of mortgage pools.

A Brief History of Mortgage-Backed Securities

- Traditionally, local banks wrote most home mortgages and then held the mortgages in their portfolios of interest-earning assets.
- Then, when market interest rates climbed to near 20% in the early 1980s, bank customers flocked to withdraw funds from their savings deposits to invest in money market funds.
- Today, an originator usually sells the mortgage to a mortgage repackager, who accumulates them into mortgage pools.

A Brief History of Mortgage-Backed Securities

- Financed by *mortgage-backed bonds* (also called *mortgage pass-throughs*), each mortgage pool is set up as a trust fund. A servicing agent collects the mortgage payments and then *passes* the cash flows *through* to the bondholders.
- The transformation from mortgages to *mortgage-backed securities (MBSs)* is called *mortgage securitization*.

Work the Web

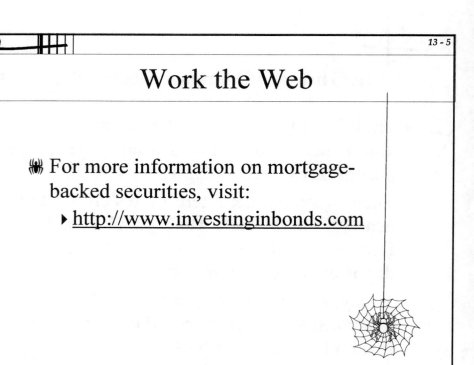

For more information on mortgage-backed securities, visit:

▸ http://www.investinginbonds.com

Fixed-Rate Mortgages

Fixed-rate mortgage
Loan that specifies constant monthly payments at a fixed interest rate over the life of the mortgage.

◆ The size of the monthly payment is determined by the requirement that the present value of all monthly payments, based on the financing rate specified in the mortgage contract, be equal to the original loan amount.

Fixed-Rate Mortgages

$$\text{Monthly payment} = \frac{\text{loan amount} \times \frac{r}{12}}{1 - \frac{1}{\left(1 + \frac{r}{12}\right)^{T \times 12}}}$$

where r = annual mortgage financing rate
T = mortgage term in years

TABLE 13.1

$100,000 Mortgage Loan Monthly Payments

Interest Rate	Mortgage Maturity				
	30-Year	20-Year	15-Year	10-Year	5-Year
5.0%	$ 536.82	$ 659.96	$ 790.79	$1,060.66	$1,887.12
5.5	567.79	687.89	817.08	1,085.26	1,910.12
6.0	599.55	716.43	843.86	1,110.21	1,933.28
6.5	632.07	745.57	871.11	1,135.48	1,956.61
7.0	665.30	775.30	898.83	1,161.08	1,980.12
7.5	699.21	805.59	927.01	1,187.02	2,003.79
8.0	733.76	836.44	955.65	1,213.28	2,027.64
8.5	768.91	867.82	984.74	1,239.86	2,051.65
9.0	804.62	899.73	1,014.27	1,266.76	2,075.84
9.5	840.85	932.13	1,044.22	1,293.98	2,100.19
10.0	877.57	965.02	1,074.61	1,321.51	2,124.70
10.5	914.74	998.38	1,105.40	1,349.35	2,149.39
11.0	952.32	1,032.19	1,136.60	1,377.50	2,174.24
11.5	990.29	1,066.43	1,168.19	1,405.95	2,199.26
12.0	1,028.61	1,101.09	1,200.17	1,434.71	2,224.44
12.5	1,067.26	1,136.14	1,232.52	1,463.76	2,249.79
13.0	1,106.20	1,171.58	1,265.24	1,493.11	2,275.31
13.5	1,145.41	1,207.37	1,298.32	1,522.74	2,300.98
14.0	1,184.87	1,243.52	1,331.74	1,552.66	2,326.83
14.5	1,224.56	1,280.00	1,365.50	1,582.87	2,352.83
15.0	1,264.44	1,316.79	1,399.59	1,613.35	2,378.99

Fixed-Rate Mortgage Amortization

- ◆ Each monthly mortgage payment has two separate components:
  - ① payment of interest on outstanding *mortgage principal*
  - ② pay-down, or *amortization*, of mortgage principal
- ◆ The relative amounts of each component change throughout the life of the mortgage.

Fixed-Rate Mortgage Amortization

- ◆ Suppose a 30-year $100,000 mortgage loan is financed at a fixed interest rate of 8%.
  - ✧ Monthly payment $= \dfrac{\$100{,}000 \times .08/12}{1 - 1/\left(1 + .08/12\right)^{30 \times 12}} = \$733.76$
  - ✧ In the first month,
    Interest payment $= \$100{,}000 \times .08/12 = \$666.67$
    Principal payment $= \$733.76 - \$666.67 = \$67.09$
    New principal $= \$100{,}000 - \$67.09 = \$99{,}932.91$
  - ✧ In the second month,
    Interest payment $= \$99{,}932.91 \times .08/12 = \$666.22$
    Principal payment $= \$733.76 - \$666.22 = \$67.54$
    New principal $= \$99{,}932.91 - \$67.54 = \$99{,}865.37$

Fixed-Rate Mortgage Amortization

♦ Mortgage amortization can be described by an *amortization schedule*, which states the scheduled principal payment, interest payment, and remaining principal owed in any month.

McGraw Hill / Irwin

TABLE 13.2   **$100,000 Mortgage Loan Amortization Schedules for 15-year and 30-year Mortgages**

	30-Year Mortgage $733.76 Monthly Payment				15-Year Mortgage $955.65 Monthly Payment		
Payment Month	Remaining Principal	Principal Reduction	Interest Payment	Payment Month	Remaining Principal	Principal Reduction	Interest Payment
1	$99,932.90	$ 67.10	$666.67	1	$99,711.01	$288.99	$666.67
12	99,164.64	72.19	661.58	12	96,402.15	310.90	644.75
24	98,259.94	78.18	655.59	24	92,505.69	336.70	618.95
36	97,280.15	84.67	649.10	36	88,285.81	364.65	591.00
48	96,219.04	91.69	642.07	48	83,715.70	394.91	560.74
60	95,069.86	99.30	634.46	60	78,766.26	427.69	527.96
72	93,825.29	107.55	626.22	72	73,406.02	463.19	492.46
84	92,477.43	116.47	617.29	84	67,600.89	501.64	454.02
96	91,017.70	126.14	607.63	96	61,313.93	543.27	412.38
108	89,436.81	136.61	597.16	108	54,505.16	588.36	367.29
120	87,724.70	147.95	585.82	120	47,131.26	637.20	318.46
132	85,870.50	160.23	573.54	132	39,145.34	690.08	265.57
144	83,862.39	173.53	560.24	144	30,496.58	747.36	208.29
156	81,687.61	187.93	545.84	156	21,129.99	809.39	146.26
168	79,332.33	203.53	530.24	168	10,985.97	876.57	79.08
180	76,781.56	220.42	513.35	180	0.00	949.32	6.33
192	74,019.08	238.71	495.05				
204	71,027.31	258.53	475.24				
216	67,787.23	279.98	453.78				
228	64,278.22	303.22	430.54				
240	60,477.96	328.39	405.38				
252	56,362.29	355.65	378.12				
264	51,905.02	385.16	348.60				
276	47,077.79	417.13	316.63				
288	41,849.91	451.75	282.01				
300	36,188.12	489.25	244.52				
312	30,056.40	529.86	203.91				
324	23,415.75	573.83	159.93				
336	16,223.93	621.46	112.30				
348	8,435.20	673.04	60.72				
360	0.00	728.91	4.86				

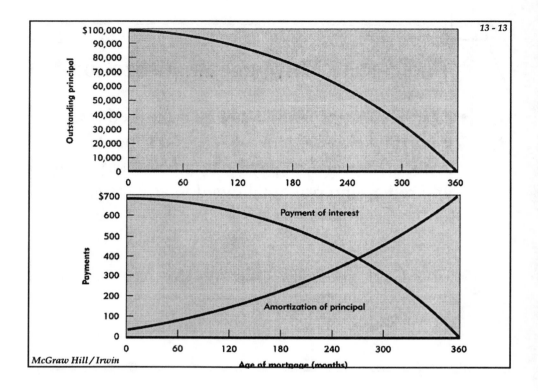

McGraw Hill / Irwin

Age of mortgage (months)

Fixed-Rate Mortgage Prepayment & Refinancing

- ◆ A mortgage borrower has the right to pay off all or part of the mortgage ahead of its amortization schedule. This is similar to the call feature of corporate bonds and is known as *mortgage prepayment*.

- ◆ During periods of falling interest rates, *mortgage refinancings* are an important reason for mortgage prepayments.

- ◆ Hence, mortgage investors face the risk of a reduced rate of return.

McGraw Hill / Irwin

Government National Mortgage Association

- The Government National Mortgage Association (GNMA), or "Ginnie Mae," is a government agency charged with the mission of promoting liquidity in the secondary market for home mortgages.

- GNMA mortgage pools are based on mortgages issued under programs administered by the Federal Housing Administration (FHA), the Veteran's Administration (VA), and the Farmer's Home Administration (FmHA).

Government National Mortgage Association

- Mortgages in GNMA pools are said to be *fully modified* because GNMA guarantees bondholders full and timely payment of both principal and interest.

- Note that although investors in GNMA pass-throughs do not face default risk, they still face prepayment risk.
  - → Prepayments are passed through to bondholders.
  - → If a default occurs, GNMA fully "prepays" the bondholders.

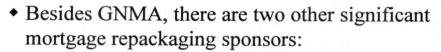

GNMA Clones

- Besides GNMA, there are two other significant mortgage repackaging sponsors:

① Federal Home Loan Mortgage Corporation (FHLMC), or "Freddie Mac," and

② Federal National Mortgage Association (FNMA), or "Fannie Mae."

- Both are government-sponsored enterprises (GSEs) and trade on the New York Stock Exchange.

GNMA Clones

- Like GNMA, both FHLMC and FNMA operate with qualified underwriters who accumulate mortgages into pools financed by an issue of bonds.

- However, since FHLMC and FNMA are only GSEs, their fully modified pass-throughs do not carry the same default protection as GNMA fully modified pass-throughs.

Work the Web

- Visit the GNMA website at:
  - http://www.ginniemae.gov
- Check out the FNMA and FHLMC websites at:
  - http://www.fanniemae.com
  - http://www.freddiemac.com

PSA Mortgage Prepayment Model

- Mortgage prepayments are typically described by stating a *prepayment rate*, which is the probability that a mortgage will be prepaid in a given year.
- Conventional industry practice states prepayment rates using a model specified by the Public Securities Association (PSA).
  - Prepayment rates are stated as a percentage of a PSA benchmark.

PSA Mortgage Prepayment Model

- ◆ In the PSA model, the rates are conditional on the age of the mortgages in the pool. They are *conditional prepayment rates (CPRs)*.

- ◆ For *seasoned* (> 30 months old) *mortgages*, the CPR is a constant (6% annually for 100% of the PSA benchmark (100 PSA)).

- ◆ For *unseasoned* (< 30 months old) *mortgages*, the CPR rises steadily in each month until it reaches an annual rate of 6% (for 100 PSA) in month 30.

PSA Mortgage Prepayment Model

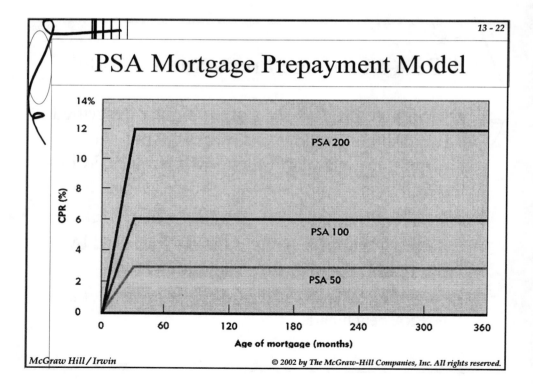

PSA Mortgage Prepayment Model

- By convention, the probability of prepayment in a given month is stated as a *single monthly mortality (SMM)*.

$$SMM = 1 - (1 - CPR)^{1/12}$$

PSA Mortgage Prepayment Model

- The *average life* of a mortgage in a pool is the average time for a single mortgage in the pool to be paid off, either by prepayment or by making scheduled payments until maturity.

- For a pool of 30-year mortgages,

Prepayment Schedule	Average Mortgage Life (years)
50 PSA	20.40
100 PSA	14.68
200 PSA	8.87
400 PSA	4.88

Work the Web

Visit the Public Securities Association at:

- http://www.psa.com

Cash Flow Analysis
GNMA Fully Modified Mortgage Pools

- Each month, GNMA mortgage-backed bond investors receive pro rata shares of cash flows derived from fully modified mortgage pools.

- Each monthly cash flow has three components (less the servicing and guarantee fees):
  1. Payment of interest on outstanding mortgage principal.
  2. Scheduled amortization of mortgage principal.
  3. Mortgage principal prepayments.

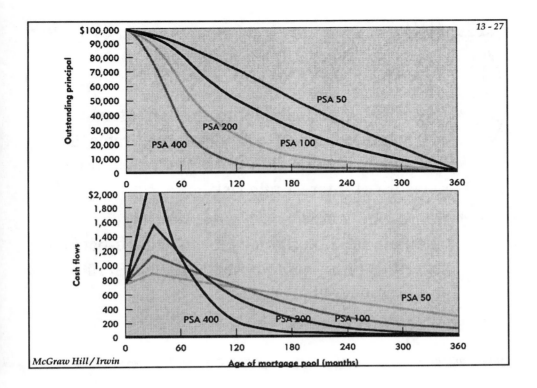

Age of mortgage pool (months)

Macaulay Durations
for GNMA Mortgage-Backed Bonds

- The interest rate risk for a bond is often measured by Macaulay duration, which assumes a fixed schedule of cash flow payments.

- However, the schedule of cash flow payments for mortgage-backed bonds is not fixed.
  - With falling interest rates, prepayments speed up, and vice versa.

Macaulay Durations
for GNMA Mortgage-Backed Bonds

- ◆ Historical experience indicates that interest rates significantly affect prepayment rates, and that Macaulay duration is a very conservative measure of interest rate risk.

- ◆ In practice, *effective duration* is used to calculate predicted prices for mortgage-backed securities based on hypothetical interest rate and prepayment scenarios.

Collateralized Mortgage Obligations

Collateralized mortgage obligations (CMOs)
Securities created by splitting mortgage pool cash flows according to specific allocation rules.

- ◆ The three best-known types of CMOs are:
  - ① interest-only (IOs) and principal-only (POs) strips,
  - ② sequential CMOs, and
  - ③ protected amortization class securities (PACs).

Interest-Only and Principal-Only Strips

- *Interest-only strips (IOs)* pay only the interest cash flows to investors, while *principal-only strips (POs)* pay only the principal cash flows to investors.

- IO strips and PO strips behave quite differently in response to changes in prepayment rates and interest rates.

  → Faster prepayments imply *lower* IO strip values and *higher* PO strip values, and vice versa.

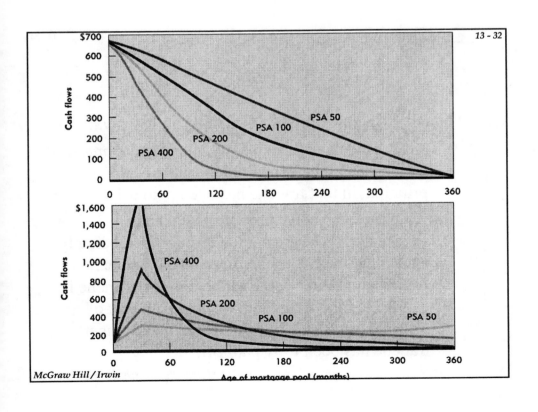

Sequential CMOs

- *Sequential CMOs* carve a mortgage pool into a number of tranches (slices).
  - → For example, A, B, C, and Z-tranches.
- Each tranche is entitled to a share of mortgage pool principal and interest on that share of principal.
- However, cash flows are distributed sequentially, so as to create securities with a range of maturities.

Sequential CMOs

- Cash flows are passed through as follows:
  - → All payments of principal will go to the topmost tranche (in alphabetical order), until all the principal in that tranche has been paid off.
  - → All tranches receive proportionate interest payments. These are passed through immediately, except for the Z-tranche. Interest on Z-tranche principal is paid as cash to the topmost tranche in exchange for a transfer of an equal amount of principal, until all the principal in the topmost tranche has been fully paid off.

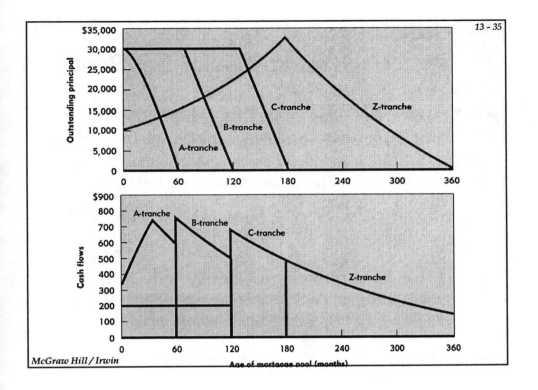

Age of mortgage pool (months)

Protected Amortization Class Bonds

- *Protected amortization class (PAC) bonds* take priority for scheduled payments of principal. The residual cash flows are paid to *PAC support (or companion) bonds*.

- PAC cash flows are predictable as long as prepayments remain within a specified band.

Protected Amortization Class Bonds

- ◆ Creating a PAC bond entails three steps.
  - ① Specify two PSA prepayment schedules that form the upper and lower prepayment bounds of the PAC bond. These bounds define a *PAC collar*.
  - ② Calculate principal-only (PO) cash flows for the two prepayment schedules specified in ①.
  - ③ On a priority basis, at any point in time, PAC bondholders receive payments of principal according to the PSA prepayment schedule with the lower PO cash flow as calculated in ②.

McGraw Hill / Irwin

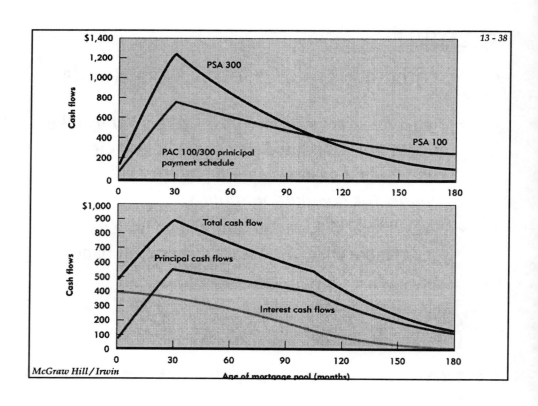

McGraw Hill / Irwin

Work the Web

Check out the CMO section at:
  ▸ http://www.bondresources.com

Yields for MBSs and CMOs

- The yield to maturity for a mortgage-backed security conditional on an assumed prepayment pattern is called the *cash flow yield*.
- Essentially, cash flow yield is the interest rate that equates the present value of all future cash flows on the mortgage pool to the current price of the pool, assuming a particular prepayment rate.

Chapter Review

- A Brief History of Mortgage-Backed Securities
- Fixed-Rate Mortgages
  - → Fixed-Rate Mortgage Amortization
  - → Fixed-Rate Mortgage Prepayment and Refinancing
- Government National Mortgage Association
  - → GNMA Clones
- Public Securities Association Mortgage Prepayment Model

Chapter Review

- Cash Flow Analysis of GNMA Fully Modified Mortgage Pools
  - → Macaulay Durations for GNMA Mortgage-Backed Bonds
- Collateralized Mortgage Obligations
  - → Interest-Only and Principal-Only Mortgage Strips
  - → Sequential Collateralized Mortgage Obligations
  - → Protected Amortization Class Bonds
- Yields for Mortgage-Backed Securities and Collateralized Mortgage Obligations

14
Chapter

Stock Options

Fundamentals
of Investments
Valuation & Management
second edition

Charles J. Corrado   Bradford D. Jordan

McGraw Hill / Irwin

Slides by Yee-Tien (Ted) Fu

Stock Options

Goal

In this chapter, we will discuss options generally, but with a focus on options on individual common stocks. We will see the tremendous flexibility that options offer investors in designing investment strategies.

McGraw Hill / Irwin

Option Basics

- ◆ A stock option is a *derivative security,* because the value of the option is "derived" from the value of the underlying common stock.

- ◆ There are two basic option types. *Call options* are options to buy, while *put options* are options to sell.

- ◆ Option contracts are standardized to facilitate trading and price reporting.
  - → A single standard option is an option to buy/sell 100 shares of stock.

Option Basics

- ◆ In general, options on common stock must stipulate at least the following terms:
  - ① The identity of the underlying stock.
  - ② The strike price, or exercise price.
  - ③ The option contract size.
  - ④ The option expiration date, or option maturity.
  - ⑤ The option exercise style (*American* or *European*).
  - ⑥ The delivery or settlement procedure.

- ◆ There are organized options exchanges as well as over-the-counter (OTC) options markets where stock options may be traded.

Work the Web

- Visit these options exchanges:
  - http://www.cboe.com
  - http://www.amex.com
  - http://www.phlx.com
  - http://www.nyse.com
  - http://www.pacificex.com

Option Price Quotes

Thursday, August 9, 2001

Composite volume and close for actively traded equity and LEAPS, or long-term options, with results for the corresponding put or call contract. Volume figures are unofficial. Open interest is total outstanding, for all exchanges and reflects previous trading day. Close when possible is shown for the underlying stock or primary market. **CB**-Chicago Board Options Exchange. **AM**-American Stock Exchange. **PB**-Philadelphia Stock Exchange. **PC**-Pacific Stock Exchange. **XC**-Composite. **p**-Put. **o**-Strike price adjusted for split.

MOST ACTIVE CONTRACTS

Journal Link: Complete equity option listings and data are available in the online Journal at **WSJ.com/JournalLinks**

Option Price Quotes

- ◆ A list of available option contracts and their prices for a particular security arrayed by strike price and maturity is known as an *option chain*.

Work the Web

- ☸ For information on options ticker symbols, see:
  - ▸ http://www.cboe.com
  - ▸ http://www.optionsites.com

Why Options?

- Should you buy 100 IBM shares at $90 each ($9,000 investment), or should you buy a call option with a strike price of $90 expiring in three months at $500 ($5 per share)?

- Three months later,

	Buy Shares		Buy Option	
	Profit	Return	Profit	Return
Case 1: $100	$1,000	11.11%	$500	100%
Case 2: $90	$0	0%	-$500	-100%
Case 3: $80	-$1,000	-11.11%	-$500	-100%

Why Options?

- Whether one strategy is preferred over another is a matter for each individual investor to decide.

- What is important is the fact that options offer an alternative means of formulating investment strategies.

Work the Web

For more information on options education, see:

- http://www.optionscentral.com

Option Writing

- The seller of a call/put option is called the call/put "writer," and the act of selling an option is referred to as *option writing*.
- Option writing involves receiving the option price and, in exchange, assuming the obligation to satisfy the buyer's exercise rights if the option is exercised.

Option Payoffs

- ◆ It is useful to think about option investment strategies in terms of their initial and terminal cash flows.
- ◆ The initial cash flow of an option is the price of the option, also called the option premium.
- ◆ The terminal cash flow of an option is the option's payoff that can be realized from the exercise privilege.

Payoff Diagrams

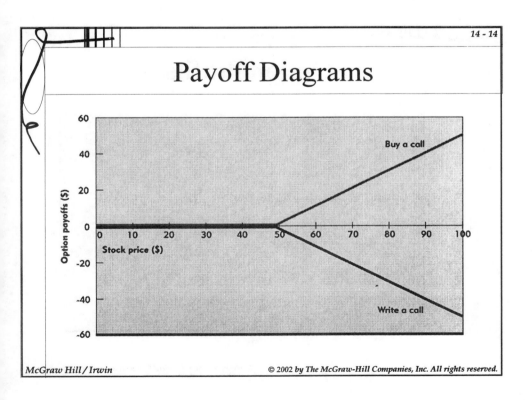

Payoff Diagrams

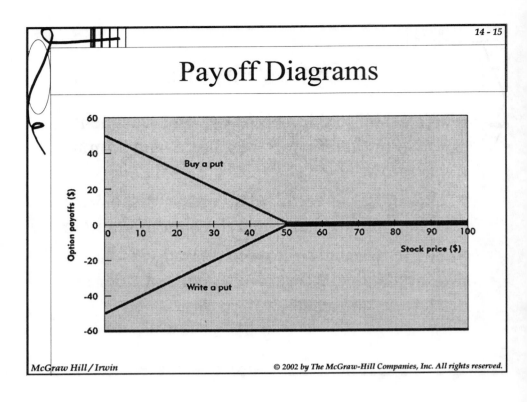

Option Profits

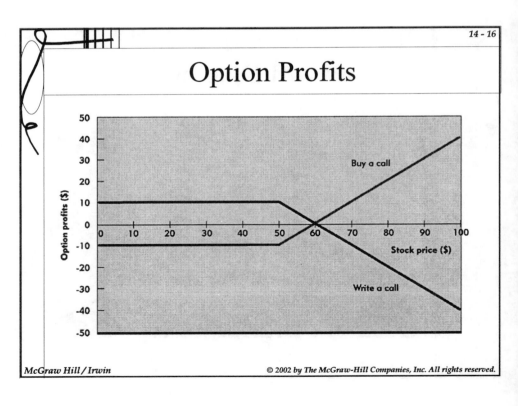

Option Profits

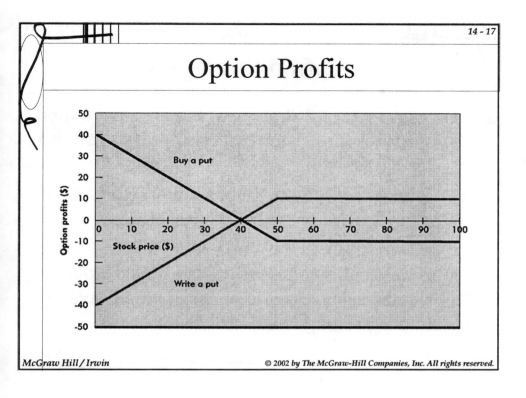

Work the Web

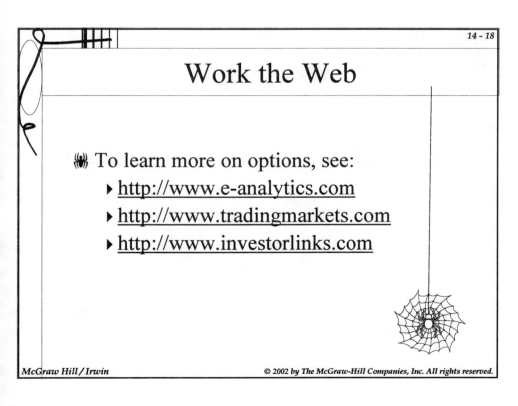

🕷 To learn more on options, see:
- ▸ http://www.e-analytics.com
- ▸ http://www.tradingmarkets.com
- ▸ http://www.investorlinks.com

Option Strategies

- *Protective put* - Strategy of buying a put option on a stock already owned. This protects against a decline in value.
- *Covered call* - Strategy of selling a call option on stock already owned. This exchanges "upside" potential for current income.
- *Straddle* - Buying or selling a call and a put with the same exercise price. Buying is a *long* straddle; selling is a *short* straddle.

Work the Web

For ideas on option trading strategies, see:
- http://www.commodityworld.com
- http://www.writecall.com
- http://www.giscor.com

Option Prices, Intrinsic Values, and Arbitrage

- ◆ call option price < stock price
  - ➔ Otherwise, arbitrage will be possible.
- ◆ put option price < strike price
  - ➔ Otherwise, arbitrage will be possible.
- ◆ option price ≥ 0
  - ➔ By definition, an option can simply be discarded.

Option Prices, Intrinsic Values, and Arbitrage

- ◆ The *intrinsic value* of an option is the payoff that an option holder receives if the underlying stock price does not change from its current value.

- ◆ Call option intrinsic value = max $[0, S-K]$

  Put option intrinsic value = max $[0, K-S]$

  where S = current stock price

  K = option's strike price

Option Prices, Intrinsic Values, and Arbitrage

- option price ≥ option's intrinsic value
  - → Otherwise, arbitrage will be possible.

- So,

> Call option price $\geq$ max $[0, S-K]$
> Put option price $\geq$ max $[0, K-S]$
> where S = current stock price
> K = option's strike price

Stock Index Options

- A stock index option is an option on a stock market index.
- The most popular stock index options are options on the S&P 100, S&P 500, and Dow Jones Industrial Average.
- Since the actual delivery of all stocks comprising a stock index is impractical, a cash settlement procedure is adopted for stock index options.

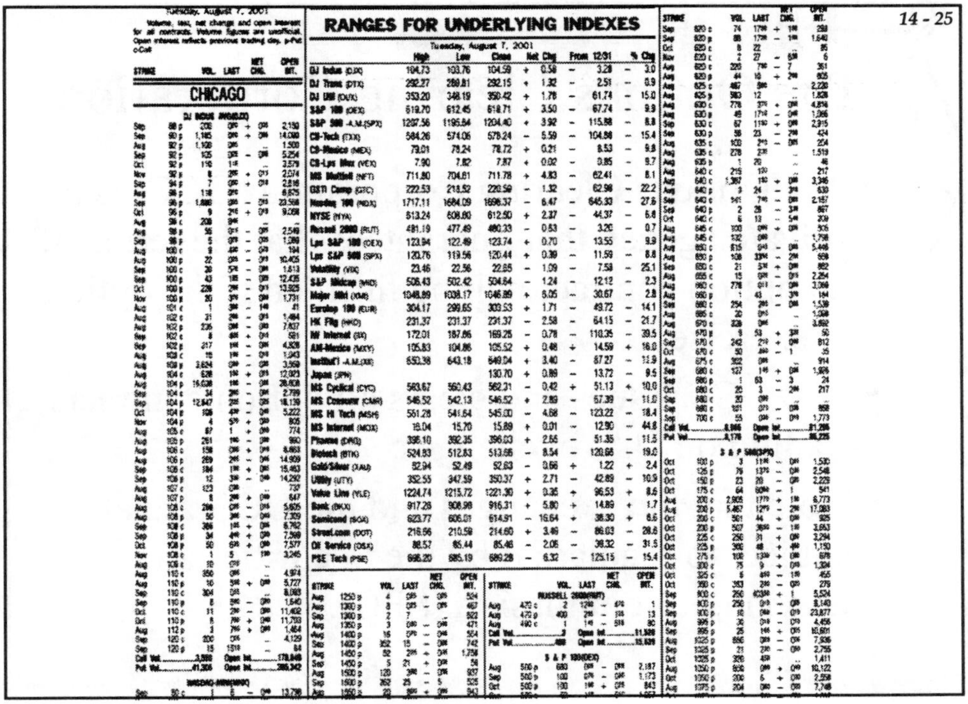

Tuesday, August 7, 2001

Volume, last, net change and open interest for all contracts. Volume figures are unofficial. Open interest reflects previous trading day. p-Put c-Call

CHICAGO

RANGES FOR UNDERLYING INDEXES

Tuesday, August 7, 2001

	High	Low	Close	Net Chg	From 12/31	% Chg
DJ Indus (DJX)	104.73	103.76	104.59	+ 0.58	− 3.28	− 3.0
DJ Trans (DTX)	292.27	289.81	292.15	+ 1.32	− 2.51	− 0.9
DJ Util (DUX)	353.20	348.19	350.42	+ 1.78	− 61.74	− 15.0
S&P 100 (OEX)	619.70	612.45	618.71	+ 3.50	− 67.74	− 9.9
S&P 500 -A.M.(SPX)	1207.56	1195.84	1204.40	+ 3.92	− 115.88	− 8.8
CB-Tech (TXX)	584.26	574.06	578.24	− 5.59	− 104.88	− 15.4
CB-Mexico (MEX)	79.01	78.24	78.72	+ 0.21	− 8.53	− 9.8
CB-Lps Mex (VEX)	7.90	7.82	7.87	+ 0.02	− 0.85	− 9.7
MS Multint (NFT)	711.80	704.81	711.78	+ 4.83	− 62.41	− 8.1
GSTI Comp (GTC)	222.53	218.52	220.59	− 1.32	− 62.98	− 22.2
Nasdaq 100 (NDX)	1717.11	1684.09	1696.37	− 6.47	− 645.33	− 27.6
NYSE (NYA)	613.24	608.80	612.50	+ 2.37	− 44.37	− 6.8
Russell 2000 (RUT)	481.19	477.49	480.33	− 0.53	− 3.20	− 0.7
Lps S&P 100 (OEX)	123.94	122.49	123.74	+ 0.70	− 13.55	− 9.9
Lps S&P 500 (SPX)	120.76	119.56	120.44	+ 0.39	− 11.59	− 8.8
Volatility (VIX)	23.46	22.56	22.65	− 1.09	− 7.58	− 25.1
S&P Midcap (MID)	506.43	502.42	504.64	− 1.24	− 12.12	− 2.3
Major Mkt (XMI)	1048.89	1038.17	1046.89	+ 6.05	− 30.67	− 2.8
Eurotop 100 (EUR)	304.17	299.65	303.53	+ 1.71	− 49.72	− 14.1
HK Fltg (HKO)	231.37	231.37	231.37	− 2.58	− 64.15	− 21.7
IW Internet (IIX)	172.01	167.66	169.25	− 0.78	− 110.35	− 39.5
AM-Mexico (MXY)	105.83	104.86	105.52	+ 0.48	+ 14.59	+ 16.0
Institut'l -A.M.(XII)	650.38	643.18	649.04	+ 3.40	− 87.27	− 11.9
Japan (JPN)			130.70	+ 0.89	− 13.72	− 9.5
MS Cyclical (CYC)	563.67	560.43	562.31	− 0.42	+ 51.13	+ 10.0
MS Consumr (CMR)	546.52	542.13	546.52	+ 2.89	− 67.39	− 11.0
MS Hi Tech (MSH)	561.28	541.64	545.00	− 4.68	− 123.22	− 18.4
MS Internet (MOX)	16.04	15.70	15.89	+ 0.01	− 12.90	− 44.8
Pharma (DRG)	396.10	392.35	396.03	+ 2.65	− 51.35	− 11.5
Biotech (BTK)	524.83	512.83	513.66	− 8.54	− 120.68	− 19.0
Gold/Silver (XAU)	52.94	52.49	52.63	− 0.66	+ 1.22	+ 2.4
Utility (UTY)	352.55	347.59	350.37	+ 2.71	− 42.89	− 10.9
Value Line (VLE)	1224.74	1215.72	1221.30	+ 0.35	+ 96.53	+ 8.6
Bank (BKX)	917.28	908.98	916.31	+ 5.80	+ 14.89	+ 1.7
Semicond (SOX)	623.77	606.01	614.91	− 16.64	+ 38.30	+ 6.6
Street.com (DOT)	218.66	210.58	214.60	+ 3.46	− 86.03	− 28.6
Oil Service (OSX)	88.57	85.44	85.46	− 2.08	− 38.32	− 31.5
PSE Tech (PSE)	696.20	685.19	689.28	− 6.32	− 125.15	− 15.4

RUSSELL 2000(RUT)

S & P 100(OEX)

S & P 500(SPX)

Work the Web

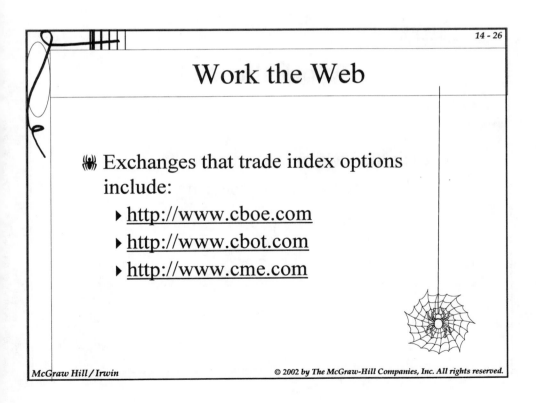

- Exchanges that trade index options include:
  - http://www.cboe.com
  - http://www.cbot.com
  - http://www.cme.com

The Options Clearing Corporation

- ◆ The Options Clearing Corporation (OCC) is a private agency that guarantees that the terms of an option contract will be fulfilled if the option is exercised.
- ◆ The OCC issues and clears all option contracts trading on U.S. exchanges.
- ◆ Note that the exchanges and the OCC are all subject to regulation by the Securities and Exchange Commission (SEC).

Work the Web

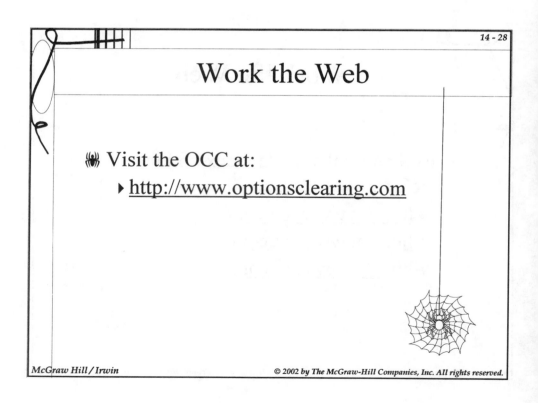

- 🕷 Visit the OCC at:
  - ▸ http://www.optionsclearing.com

Chapter Review

- ◆ Options on Common Stocks
  - → Option Basics
  - → Option Price Quotes
- ◆ Why Options?
- ◆ Option Payoffs and Profits
  - → Option Writing
  - → Option Payoffs
  - → Payoff Diagrams
  - → Option Profits

Chapter Review

- ◆ Option Strategies
  - → The Protective Put Strategy
  - → The Covered Call Strategy
  - → Straddles
- ◆ Option Prices, Intrinsic Values, and Arbitrage
  - → The Upper Bound for a Call Option Price
  - → The Upper Bound for a Put Option Price
  - → The Lower Bounds on Option Prices

Chapter Review

- Stock Index Options
    - Features and Settlement
    - Index Option Price Quotes
- The Options Clearing Corporation

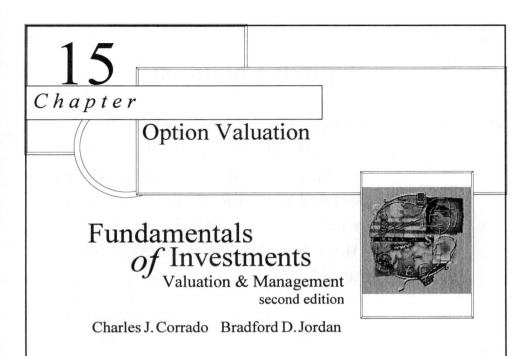

15
Chapter

Option Valuation

Fundamentals
of Investments
Valuation & Management
second edition

Charles J. Corrado   Bradford D. Jordan

McGraw Hill / Irwin   *Slides by Yee-Tien (Ted) Fu*

Just What is an Option Worth?

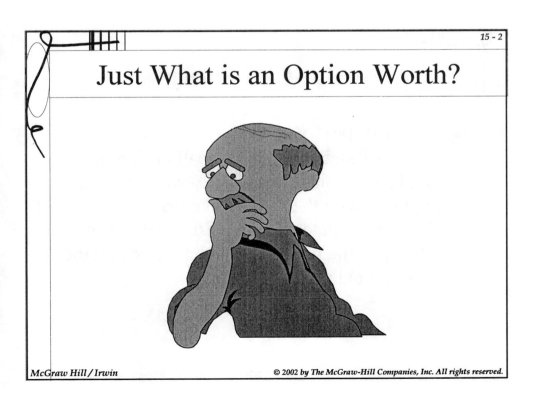

McGraw Hill / Irwin

Option Valuation

Goal Our goal in this chapter is to discuss stock option prices. We will look at the fundamental relationship between call and put option prices and stock prices. Then we will discuss the Black-Scholes-Merton option pricing model.

Put-Call Parity

Put-call parity
The difference between a call option price and a put option price for European-style options with the same strike price and expiration date is equal to the difference between the underlying stock price and the discounted strike price.

Put-Call Parity

$$C - P = S - Ke^{-rT}$$

C = call option price
P = put option price
S = current stock price
K = option strike price
r = risk-free interest rate
T = time remaining until option expiration

Put-Call Parity

- Put-call parity is based on the fundamental principle of finance stating that two securities with the same riskless payoff on the same future date must have the same price.

- Suppose we create the following portfolio:
  ① Buy 100 shares of stock X.
  ② Write one stock X call option contract.
  ③ Buy one stock X put option contract.

Put-Call Parity

Put-Call Parity

	Expiration Date Payoffs	
Expiration Date Stock Price	$S_T > K$	$S_T < K$
Buy stock	S_T	S_T
Write one call option	$-(S_T - K)$	0
Buy one put option	0	$(K - S_T)$
Total portfolio expiration date payoff	K	K

Put-Call Parity

+ Since the payoff for the portfolio is always equal to the strike price, it is risk-free, and therefore comparable to a U.S. T-bill.
+ So, cost of portfolio = discounted strike price

$$S + P - C = Ke^{-rT}$$

$$\Rightarrow \quad C - P = S - Ke^{-rT}$$

+ If the stock pays a dividend before option expiration, then $C - P = S - Ke^{-rT} - PV(D)$, where $PV(D)$ represents the present value of the dividend payment.

Work the Web

To learn more about trading options, see:
  - http://www.ino.com
  - http://www.optionetics.com

The Black-Scholes-Merton Option Pricing Model

- Option pricing theory made a great leap forward in the early 1970s with the development of the Black-Scholes option pricing model by Fischer Black and Myron Scholes.

- Recognizing the important theoretical contributions by Robert Merton, many finance professionals refer to an extended version of the model as the Black-Scholes-Merton option pricing model.

The Black-Scholes-Merton Option Pricing Model

- The Black-Scholes-Merton option pricing model states the value of a stock option as a function of six input factors:

① S, the current price of the underlying stock

② y, the dividend yield of the underlying stock

③ K, the strike price specified in the option contract

④ r, the risk-free interest rate over the life of the option contract

⑤ T, the time remaining until the option contract expires

⑥ σ, the price volatility of the underlying stock

The Black-Scholes-Merton Option Pricing Model

- The price of a call option on a single share of common stock, $C = Se^{-yT}N(d_1) - Ke^{-rT}N(d_2)$
- The price of a put option on a share of common stock, $P = Ke^{-rT}N(-d_2) - Se^{-yT}N(-d_1)$

where $d_1 = \dfrac{\ln(S/K) \times (r - y + \sigma^2/2)T}{\sigma\sqrt{T}}$

$$d_2 = d_1 - \sigma\sqrt{T}$$

$N(x)$ denotes the standard normal probability of the value of x

The Black-Scholes-Merton Option Pricing Model

		Standard Normal Probability Values									
Z-value	P-value	Z-value	P-value	Z-value	P-value	Z-value	P-value	Z-value	P-value	Z-value	P-value
−3	0.0013	−2	0.0228	−1	0.1587	0	0.5000	1	0.8413	2	0.9772
−2.95	0.0016	−1.95	0.0256	−0.95	0.1711	0.05	0.5199	1.05	0.8531	2.05	0.9798
−2.9	0.0019	−1.9	0.0287	−0.9	0.1841	0.1	0.5398	1.1	0.8643	2.1	0.9821
−2.85	0.0022	−1.85	0.0322	−0.85	0.1977	0.15	0.5596	1.15	0.8749	2.15	0.9842
−2.8	0.0026	−1.8	0.0359	−0.8	0.2119	0.2	0.5793	1.2	0.8849	2.2	0.9861
−2.75	0.0030	−1.75	0.0401	−0.75	0.2266	0.25	0.5987	1.25	0.8944	2.25	0.9878
−2.7	0.0035	−1.7	0.0446	−0.7	0.2420	0.3	0.6179	1.3	0.9032	2.3	0.9893
−2.65	0.0040	−1.65	0.0495	−0.65	0.2578	0.35	0.6368	1.35	0.9115	2.35	0.9906
−2.6	0.0047	−1.6	0.0548	−0.6	0.2743	0.4	0.6554	1.4	0.9192	2.4	0.9918
−2.55	0.0054	−1.55	0.0606	−0.55	0.2912	0.45	0.6736	1.45	0.9265	2.45	0.9929
−2.5	0.0062	−1.5	0.0668	−0.5	0.3085	0.5	0.6915	1.5	0.9332	2.5	0.9938
−2.45	0.0071	−1.45	0.0735	−0.45	0.3264	0.55	0.7088	1.55	0.9394	2.55	0.9946
−2.4	0.0082	−1.4	0.0808	−0.4	0.3446	0.6	0.7257	1.6	0.9452	2.6	0.9953
−2.35	0.0094	−1.35	0.0885	−0.35	0.3632	0.65	0.7422	1.65	0.9505	2.65	0.9960
−2.3	0.0107	−1.3	0.0968	−0.3	0.3821	0.7	0.7580	1.7	0.9554	2.7	0.9965
−2.25	0.0122	−1.25	0.1056	−0.25	0.4013	0.75	0.7734	1.75	0.9599	2.75	0.9970
−2.2	0.0139	−1.2	0.1151	−0.2	0.4207	0.8	0.7881	1.8	0.9641	2.8	0.9974
−2.15	0.0158	−1.15	0.1251	−0.15	0.4404	0.85	0.8023	1.85	0.9678	2.85	0.9978
−2.1	0.0179	−1.1	0.1357	−0.1	0.4602	0.9	0.8159	1.9	0.9713	2.9	0.9981
−2.05	0.0202	−1.05	0.1469	−0.05	0.4801	0.95	0.8289	1.95	0.9744	2.95	0.9984
−2	0.0228	−1	0.1587	0	0.5000	1	0.8413	2	0.9772	3	0.9987

TABLE 15.2

McGraw Hill / Irwin

Work the Web

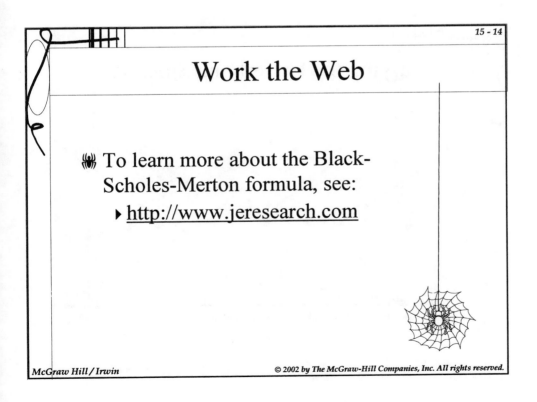

To learn more about the Black-Scholes-Merton formula, see:
- http://www.jeresearch.com

McGraw Hill / Irwin

Varying the Option Price Input Values

Six Inputs Affecting Option Prices

Input	Sign of Input Effect		Common Name
	Call	Put	
Underlying stock price (S)	+	–	Delta
Strike price of the option contract (K)	–	+	
Time remaining until option expiration (T)	+	+	Theta
Volatility of the underlying stock price (σ)	+	+	Vega
Risk-free interest rate (r)	+	–	Rho
Dividend yield of the underlying stock (y)	–	+	

Varying the Underlying Stock Price

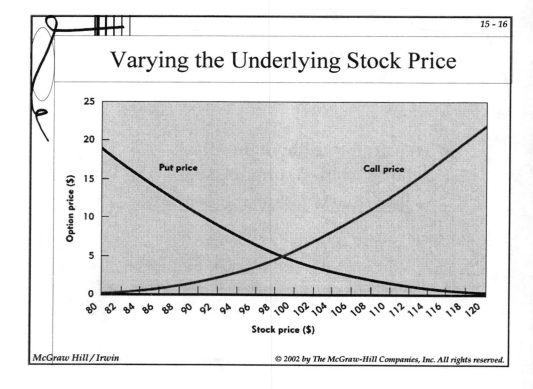

Varying the Time to Option Expiration

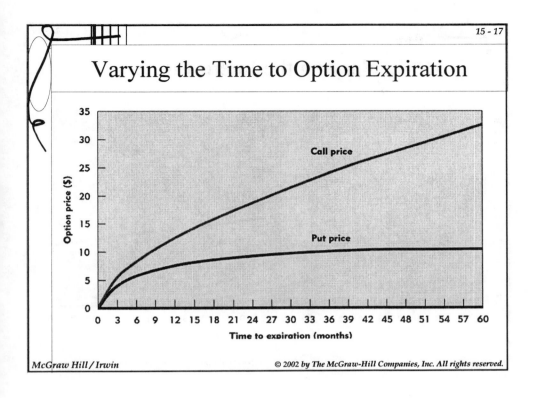

Varying the Volatility of the Stock Price

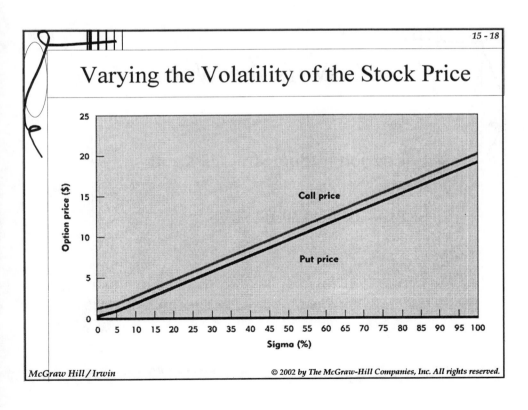

Varying the Interest Rate

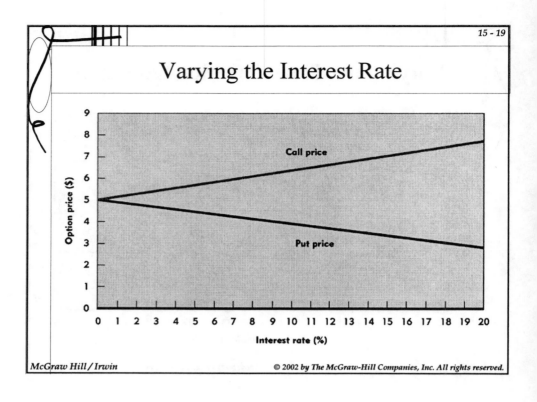

Work the Web

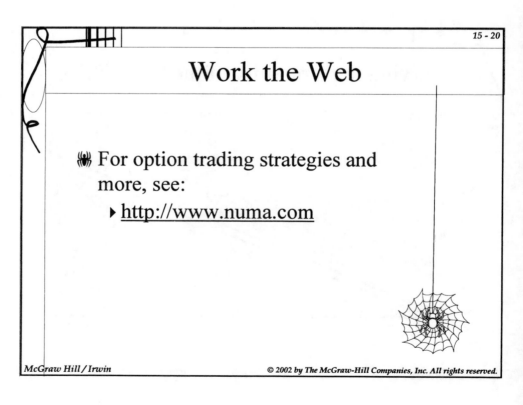

🕷 For option trading strategies and more, see:
  ‣ http://www.numa.com

Measuring the Impact of Input Changes

- *Delta* measures the *dollar* impact of a change in the underlying stock price on the value of a stock option.

    Call option delta $= e^{-yT}N(d_1) > 0$

    Put option delta $= -e^{-yT}N(-d_1) < 0$

- A \$1 change in the stock price causes an option price to change by approximately delta dollars.

Measuring the Impact of Input Changes

- *Eta* measures the *percentage* impact of a change in the underlying stock price on the value of a stock option.

    Call option eta $= e^{-yT}N(d_1)S/C > 1$

    Put option eta $= -e^{-yT}N(-d_1)S/P < -1$

- A 1% change in the stock price causes an option price to change by approximately eta%.

Measuring the Impact of Input Changes

- *Vega* measures the impact of a change in stock price volatility on the value of a stock option.

- Vega is the same for both call and put options.

$$Vega = Se^{-yT}n(d_1)\sqrt{T} > 0$$

where $n(x)$ represents a standard normal density

- A 1% change in sigma changes an option price by approximately the amount vega.

Measuring the Impact of Input Changes

- *Gamma* measures delta sensitivity to a stock price change. A $1 stock price change causes delta to change by approximately the amount gamma.

- *Theta* measures option price sensitivity to a change in time remaining until option expiration. A one-day change causes the option price to change by approximately the amount theta.

Measuring the Impact of Input Changes

- *Rho* measures option price sensitivity to a change in the interest rate. A 1% interest rate change causes the option price to change by approximately the amount rho.

Implied Standard Deviations

- Of the six input factors for the Black-Scholes-Merton stock option pricing model, only the stock price volatility is not directly observable.

- A stock price volatility estimated from an option price is called an *implied standard deviation (ISD)* or *implied volatility (IVOL)*.

- Calculating an implied volatility requires that all input factors (except sigma) and either a call or put option price be known.

Implied Standard Deviations

- ◆ Sigma can be found by trial and error, or by using the following formula, which yields accurate implied volatility values as long as the stock price is not too far from the strike price of the option contract.

$$\sigma \approx \frac{\sqrt{2\delta/T}}{Y+X}\left(C-\frac{Y-X}{2}+\sqrt{\left(C-\frac{Y-X}{2}\right)^2-\frac{(Y-X)^2}{\delta}}\right)$$

$$Y = Se^{-yT} \qquad X = Ke^{-rT}$$

McGraw Hill / Irwin

Work the Web

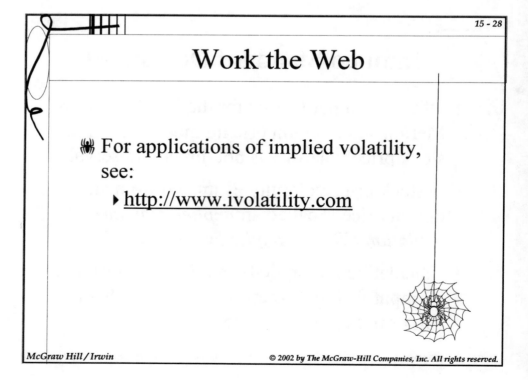

- 🕷 For applications of implied volatility, see:
  - ▸ http://www.ivolatility.com

McGraw Hill / Irwin

Hedging a Portfolio with Index Options

- Many institutional money managers make some use of stock index options to hedge the equity portfolios they manage.

- To form an effective hedge, the number of option contracts needed =

$$\frac{\text{Portfolio beta} \times \text{Portfolio value}}{\text{Option delta} \times \text{Option contract value}}$$

- Note that regular rebalancing is needed to maintain an effective hedge over time.

Work the Web

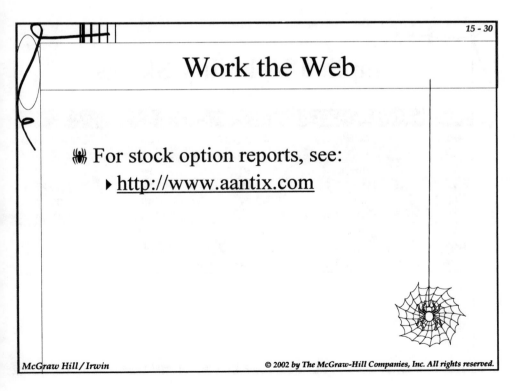

🕷 For stock option reports, see:
- http://www.aantix.com

Implied Volatility Skews

- *Volatility skews* (or *volatility smiles*) describe the relationship between implied volatilities and strike prices for options.
  - → Recall that implied volatility is often used to estimate a stock's price volatility over the period remaining until option expiration.

Implied Volatility Skews

Volatility Skews for MSFT Options

Strikes	Calls	Call ISD (%)	Puts	Put ISD (%)
65	14⅞	58.06	⅝	50.46
70	10⅜	49.10	1	42.19
75	6⅜	42.25	2¼	40.27
80	3½	39.79	4⅜	38.31
85	1¹⁵⁄₁₆	41.43	7¼	40.80
90	¹⁵⁄₁₆	41.46	12	42.96
95	¼	36.89	16⅜	47.40

Other information: $S = 78.5$, $y = .0\%$, $T = 37$ days, $r = 5.9\%$

Implied Volatility Skews

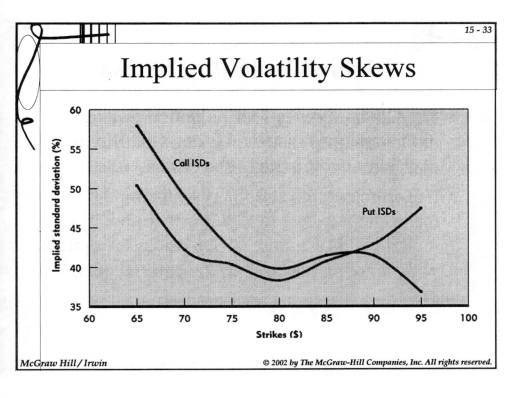

Implied Volatility Skews

- Logically, there can be only one stock price volatility, since price volatility is a property of the underlying stock.

- However, volatility skews do exist. There is widespread agreement that the major cause factor is stochastic volatility.

- *Stochastic volatility* is the phenomenon of stock price volatility changing randomly over time.

Implied Volatility Skews

- The Black-Scholes-Merton option pricing model assumes that stock price volatility is constant over the life of the option.
- Nevertheless, the simplicity of the model makes it an excellent tool. Furthermore, the model yields accurate option prices for options with strike prices close to the current stock price.

Work the Web

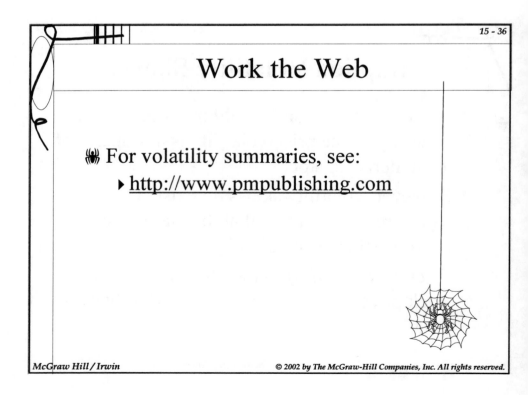

🕷 For volatility summaries, see:
  ▸ http://www.pmpublishing.com

Chapter Review

- Put-Call Parity
- The Black-Scholes-Merton Option Pricing Model

Chapter Review

- Varying the Option Price Input Values
  - Varying the Underlying Stock Price
  - Varying the Option's Strike Price
  - Varying the Time Remaining until Option Expiration
  - Varying the Volatility of the Stock Price
  - Varying the Interest Rate
  - Varying the Dividend Yield

Chapter Review

- ◆ Measuring the Impact of Input Changes on Option Prices
  - → Interpreting Option Deltas
  - → Interpreting Option Etas
  - → Interpreting Option Vegas
  - → Interpreting an Option's Gamma, Theta, and Rho
- ◆ Implied Standard Deviations
- ◆ Hedging a Stock Portfolio with Stock Index Options

Chapter Review

- ◆ Implied Volatility Skews

16

Chapter

Futures Contracts

Fundamentals
of Investments
Valuation & Management
second edition

Charles J. Corrado   Bradford D. Jordan

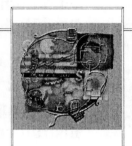

Slides by Yee-Tien (Ted) Fu

Futures Contracts

Goal

Our goal in this chapter is to discuss the basics of futures contracts and how their prices are quoted in the financial press. We will also look at how futures contracts are used and the relationship between current cash prices and futures prices.

Futures Contracts Basics

 Forward contract
Agreement between a buyer and a seller, who both commit to a transaction at a future date at a price set by negotiation today.

 Futures contract
Contract between a seller and a buyer specifying a commodity or financial instrument to be delivered and paid for at contract maturity. The specified price is called the *futures price*.

Futures Contracts Basics

- ◆ While a forward contract can be struck between any two parties, futures contracts are managed through an organized futures exchange.

Futures Contracts Basics

- Established in 1848, the Chicago Board of Trade (CBOT) is the oldest organized futures exchange in the United States.
- It grew with the westward expansion of American ranching and agriculture, and is today, the largest, most active futures exchange in the world.
- In the 1970s, financial futures were introduced. They are so successful that they now constitute the bulk of all futures trading.

Futures Contracts Basics

- In general, futures contracts must stipulate at least the following five terms:
  ① The identity of the underlying commodity or financial instrument.
  ② The futures contract size.
  ③ The futures maturity date, also called the expiration date.
  ④ The delivery or settlement procedure.
  ⑤ The futures price.

Futures Contracts Basics

Monday, February 22, 1999

Open Interest Reflects Previous Trading Day.

GRAINS AND OILSEEDS

	Open	High	Low	Settle	Change	Lifetime High	Low	Open Interest

CORN (CBT) 5,000 bu.; cents per bu.

OATS (CBT) 5,000 bu.; cents per bu.

SOYBEANS (CBT) 5,000 bu.; cents per bu.

SOYBEAN MEAL (CBT) 100 tons; $ per ton.

SOYBEAN OIL (CBT) 60,000 lbs.; cents per lb.

WHEAT (CBT) 5,000 bu.; cents per bu.

WHEAT (KC) 5,000 bu.; cents per bu.

WHEAT (MPLS) 5,000 bu.; cents per bu.

METALS AND PETROLEUM

COPPER-HIGH (Cmx.Div.NYM)-25,000 lbs.; cents per lb.

GOLD (Cmx.Div.NYM)-100 troy oz.; $ per troy oz.

(tables of numeric price data — Open, High, Low, Settle, Change, Lifetime High, Low, Open Interest)

HEATING OIL. NO. 2 (NYM) 42,000 gal.; $ per gal.

GASOLINE-NY Unleaded (NYM) 42,000 gal.; $ per gal.

NATURAL GAS. (NYM) 10,000 MMBtu.; $ per MMBtu's

BRENT CRUDE (IPE) 1,000 net bbls.; $ per bbl.

CURRENCY

	Open	High	Low	Settle	Change	Lifetime High	Low	Open Interest

JAPAN YEN (CME)-12.5 million yen.; $ per yen (.00)

DEUTSCHEMARK (CME)-125,000 marks; $ per mark

CANADIAN DOLLAR (CME)-100,000 dlrs.; $ per Can $

BRITISH POUND (CME)-62,500 pds.; $ per pound

SWISS FRANC (CME)-125,000 francs.; $ per franc

AUSTRALIAN DOLLAR (CME)-100,000 dlrs.; $ per A.$

MEXICAN PESO (CME)-500,000 new Mexico. pesos; $ per MP

BRAZILIAN REAL (CME)-100,000 Braz. reals; $ per reals

INTEREST RATE

TREASURY BONDS (CBT)-$100,000; pts. 32nds of 100%

	Open	High	Low	Settle	Change	Lifetime High	Low	Open Interest

TREASURY BONDS (MCE)-$50,000; pts. 32nds of 100%

TREASURY NOTES (CBT)-$100,000; pts. 32nds of 100%

5 YR TREAS NOTES (CBT)-$100,000; pts. 32nds of 100%

2 YR TREAS NOTES (CBT)-$200,000; pts. 32nds of 100%

30-DAY FEDERAL FUNDS (CBT)-$5 million.; pts. of 100%

MUNI BOND INDEX (CBT)-$1,000; Home Bond Buyer MBI

The Index: Close 125-07; Yield 5.28.

TREASURY BILLS (CME)-$1 mil.; pts. of 100%

	Open	High	Low	Settle	Chg	Discount Settle	Chg	Open Interest

LIBOR-1 MO. (CME)-$3,000,000; points of 100%

INDEX

DJ INDUSTRIAL AVERAGE (CBOT)-$10 times average

INDEX

DJ INDUSTRIAL AVERAGE (CBOT)-$10 times average

	Open	High	Low	Settle	Chg	High	Low	Open Interest

S&P 500 INDEX (CME)-$250 times index

MINI S&P 500 (CME)-$50 times index

S&P MIDCAP 400 (CME)-$500 times index

EXCHANGE ABBREVIATIONS
(for commodity futures and futures options)

CBT-Chicago Board of Trade; CME-Chicago Mercantile Exchange; CSCE-Coffee, Sugar & Cocoa Exchange, New York; CMX-COMEX (Div. of New York Mercantile Exchange); CTN-New York Cotton Exchange; EUREX-European Exchange; FINEX-Financial Exchange (Div. of New York Cotton Exchange); IPE-International Petroleum Exchange; KC-Kansas City Board of Trade; LIFFE-London International Financial Futures Exchange; MATIF-Marche a Terme International de France; ME-Montreal Exchange; MCE-MidAmerica Commodity Exchange; MPLS-Minneapolis Grain Exchange; NYFE-New York Futures Exchange (Sub. of New York Cotton Exchange); NYM-New York Mercantile Exchange; SIMEX-Singapore International Monetary Exchange Ltd.; SFE-Sydney Futures Exchange; TFE-Toronto Futures Exchange; WPG-Winnipeg CommodityExchange. CBT, CME, NYMX/CMX, CTN, FINEX, NYFE reflect overnight trading.

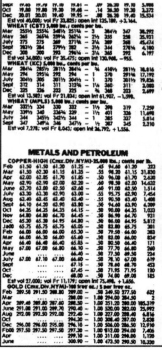

Work the Web

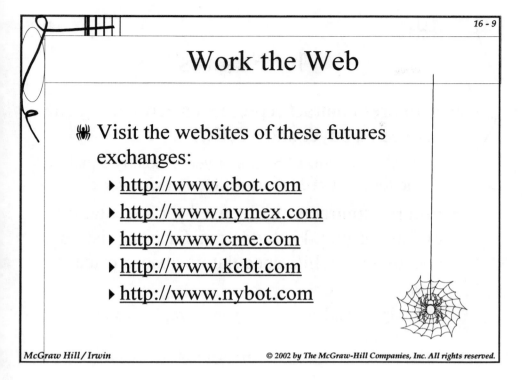

- ⚜ Visit the websites of these futures exchanges:
  - ▸ http://www.cbot.com
  - ▸ http://www.nymex.com
  - ▸ http://www.cme.com
  - ▸ http://www.kcbt.com
  - ▸ http://www.nybot.com

Work the Web

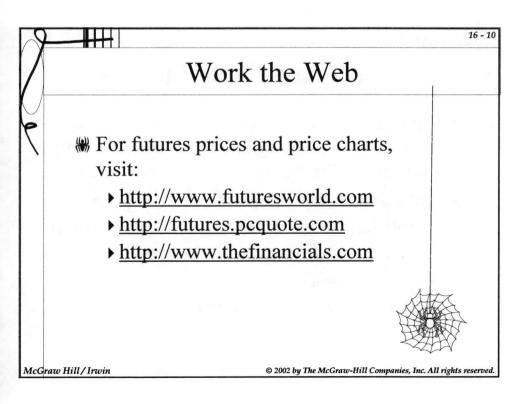

- ⚜ For futures prices and price charts, visit:
  - ▸ http://www.futuresworld.com
  - ▸ http://futures.pcquote.com
  - ▸ http://www.thefinancials.com

Why Futures?

- A futures contract represents a zero-sum game between a buyer and a seller.
  - → Any gain realized by the buyer is exactly equal to the loss realized by the seller, and vice versa.
- Futures contracts can be used for speculation or for hedging. Hedgers transfer price risk to speculators, while speculators absorb price risk.
  - → Hedging and speculating are complementary activities.

Speculating with Futures

- Buying futures is often referred to as "going long," or establishing a *long position*. A long position profits from a futures price increase.
- Selling futures is often called "going short," or establishing a *short position*. A short position profits from a futures price decrease.
- A *speculator* accepts price risk by going long or short to bet on the future direction of prices.

Hedging with Futures

- A *hedger* is a trader who seeks to transfer price risk by taking a futures position opposite to an existing position in the underlying commodity or financial instrument.
- Suppose a large operating inventory is needed. The sale of futures to offset potential losses from falling prices is called a *short hedge*.
- When some commodity is needed in the future, the purchase of futures to offset potential losses from rising prices is called a *long hedge*.

Work the Web

- To learn more about futures, visit:
  - http://www.futurewisetrading.com
  - http://www.usafutures.com

Futures Trading Accounts

- ◆ A futures exchange, like a stock exchange, allows only exchange members to trade on the exchange.
- ◆ Exchange members may be firms or individuals trading for their own accounts, or they may be brokerage firms handling trades for customers.

Futures Trading Accounts

- ◆ There are several essential things to know about futures trading accounts.
- ① Margin is required - *initial margin* as well as *maintenance margin.*
- ② The contract values are *marked to market* on a daily basis, and a *margin call* will be issued if necessary.
- ③ A futures position can be closed out at any time. This is done by entering a *reverse trade.*

Work the Web

🕷 For a list of online futures brokers, visit the *Commodities & Futures* section of *Investor Links* at:

  ▸ http://www.investorlinks.com

Cash Prices

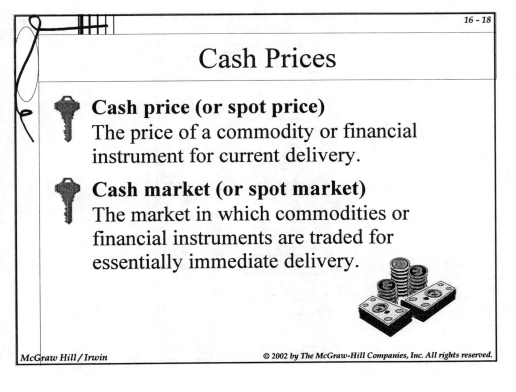

Cash price (or spot price)
The price of a commodity or financial instrument for current delivery.

Cash market (or spot market)
The market in which commodities or financial instruments are traded for essentially immediate delivery.

16 - 19

CASH PRICES

Monday, February 22, 1999
(Closing Market Quotations)

	Mon	Fri	Year Ago
GRAINS AND FEEDS			
Barley, top-quality Mpls., bu	u220-25	220-25	z
Bran, wheat middlings, KC ton	u54-7	51-55	71.50
Corn, No. 2 yel. Cent. Ill. bu	bpu2.04½	2.05	2.57½
Corn Gluten Feed, Midwest, ton	53.00	55-69	71.50
Cottonseed Meal, Clksdle, Miss. ton	100.00	97.50	127.50
Hominy Feed, Cent. Ill. ton	52.00	54.00	77.00
Meat-Bonemeal, 50% pro. Ill. ton.	140-45	145.00	170.00
Oats, No. 2 milling, Mpls., bu	u1.16½	1.16¾	1.69¾
Sorghum, (Milo) No. 2 Gulf cwt	u407-13	408-14	5.02½
Soybean Meal, Cent. Ill., rail, ton 44%	u122-4	123-5	173.50
Soybean Meal, Cent. Ill., rail, ton 48%	u129-32	131-3	183.00
Soybeans, No. 1 yel Cent.-Ill. bu	bpu4.64	4.78	6.57½
Wheat, Spring 14%-pro Mpls. bu	u354-72	3.72	4.14¾
Wheat, No. 2 sft red, St.Lou. bu	bpu2.26	2.29½	3.23
Wheat, hard KC, bu	2.85¾	2.86½	3.56½
Wheat, No. 1 sft wht, del Port Ore	u3.08	3.11	3.53
FOODS			
Beef, Carcass, Equiv.Index Value, choice 1-3,550-700lbs.	u94.04	94.17	89.90
Beef, Carcass, Equiv.Index Value, select 1-3,550-700lbs.	u91.12	90.81	87.31
Broilers, Dressed "A" lb.	ux.5745	.5581	.5408
Broilers, 12-Cty Comp Wtd Av	u.5789	.5816	.5772
Butter, AA, Chgo., lb.	u1.34	1.34	1.40
Cheddar Cheese, barrels, Chgo lb.	n129.50	129.50	143.00
Cheddar Cheese, blocks, Chgo lb.	n133.00	133.00	142.75
Cocoa, Ivory Coast, $metric ton	1,491	1,502	1,711
Coffee, Brazilian, NY lb.	n1.00½	1.01½	1.91½
Coffee, Colombian, NY lb.	n1.10½	1.11½	2.01½
Eggs, Lge white, Chgo doz.	u.58-63	.58-63	.61½
Flour, hard winter KC cwt	8.60	8.65	9.75
Hams, 17-20 lbs, Mid-US lb fob	u.48-51	.48	.58½
Hogs, Iowa-S.Minn. avg. cwt	u27.26	25.50	34.00
Hogs, S. Dakota avg. cwt	u28.26	27.63	33.00
Pork Bellies, 12-14 lbs Mid-US lb	u.47	z	.44¾
Pork Loins, 13-19 lbs. Mid-US lb	u.85-90	.82-91	1.01
Steers, Tex.-Okla. ch avg cwt	uz	z	z
Steers, Feeder, Okl Cty, av cwt	u82.13	83.38	87.00
Sugar, cane, raw, world, lb, fob	7.08	7.02	10.59
FATS AND OILS			
Coconut Oil, crd, N. Orleans lb.	xxn.35	.35	.26½
Corn Oil, crd wet/dry mill, Chgo.	u24¾-5¼	24¾-5¼	.28
Grease, choice white, Chgo lb.	z	z	.12½
Lard, Chgo lb.	.14¼	.14¼	.16
Palm Oil, ref. bl. deod. N.Orl. lb.	n.28½	.28½	.32½
Soybean Oil, crd, Central Ill. lb.	u1869-79	1871-81	.2691
Tallow, bleachable, Chgo lb.	.11	.11	.16
Tallow, edible, Chgo lb.	.14	.14	.18
METALS			
Aluminum ingot lb. del. Midwest	p.58½-9½	.58½-9½	.70¼
Copper high gr lb., Cmx sp price	.61	.62	.73
Copper Scrap, No 2 wire NY lb	h.50	.50	.60
Lead, lb.	p.43769	.43784	.44876
Mercury 76 lb. flask NY	q155-80	155-80	170
Steel Scrap 1 hvy mlt EC ton	79-80	79-80	140.5
Tin composite lb.	q3.5649	3.5773	3.6034
Zinc Special High grade lb	q.52332	.52332	.50250
PRECIOUS METALS			
Gold, troy oz			
Engelhard indust bullion	288.34	287.49	293.85
Engelhard fabric prods	302.76	301.86	308.54
Handy & Harman base price	287.20	286.35	292.70
Handy & Harman fabric price	301.56	300.67	307.34
London fixing AM 287.20 PM	287.20	286.35	292.70
Krugerrand, whol	a296.00	297.00	300.00
Maple Leaf, troy oz.	a297.00	298.00	304.00
American Eagle, troy oz.	a297.00	298.00	304.00
Platinum, (Free Mkt.)	374.50	377.00	377.00
Platinum, indust (Engelhard)	376.00	381.00	377.00
Platinum, fabric prd (Engelhard)	476.00	481.00	477.00
Palladium, indust (Engelhard)	355.00	360.00	238.00
Palladium, fabrc prd (Englhard)	370.00	375.00	253.00
Silver, troy ounce			
Engelhard indust bullion	5.540	5.580	6.500
Engelhard fabric prods	6.205	6.250	7.280
Handy & Harman base price	5.570	5.590	6.480
Handy & Harman fabric price	6.238	6.261	7.258
London Fixing (in pounds)			
Spot (U.S. equiv.$5.5750)	3.4414	3.4282	3.9565
Coins, whol $1,000 face val	a5,255	5,350	4,423

a-Asked. b-Bid. bp-Country elevator bids to producers. c-Corrected. h-Reuters. n-Nominal. na-Not available. p-Producer price via Platt's Metals Week. q-Platt's Metals Week. r-Rail bids. u-U.S. Dept. of Agriculture. x-Less than truckloads. z-Not quoted. xx-f.o.b. tankcars.

16 - 20

OIL PRICES

Monday, February 22, 1999

CRUDE GRADES	Mon	Fri	Yr. Ago
OFFSHORE-d			
European "spot" or free market prices			
Arab lt.	8.55	8.66	12.12
Arab hvy.	7.75	7.86	10.02
Iran, lt.	9.75	9.86	12.72
Forties	10.00	10.11	14.30
Brent	10.10	10.21	14.02
Bonny lt.	10.10	10.21	14.02
Urals-Medit.	9.35	9.46	13.02
DOMESTIC-f			
Spot market			
W. Tex. Int Cush (900-1125) (Mar)	11.98	11.78	15.18
W.Tx.sour, Midl (575-1000) ..	10.63	10.40	13.18
La. sw. St.Ja (800-1076)	11.20	10.98	14.88
Al. No. Slope Pacific Del	10.48	10.28	12.40

Open-market crude oil values in Northwest Europe around 17:50 GMT in dlrs per barrel, for main loading ports in country of origin for prompt loading, except as indicated.

REFINED PRODUCTS	Mon	Fri	Yr. Ago
Fuel Oil, No. 2 NY gal.	.3025	.2912	.4193
Diesel Fuel, 0.05 S. NY harbor low sulfur	.3185	.3072	.4398
Gasoline, unlded, premium NY gal. non-oxygenated ...	.3633	.3572	.4781
Gasoline, unlded, premium NY gal. oxygenated	.3683	.3622	.4894
Gasoline, unlded, reg. NY gal. non-oxygenated ...	.3108	.3072	.4424
Gasoline, unlded, reg. NY gal. oxygenated	.3208	.3147	.4646
Propane, non-tet, Mont Belvieu, Texas, gal.	.2263	.2238	.3005
Propane, wet-tet, Mont Belvieu, Texas, gal.	.2578	.2238	.2981
Butane, normal, Mont Belvieu, Texas, gal.	.2875	.2875	.3650
RAW PRODUCTS			
Natural Gas Henry Hub, $ per mmbtu .	1.775	1.785	2.185

a-Asked. b-Bid. c-Corrected. d-as of 11 a.m. est in Northwest Europe. f-As of 4 p.m. est. Refiners' posted buying prices are in parentheses. n.a.-Not available, z-Not quoted. n-Nominal. r-Revised. Source: Dow Jones Energy Service

Cash-Futures Arbitrage

- Earning risk-free profits from an unusual difference between cash and futures prices is called *cash-futures arbitrage*.
  - → In a competitive market, cash-futures arbitrage has very slim profit margins.
- Cash prices and futures prices are seldom equal. The difference between the cash price and the futures price for a commodity is known as *basis*.

  basis = cash price − futures price

Cash-Futures Arbitrage

- For commodities with storage costs, the cash price is usually less than the futures price, i.e. basis < 0. This is referred to as a *carrying-charge market*.
- Sometimes, the cash price is greater than the futures price, i.e. basis > 0. This is referred to as an *inverted market*.
- Basis is kept at an economically appropriate level by arbitrage.

Spot-Futures Parity

- The relationship between spot prices and futures prices that holds in the absence of arbitrage opportunities is known as the *spot-futures parity* condition.

- Let F be the futures price, and S be the spot price. If r is the risk-free rate per period, and the futures contract matures in T periods, then the spot-futures parity condition is:

$$F_T = S(1+r)^T$$

More on Spot-Futures Parity

- Let D be the dividend (or coupon payment) paid in one period, at or near the end of the futures contract's life. Then, the spot-futures parity condition becomes $F = S(1 + r) - D$.

- Alternatively, we can write the dividend-adjusted parity result as $F = S(1 + r - d)$, where dividend yield $d = D/S$. Then

$$F_T = S(1+r-d)^T$$

Stock Index Futures

- There are a number of futures contracts on stock market indexes. The S&P 500 contract is one of the most important ones.

- Because of the difficulty of actual delivery, stock index futures are usually settled in cash.

Index Arbitrage

- *Index arbitrage* refers to the strategy of monitoring the futures price on a stock index and the level of the underlying index to exploit deviations from parity.

- Index arbitrage is often implemented as a *program trading* strategy. Program trading accounts for about 15% of total trading volume on the NYSE, and about 20% of all program trading involves stock-index arbitrage.

Index Arbitrage

- ◆ Another phenomenon often associated with index arbitrage (and more generally, futures and options trading) is the *triple witching hour* effect.

- ◆ S&P 500 futures contracts and options, and various stock options, all expire on the third Friday of four particular months per year. The closing out of all the positions held sometimes lead to unusual price behavior.

Work the Web

- 🕷 For more information on stock index futures, visit the CBOT website at:
  - ▸ http://www.cbot.com

- 🕷 For information on program trading, visit:
  - ▸ http://www.programtrading.com

Hedging Stock Market Risk with Futures

- *Cross-hedging* refers to hedging a particular spot position with futures contracts on a related, but not identical, commodity or financial instrument.
- For example, you may decide to protect your stock portfolio from a fall in value (caused by a falling stock market) by establishing a short hedge using stock index futures.

Hedging Stock Market Risk with Futures

- The number of stock index futures contracts needed to hedge a stock portfolio effectively can be determined as follows:

$$\text{Number of contracts} = \frac{\hat{a}_P \times V_P}{V_F}$$

where β_P = beta of the stock portfolio
V_P = value of the stock portfolio
V_F = value of a single futures contract

Hedging Interest Rate Risk with Futures

- The protect a bond portfolio against changing interest rates, we may cross-hedge using futures contracts on U.S. Treasury notes.
- A short hedge will protect your bond portfolio against the risk of a general rise in interest rates during the life of the futures contracts.

Hedging Interest Rate Risk with Futures

- To hedge a bond portfolio effectively,

$$\text{Number of contracts needed} = \frac{D_P \times V_P}{D_F \times V_F}$$

where D_P = duration of the bond portfolio
V_P = value of the bond portfolio
D_F = duration of the futures contract
V_F = value of a single futures contract

Hedging Interest Rate Risk with Futures

- As a useful rule of thumb, the duration of an interest rate futures contract is equal to the duration of the underlying instrument plus the time remaining until contract maturity.

$$D_F = D_U + M_F$$

where D_F = duration of the futures contract
D_U = duration of the underlying instrument
M_F = time remaining until contract maturity

Futures Contract Delivery Options

- The *cheapest-to-deliver option* refers to the seller's option to deliver the cheapest instrument when a futures contract allows several instruments for delivery.

- For example, U.S. Treasury note futures allow delivery of any Treasury note with a maturity between 6 1/2 and 10 years. Note that the cheapest-to-deliver note may vary over time.

Chapter Review

- ◆ Futures Contracts Basics
  - → Modern History of Futures Trading
  - → Futures Contract Features
  - → Futures Prices
- ◆ Why Futures?
  - → Speculating with Futures
  - → Hedging with Futures
- ◆ Futures Trading Accounts

Chapter Review

- ◆ Cash Prices versus Futures Prices
  - → Cash Prices
  - → Cash-Futures Arbitrage
  - → Spot-Futures Parity
  - → More on Spot-Futures Parity

Chapter Review

- Stock Index Futures
  - Basics of Stock Index Futures
  - Index Arbitrage
  - Hedging Stock Market Risk with Futures
  - Hedging Interest Rate Risk with Futures
  - Futures Contract Delivery Options

17
Chapter

Diversification & Asset Allocation

Fundamentals
of Investments
Valuation & Management
second edition

Charles J. Corrado   Bradford D. Jordan

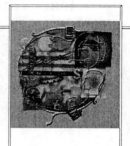

McGraw Hill / Irwin

Slides by Yee-Tien (Ted) Fu

Don't Put All Your Eggs in One Basket

McGraw Hill / Irwin

Diversification and Asset Allocation

Goal Our goal in this chapter is to examine the role of diversification and asset allocation in investing.

- The role and impact of diversification were first formally explained in the early 1950s by Harry Markowitz.

- Based on his work, we will look at how diversification works, and how we can be sure we have an efficiently diversified portfolio.

Expected Returns

Expected return
Average return on a risky asset expected in the future. This is calculated as the sum of the possible returns multiplied by their probabilities.

$$\text{expected return} = \sum_i \left[p_i \times \text{return}_i \right]$$

- Recall that
risk premium = expected return – risk-free rate

Expected Returns

States of the Economy and Stock Returns

State of Economy	Probability of State of Economy	Security Returns if State Occurs	
		Netcap	Jmart
Recession	.50	−20%	30%
Boom	.50	70	10
	1.00		

Calculating Expected Returns

		Netcap		Jmart	
(1)	(2)	(3)	(4)	(5)	(6)
		Return if		Return if	
State of Economy	Probability of State of Economy	State Occurs	Product (2) × (3)	State Occurs	Product (2) × (5)
Recession	.50	−20%	−.10	30%	.15
Boom	.50	70	.35	10	.05
	1.00		$E(R_N) = 25\%$		$E(R_J) = 20\%$

Calculating the Variance

- *Variance* is calculated as the sum of the squared deviations from the expected return multiplied by their probabilities.

$$\text{variance} = \sum_{i}\left[p_i \times \left(\text{return}_i - \text{expected return}\right)^2\right]$$

- The standard deviation is the square root of the variance. Standard deviation = $\sigma = \sqrt{\text{variance}}$.

Calculating the Variance

Expected Returns and Variances			
		Netcap	Jmart
Expected return, $E(R)$		25%	20%
Variance, σ^2		.2025	.0100
Standard deviation, σ		45%	10%

Portfolios

Portfolios

Group of assets such as stocks and bonds held by an investor.

♦ One convenient way of describing a portfolio is to list the percentages of the portfolio's total value that are invested in each portfolio asset. We call these percentages the *portfolio weights*.

Portfolios

• The expected return on a portfolio is a linear combination of the expected returns on the assets in that portfolio.

$$E(R_P) = \sum_i \left[w_i \times E(R_i) \right]$$

where $E(R_P)$ = expected portfolio return

w_i = portfolio weight of portfolio asset i

$E(R_i)$ = expected return on portfolio asset i

Portfolios

$$VAR(R_P) = \sum_s \left[p_s \times \{ E(R_s) - E(R_P) \}^2 \right]$$

where $VAR(R_P)$ = variance of portfolio return

p_s = probability of state of economy s

$E(R_s)$ = expected portfolio return given state s

• Note that portfolio variance is *not* generally a simple combination of the variances of the portfolio assets.

• Moreover, it may be possible to construct a portfolio of risky assets with zero portfolio variance!

Diversification and Portfolio Risk

Portfolio Standard Deviations		
(1)	(2)	(3)
Number of Stocks in Portfolio	Average Standard Deviation of Annual Portfolio Returns	Ratio of Portfolio Standard Deviation to Standard Deviation of a Single Stock
1	49.24%	1.00
2	37.36	.76
4	29.69	.60
6	26.64	.54
8	24.98	.51
10	23.93	.49
20	21.68	.44
30	20.87	.42
40	20.46	.42
50	20.20	.41
100	19.69	.40
200	19.42	.39
300	19.34	.39
400	19.29	.39
500	19.27	.39
1,000	19.21	.39

Source: These figures are from Table 1 in Meir Statman, "How Many Stocks Make a Diversified Portfolio?"
Journal of Financial and Quantitative Analysis 22 (September 1987), pp. 353–64. They were derived from
E. J. Elton and M. J. Gruber, "Risk Reduction and Portfolio Size: An Analytic Solution," *Journal of
Business* 50 (October 1977), pp. 415–37.

McGraw Hill / Irwin

The Principle of Diversification

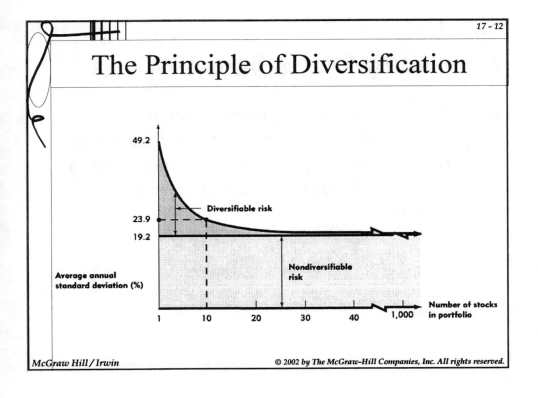

McGraw Hill / Irwin

Why Diversification Works

 Correlation

The tendency of the returns on two assets to move together. Imperfect correlation is the key reason why diversification reduces portfolio risk as measured by the portfolio standard deviation.

- *Positively* correlated assets tend to move up and down together, while *negatively* correlated assets tend to move in opposite directions.

Why Diversification Works

- The *correlation coefficient* is denoted by Corr(R_A, R_B) or ρ. It measures correlation and ranges from -1 (perfect negative correlation) to 0 (uncorrelated) to +1 (perfect positive correlation).

Why Diversification Works

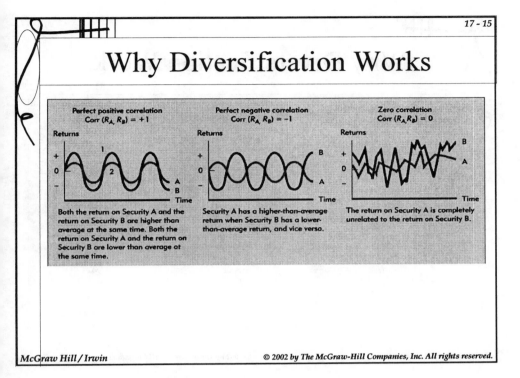

Why Diversification Works

Annual Returns on Stocks A and B			
Year	Stock A	Stock B	Portfolio AB
1997	10%	15%	12.5%
1998	30%	−10%	10%
1999	−10%	25%	7.5%
2000	5%	20%	12.5%
2001	10%	15%	12.5%
Average returns	9%	13%	11%
Standard deviations	14.3%	13.5%	2.2%

Why Diversification Works

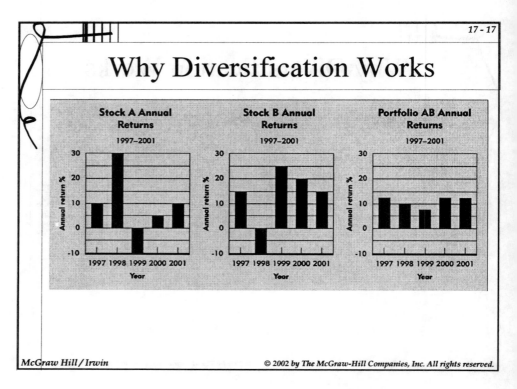

Calculating Portfolio Risk

- For a portfolio of two assets, A and B, the variance of the return on the portfolio is:

$$\sigma_p^2 = w_A^2 \sigma_A^2 + w_B^2 \sigma_B^2 + 2 w_A w_B \sigma_A \sigma_B Corr(R_A R_B)$$

where w_A = portfolio weight of asset A
w_B = portfolio weight of asset B
such that $w_A + w_B = 1$

Correlation and Diversification

- ◆ Suppose that as a very conservative, risk-averse investor, you decide to invest all of your money in a bond mutual fund. Is this decision a wise one?

Correlation and Diversification

Risk and Return with Stocks and Bonds			
Portfolio Weights			
Stocks	Bonds	Expected Return	Standard Deviation
1.00	.00	12.00%	15.00%
.95	.05	11.70	14.31
.90	.10	11.40	13.64
.85	.15	11.10	12.99
.80	.20	10.80	12.36
.75	.25	10.50	11.77
.70	.30	10.20	11.20
.65	.35	9.90	10.68
.60	.40	9.60	10.28
.55	.45	9.30	9.78
.50	.50	9.00	9.42
.45	.55	8.70	9.12
.40	.60	8.40	8.90
.35	.65	8.10	8.75
.30	.70	7.80	8.69
.25	.75	7.50	8.71
.20	.80	7.20	8.82
.15	.85	6.90	9.01
.10	.90	6.60	9.27
.05	.95	6.30	9.60
.00	1.00	6.00	10.00

Correlation and Diversification

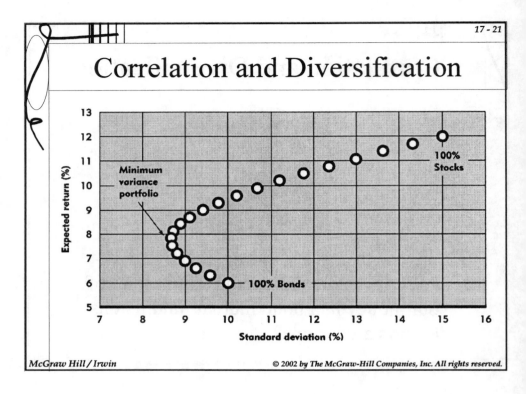

Correlation and Diversification

- ◆ The various combinations of risk and return available all fall on a smooth curve.
- ◆ This curve is called an *investment opportunity set* because it shows the possible combinations of risk and return available from portfolios of these two assets.
- ◆ A portfolio that offers the highest return for its level of risk is said to be an *efficient portfolio*.
- ◆ The undesirable portfolios are said to be *dominated* or *inefficient*.

More on Correlation & the Risk-Return Trade-Off

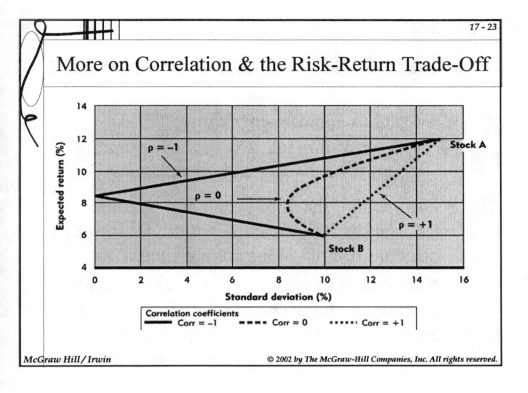

Risk and Return with Multiple Assets

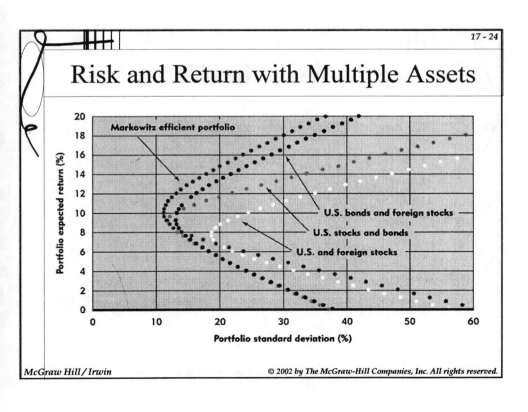

The Markowitz Efficient Frontier

 Markowitz efficient frontier
The set of portfolios with the maximum return for a given standard deviation.

- For the plot, the upper left-hand boundary is the Markowitz efficient frontier. All the other possible combinations are inefficient.

- Note that Markowitz analysis is not usually extended to large collections of individual assets because of the data requirements.

Work the Web

Perform a Markowitz-type analysis at:
- http://www.finportfolio.com

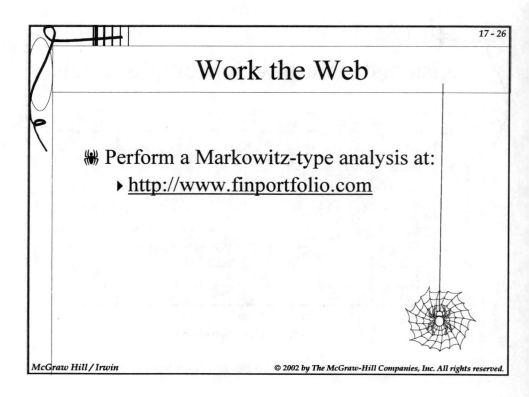

Chapter Review

- ◆ Expected Returns and Variances
  - → Expected Returns
  - → Calculating the Variance

- ◆ Portfolios
  - → Portfolio Weights
  - → Portfolio Expected Returns
  - → Portfolio Variance

Chapter Review

- ◆ Diversification and Portfolio Risk
  - → The Effect of Diversification: Another Lesson from Market History
  - → The Principle of Diversification

- ◆ Correlation and Diversification
  - → Why Diversification Works
  - → Calculating Portfolio Risk
  - → More on Correlation and the Risk-Return Trade-Off

Chapter Review

- ◆ The Markowitz Efficient Frontier
  - → Risk and Return with Multiple Assets

18
Chapter

Return, Risk, and the Security Market Line

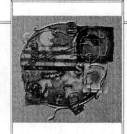

Fundamentals
of Investments
Valuation & Management
second edition

Charles J. Corrado   Bradford D. Jordan

McGraw Hill / Irwin

Slides by Yee-Tien (Ted) Fu

Return, Risk, & the Security Market Line

Goal

Our goal in this chapter is to define risk more precisely, and discuss how to measure it. Then, we will quantify the relation between risk and return in financial markets.

McGraw Hill / Irwin

Expected and Unexpected Returns

- ◆ The return on any stock traded in a financial market is composed of two parts.

  ① The normal, or expected, part of the return is the return that investors predict or expect.

  ② The uncertain, or risky, part of the return comes from unexpected information revealed during the year.

Total return − Expected return = Unexpected return

or $\qquad$ $R - E(R) = U$

Announcements and News

- ◆ The impact of an announcement depends on how much of it represents new information.

  → When the situation is not as bad as previously thought, what seems to be bad news is actually good news.

- ◆ News about the future is what matters.

  → Market participants factor predictions into the expected part of the stock return.

Announcement = Expected part + Surprise

Systematic and Unsystematic Risk

 Systematic risk
Risk that influences a large number of
assets. Also called *market risk.*

 Unsystematic risk
Risk that influences a single company or a
small group of companies. Also called
unique or *asset-specific risk.*

Total risk = Systematic risk + Unsystematic risk

Systematic & Unsystematic Components of Return

- $R - E(R) = U$

 $\quad$ = Systematic portion
 $\quad\quad$ + Unsystematic portion

 $\quad$ = m + ε

$$R - E(R) = m + ε$$

Diversification and Risk

- In a large portfolio, some stocks will go up in value because of positive company-specific events, while others will go down in value because of negative company-specific events.

- Unsystematic risk is essentially eliminated by diversification, so a portfolio with many assets has almost no unsystematic risk.

- Unsystematic risk is also called *diversifiable* risk, while systematic risk is also called *nondiversifiable* risk.

The Systematic Risk Principle

 What determines the size of the risk premium on a risky asset?

- The systematic risk principle states that the reward for bearing risk depends only on the systematic risk of an investment.

- So, no matter how much total risk an asset has, only the systematic portion is relevant in determining the expected return (and the risk premium) on that asset.

Measuring Systematic Risk

Beta coefficient (β)
Measure of the relative systematic risk of an asset. Assets with betas larger than 1.0 have more systematic risk than average, and vice versa.

◆ Because assets with larger betas have greater systematic risks, they will have greater expected returns.

◆ Note that not all betas are created equal.

Measuring Systematic Risk

Beta Coefficients	
Company	**Beta β**
Exxon	.65
AT&T	.90
IBM	.95
Wal-Mart	1.10
General Motors	1.15
Microsoft	1.30
Harley-Davidson	1.65
America Online	2.40

Source: *Value Line* Investment survey.

Work the Web

✹ Beta coefficients are widely available online. For example, check out:
  ‣ http://finance.yahoo.com

Portfolio Betas

- ◆ The riskiness of a portfolio has no simple relation to the risks of the assets in the portfolio.

- ◆ In contrast, a portfolio beta can be calculated just like the expected return of a portfolio.

  → In general, you can multiply each asset's beta by its portfolio weight and then add the results to get the portfolio's beta.

Beta and the Risk Premium

- ◆ Consider a portfolio made up of asset A and a risk-free asset. For asset A, $E(R_A) = 20\%$ and $\beta_A = 1.6$. The risk-free rate $R_f = 8\%$. Note that for a risk-free asset, $\beta = 0$ by definition.

- ✧ We can calculate some different possible portfolio expected returns and betas by varying the percentages invested in these two assets.

- ✧ Note that when the investor borrows at the risk-free rate and invests the proceeds in asset A, the investment in asset A will exceed 100%.

Beta and the Risk Premium

% of Portfolio in Asset A	Portfolio Expected Return	Portfolio Beta
0%	8%	.0
25	11	.4
50	14	.8
75	17	1.2
100	20	1.6
125	23	2.0
150	26	2.4

Beta and the Risk Premium

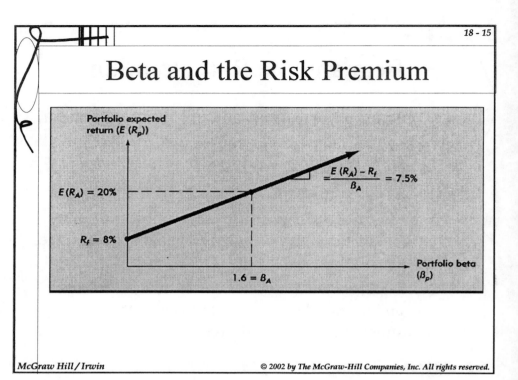

The Reward-to-Risk Ratio

- Notice that all the combinations of portfolio expected returns and betas fall on a straight line.

- Slope $= \dfrac{E(R_A) - R_f}{\hat{a}_A} = \dfrac{20\% - 8\%}{1.6} = 7.50\%$

- What this tells us is that asset A offers a *reward-to-risk* ratio of 7.50%. In other words, asset A has a risk premium of 7.50% per "unit" of systematic risk.

The Basic Argument

- Consider a second asset, asset B, with $E(R_B) = $ 16% and $\beta_A = 1.2$. Which investment is better, asset A or asset B?

The Basic Argument

% of Portfolio in Asset B	Portfolio Expected Return	Portfolio Beta
0 %	8 %	.0
25	10	.3
50	12	.6
75	14	.9
100	16	1.2
125	18	1.5
150	20	1.8

The Basic Argument

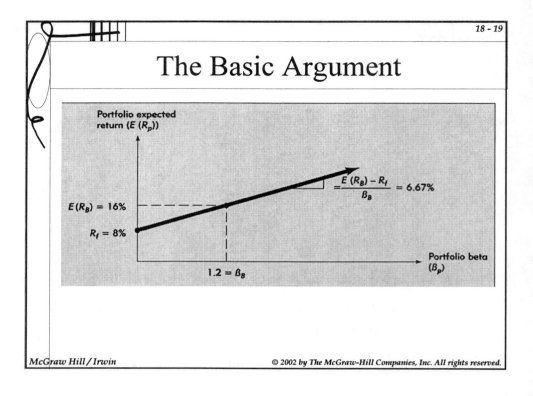

The Basic Argument

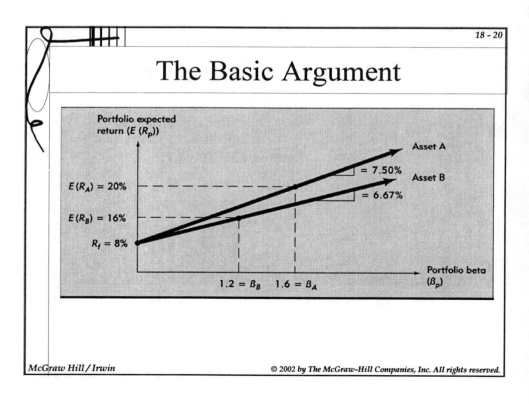

The Fundamental Result

- The situation we have described for assets A and B cannot persist in a well-organized, active market because investors will be attracted to asset A and away from asset B.
- This buying and selling will continue, and A's price will rise and B's price will fall, until the two assets plot on exactly the same line.
- So, $$\frac{E(R_A) - R_f}{\hat{a}_A} = \frac{E(R_B) - R_f}{\hat{a}_B}$$

The Fundamental Result

In general ...

- The reward-to-risk ratio must be the same for all assets in a competitive financial market.
- If one asset has twice as much systematic risk as another asset, its risk premium will simply be twice as large.
- Because the reward-to-risk ratio must be the same, all assets in the market must plot on the same line.

The Fundamental Result

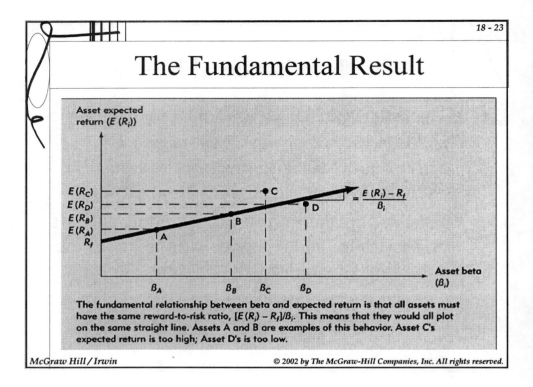

Asset expected return ($E(R_i)$)

$E(R_C)$
$E(R_D)$
$E(R_B)$
$E(R_A)$
R_f

$= \dfrac{E(R_i) - R_f}{ß_i}$

A   B   C   D

$ß_A$ $ß_B$ $ß_C$ $ß_D$

Asset beta ($ß_i$)

The fundamental relationship between beta and expected return is that all assets must have the same reward-to-risk ratio, $[E(R_i) - R_f]/ß_i$. This means that they would all plot on the same straight line. Assets A and B are examples of this behavior. Asset C's expected return is too high; Asset D's is too low.

The Security Market Line

 Security market line (SML)
Graphical representation of the linear relationship between systematic risk and expected return in financial markets.

- For a market portfolio,

$$\text{SML slope} = \frac{E(R_M) - R_f}{\hat{a}_M} = \frac{E(R_M) - R_f}{1}$$

$$= E(R_M) - R_f$$

The Security Market Line

- The term $E(R_M) - R_f$ is often called the market risk premium because it is the risk premium on a market portfolio.

- For any asset i in the market,

$$\frac{E(R_i) - R_f}{\hat{a}_i} = E(R_M) - R_f$$

$$\Rightarrow E(R_i) = R_f + [E(R_M) - R_f] \times \hat{a}_i$$

- This result is the *capital asset pricing model*.

The Security Market Line

 Capital asset pricing model (CAPM)
A theory of risk and return for securities on a competitive capital market.

$$\boxed{E(R_i) = R_f + [E(R_M) - R_f] \times \hat{a}_i}$$

- The CAPM shows that $E(R_i)$ depends on
  ① R_f, the pure time value of money.
  ② $E(R_M) - R_f$, the reward for bearing systematic risk.
  ③ β_i, the amount of systematic risk.

The Security Market Line

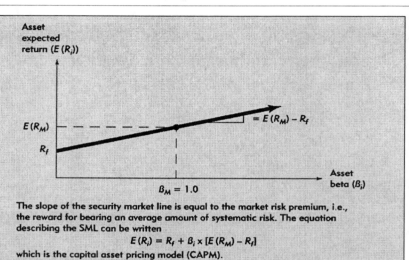

The slope of the security market line is equal to the market risk premium, i.e., the reward for bearing an average amount of systematic risk. The equation describing the SML can be written

$$E(R_i) = R_f + \beta_i \times [E(R_M) - R_f]$$

which is the capital asset pricing model (CAPM).

The Security Market Line

Risk and Return Summary

1. **Total risk.** The *total risk* of an investment is measured by the variance or, more commonly, the standard deviation of its return.

2. **Total return.** The *total return* on an investment has two components: the expected return and the unexpected return. The unexpected return comes about because of unanticipated events. The risk from investing stems from the possibility of an unanticipated event.

3. **Systematic and unsystematic risks.** *Systematic risks* (also called *market risks*) are unanticipated events that affect almost all assets to some degree because the effects are economy-wide. *Unsystematic risks* are unanticipated events that affect single assets or small groups of assets. Unsystematic risks are also called *unique* or *asset-specific risks*.

4. **The effect of diversification.** Some, but not all, of the risk associated with a risky investment can be eliminated by diversification. The reason is that unsystematic risks, which are unique to individual assets, tend to wash out in a large portfolio, but systematic risks, which affect all of the assets in a portfolio to some extent, do not.

5. **The systematic risk principle and beta.** Because unsystematic risk can be freely eliminated by diversification, the *systematic risk principle* states that the reward for bearing risk depends only on the level of systematic risk. The level of systematic risk in a particular asset, relative to the average, is given by the *beta* of that asset.

The Security Market Line

Risk and Return Summary

6. **The reward-to-risk ratio and the security market line.** The *reward-to-risk ratio* for Asset i is the ratio of its risk premium, $E(R_i) - R_f$, to its beta, β_i.

$$\frac{E(R_i) - R_f}{\beta_i}$$

In a well-functioning market, this ratio is the same for every asset. As a result, when asset expected returns are plotted against asset betas, all assets plot on the same straight line, called the *security market line* (SML).

7. **The capital asset pricing model.** From the SML, the expected return on Asset i can be written

$$E(R_i) = R_f + [E(R_M) - R_f] \times \beta_i$$

This is the *capital asset pricing model* (CAPM). The expected return on a risky asset thus has three components. The first is the pure time value of money (R_f), the second is the market risk premium, $E(R_M) - R_f$, and the third is the beta for that asset (β_i).

A Closer Look at Beta

- $R - E(R) = m + \varepsilon$, where m is the systematic portion of the unexpected return.

- $m = \beta \times [R_M - E(R_M)]$

- So, $R - E(R) = \beta \times [R_M - E(R_M)] + \varepsilon$

- In other words, a high-beta security is simply one that is relatively sensitive to overall market movements, whereas a low-beta security is one that is relatively insensitive.

A Closer Look at Beta

TABLE 18.3			**Decomposition of Total Returns into Systematic and Unsystematic Portions**			
	Actual Returns		Unexpected Returns		Systematic Portion	Unsystematic Portion (ε)
Year	R	R_M	R − E(R)	$R_M − E(R_M)$	$[R_M − E(R_M)] \times \beta$	R − $[R_M − E(R_M)] \times \beta$
1995	20%	15%	6.6%	3%	3.6%	3%
1996	−24.6	−3	−38	−15	−18	−20
1997	23	10	9.6	−2	−2.4	12
1998	36.8	24	23.4	12	14.4	9
1999	3.4	7	−10	−5	−6	−4

A Closer Look at Beta

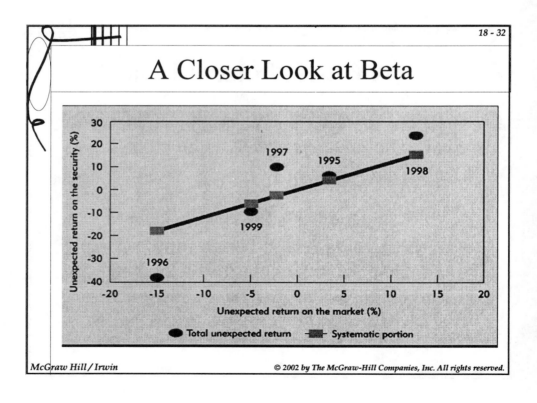

Where Do Betas Come From?

* A security's beta depends on
  ① how closely correlated the security's return is with the overall market's return, and
  ② how volatile the security is relative to the market.

* A security's beta is equal to the correlation multiplied by the ratio of the standard deviations.

$$\hat{a}_i = Corr(R_i, R_M) \times \frac{\acute{o}_i}{\acute{o}_m}$$

Where Do Betas Come From?

TABLE 18.4	Calculating Beta						
	Returns		Return Deviations		Squared Deviations		
Year	Security	Market	Security	Market	Security	Market	Product of Deviations
1997	10%	8%	.00	−.04	.0000	.0016	.0000
1998	−8	−12	−.18	−.24	.0324	.0576	.0432
1999	−4	16	−.14	.04	.0196	.0016	−.0056
2000	40	26	.30	.14	.0900	.0196	.0420
2001	12	22	.02	.10	.0004	.0100	.0020
Totals	50	60	0	0	.1424	.0904	.0816

	Average Returns	Variances	Standard Deviations
Security	50/5 = 10%	.1424/4 = .0356	$\sqrt{.0356}$ = .1887 = 18.87%
Market	60/5 = 12%	.0904/4 = .0226	$\sqrt{.0226}$ = .1503 = 15.03%

Covariance = $Cov(R_i, R_M)$ = .0816/4 = .0204
Correlation = $Corr(R_i, R_M)$ = .0204 / (.1887 × .1503) = .72
Beta = β = .72 × (.1887 / .1503) = .9031 ≈ .9

Why Do Betas Differ?

- ◆ Betas are estimated from actual data. Different sources estimate differently, possibly using different data.
  - → For data, the most common choices are three to five years of monthly data, or a single year of weekly data.
  - → To measure the overall market, the S&P 500 stock market index is commonly used.
  - → The calculated betas may be adjusted for various statistical reasons.

Chapter Review

- ◆ Announcements, Surprises, and Expected Returns
  - → Expected and Unexpected Returns
  - → Announcements and News

- ◆ Risk: Systematic and Unsystematic
  - → Systematic and Unsystematic Risk
  - → Systematic and Unsystematic Components of Return

Chapter Review

- ◆ Diversification, Systematic Risk, and Unsystematic Risk
  - → Diversification and Unsystematic Risk
  - → Diversification and Systematic Risk

- ◆ Systematic Risk and Beta
  - → The Systematic Risk Principle
  - → Measuring Systematic Risk
  - → Portfolio Betas

Chapter Review

- ◆ The Security Market Line
  - → Beta and the Risk Premium
  - → The Reward-to-Risk Ratio
  - → The Basic Argument
  - → The Fundamental Result
  - → The Security Market Line

Chapter Review

- ◆ More on Beta
  - ➔ A Closer Look at Beta
  - ➔ Where Do Betas Come From?
  - ➔ Why Do Betas Differ?

19

Chapter

Performance Evaluation and Risk Management

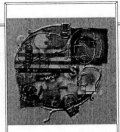

Fundamentals
of Investments
Valuation & Management
second edition

Charles J. Corrado   Bradford D. Jordan

McGraw Hill / Irwin

Slides by Yee-Tien (Ted) Fu

It is Not the Return *On* My Investment ...

*"It is not the return **on** my investment that I am concerned about. It is the return **of** my investment!"*

– Will Rogers

McGraw Hill / Irwin

Performance Evaluation & Risk Management

 Goal Our goal in this chapter is to examine the methods of ① evaluating risk-adjusted investment performance, and ② assessing and managing the risks involved with specific investment strategies.

Performance Evaluation

Can anyone consistently earn an "excess" return, thereby "beating" the market?

 Performance evaluation
Concerns the assessment of how well a money manager achieves a balance between high returns and acceptable risks.

Performance Evaluation Measures

- The *raw return* on a portfolio, R_P, is the total % return on the portfolio with no adjustment for risk or comparison to any benchmark.

- It is a naive measure of performance evaluation that does not reflect any consideration of risk. As such, its usefulness is limited.

Performance Evaluation Measures

The Sharpe Ratio

- The *Sharpe ratio* is a reward-to-risk ratio that focuses on total risk.

- It is computed as a portfolio's risk premium divided by the standard deviation for the portfolio's return.

$$\text{Sharpe ratio} = \frac{R_p - R_f}{\acute{o}_p}$$

Work the Web

🕷 Visit Professor Sharpe at:

　▸ http://www.stanford.edu/~wfsharpe

Performance Evaluation Measures

The Treynor Ratio

♦ The *Treynor ratio* is a reward-to-risk ratio that looks at systematic risk only.

♦ It is computed as a portfolio's risk premium divided by the portfolio's beta coefficient.

$$\text{Treynor ratio} = \frac{R_p - R_f}{\hat{a}_p}$$

Performance Evaluation Measures

Jensen's Alpha

- _Jensen's alpha_ is the excess return above or below the security market line. It can be interpreted as a measure of how much the portfolio "beat the market."

- It is computed as the raw portfolio return less the expected portfolio return as predicted by the CAPM.

$$\alpha_p = R_p - \left\{ R_f + \hat{a}_p \times \left[E(R_M) - R_f \right] \right\}$$

McGraw Hill / Irwin

Performance Evaluation Measures

Portfolio A plots above the Security Market Line (SML) and has a positive alpha.
Portfolio B has a zero alpha.
Portfolio C plots below the SML and has a negative alpha.

McGraw Hill / Irwin

Comparing Performance Measures

Investment Performance Data

Portfolio	R_P	σ_P	β_P
A	12%	40%	.5
B	15%	30%	.75
C	20%	22%	1.4
M	15%	15%	1
F	5%	0%	0

Portfolio Performance Measurement

Portfolio	Sharpe Ratio	Treynor Ratio	Jensen Alpha
A	.175	.14	2%
B	.333	.133	2.5%
C	.682	.107	1%
M	.667	.10	0%

Comparing Performance Measures

Since the performance rankings may be substantially different, which performance measure should we use?

Sharpe ratio

- Appropriate for the evaluation of an entire portfolio.
- Penalizes a portfolio for being undiversified, since in general, total risk ≈ systematic risk only for relatively well-diversified portfolios.

Comparing Performance Measures

Treynor ratio / Jensen's alpha

- ◆ Appropriate for the evaluation of securities or portfolios for possible inclusion in a broader or "master" portfolio.
- ◆ Both are similar, the only difference being that the Treynor ratio standardizes everything, including any excess return, relative to beta.
- ◆ Both require a beta estimate (and betas from different sources may differ a lot).

Work the Web

The performance measures we have discussed are commonly used in the evaluation of mutual funds. See, for example, the *Ratings and Risk* for various funds at:

- ▸ http://www.morningstar.com

Sharpe-Optimal Portfolios

- ◆ A funds allocation with the highest possible Sharpe ratio is said to be *Sharpe-optimal*.

- ◆ To find the Sharpe-optimal portfolio, consider the plot of the investment opportunity set of risk-return possibilities for a portfolio.

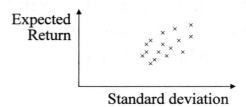

Sharpe-Optimal Portfolios

- ◆ The slope of a straight line drawn from the risk-free rate to a portfolio gives the Sharpe ratio for that portfolio.

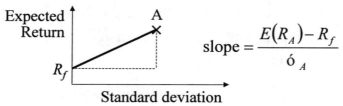

$$slope = \frac{E(R_A) - R_f}{\acute{o}_A}$$

- ◆ Hence, the portfolio on the line with the *steepest* slope is the Sharpe-optimal portfolio.

Sharpe-Optimal Portfolios

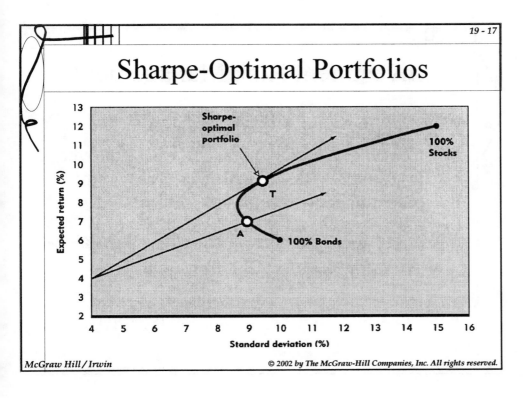

Sharpe-Optimal Portfolios

- Notice that the Sharpe-optimal portfolio is *one* of the efficient portfolios on the Markowitz efficient frontier.

Investment Risk Management

 Investment risk management
Concerns a money manager's control over
investment risks, usually with respect to
potential short-run losses.

◆ We will focus on what is known as the Value-
at-Risk approach.

Value-at-Risk (VaR)

 Value-at-Risk (VaR)
Assesses risk by stating the probability of a
loss a portfolio may experience within a
fixed time horizon.

◆ If the returns on an investment follow a normal
distribution, we can state the probability that a
portfolio's return will be within a certain range
given the mean and standard deviation of the
portfolio's return.

Value-at-Risk (VaR)

Example: VaR

◆ Suppose you own an S&P 500 index fund. Historically, $E(R_{S\&P500}) \approx 13\%$ per year, while $\sigma_{S\&P500} \approx 20\%$. What is the probability of a return of -7% or worse in a particular year?

✧ The odds of being within one σ are about 2/3 or .67. I.e. Prob $(.13-.20 \leq R_{S\&P500} \leq .13+.20) \approx .67$
or Prob $(-.07 \leq R_{S\&P500} \leq .33) \approx .67$

✧ So, Prob $(R_{S\&P500} \leq -.07) \approx 1/6$ or .17

✧ The VaR statistic is thus a return of $-.07$ or worse with a probability of 17%.

Work the Web

🕷 Learn all about VaR at:
  ▶ http://www.gloriamundi.org

More on Computing Value-at-Risk

Example: More on VaR

- For the S&P 500 index fund, what is the probability of a loss of 30% or more over the next two years?

  ◇ 2-year average return = 2×.13 = .26

  ◇ 1-year σ^2 = $.20^2$ = .04. So, 2-year σ^2 = 2×.04 = .08. So, 1-year σ = $\sqrt{.08} \approx .28$

  ◇ The odds of being within two σ's are .95.
  I.e. Prob (.26–2×.28 ≤ $R_{S\&P500}$ ≤ .26+2×.28) ≈ .95
  or Prob (−.30 ≤ $R_{S\&P500}$ ≤ .82) ≈ .95

  ◇ So, Prob ($R_{S\&P500}$ ≤ −.30) ≈ 2.5%

More on Computing Value-at-Risk

- In general, if T is the number of years,

$$E(R_{p,T}) = E(R_p) \times T$$

$$\sigma_{p,T} = \sigma_p \times \sqrt{T}$$

- So, $\text{Prob}(R_{p,T} \le E(R_p) \times T - 2.326 \times \sigma_p \sqrt{T}) = 1\%$
  $\text{Prob}(R_{p,T} \le E(R_p) \times T - 1.96 \times \sigma_p \sqrt{T}) = 2.5\%$
  $\text{Prob}(R_{p,T} \le E(R_p) \times T - 1.645 \times \sigma_p \sqrt{T}) = 5\%$

Work the Web

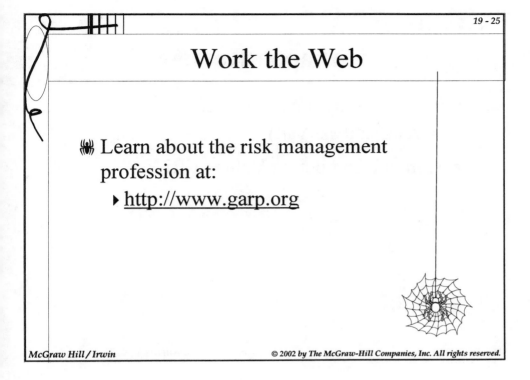

🕷 Learn about the risk management
profession at:

▸ http://www.garp.org

Chapter Review

◆ **Performance Evaluation**
  ➔ Performance Evaluation Measures
    • The Sharpe Ratio
    • The Treynor Ratio
    • Jensen's Alpha

◆ **Comparing Performance Measures**
  ➔ Sharpe-Optimal Portfolios

Chapter Review

- ◆ Investment Risk Management
  - → Value-at-Risk (VaR)
- ◆ More on Computing Value-at-Risk